Living Better in Cincinnati

The Guide to the City's Best Kept Secrets

By Lois Rosenthal

Design and Illustration by
Tina Blackburn

Writer's Digest Books
a division of F&W Publications, Inc.
Cincinnati, Ohio

Library of Congress Cataloging-in-Publication Data

Rosenthal, Lois.
    Living better in Cincinnati.

    Includes index.
    1. Shopping—Ohio—Cincinnati—Guide-books.
2. Cincinnati (Ohio)—Description—Guide-books.
3. Service industries—Ohio—Cincinnati—
Guide-books.
I. Title.
TX336.5.032C556 1987   381'.45'02577178 87-23155
ISBN 0-89879-290-8

Design and Illustration by Tina Blackburn.

Acknowledgments

It was the idea of my husband/publisher, Richard Rosenthal, that *Living Better in Cincinnati* resurface for the bicentennial. His innovative thoughts sparked every step of its rebirth.

Kudos to Vicki Klein, researcher extraordinaire; Sharon Rudd, the editor who made order from mayhem; Donna Bright, computer specialist and scout; my daughter, Jennie Rosenthal, who scoured whole areas of the city; Ruth and Jack Cowens, who covered and uncovered Northern Kentucky.

For the hot tips and heavy leads, my thanks to these ingenious, sharing people: Karla Addington, Toni Birckhead, Paul Bonner, Arthur Brand, Queen Brown, Carol Buchanan, Bruce Butler, D.V.M., Betty Cass, Sandy Chalfen, Arthur Crockett, Robert A. Dressler, Ruth Edwards, Beverly Everet, D.V.M., Bob Gervasi, Dennis Harrington, Patricia Hiett-Cogan, Rita House, Peter Huttinger, Chris Klein, Sarah and David Lewis, Carol Luppert, Mert and Chuck Ransdell, Karen Roberts, Kathy Schneider, Linda and Budge Wallis, Alyson Warner, Leo Wayne, M.D., Patty Wise.

Table of Contents

Preface

The bicentennial edition of *Living Better in Cincinnati* looks at this venerable old city with a new eye to uncover services, goods, people, and places you might never have known existed. It helps you find exactly what you especially need so that life in the Queen City is even more pleasurable.

Where can you get the best French bread in town, find a responsible baby-sitting service (or a nanny), a caring kennel for your dog, a great caterer? Where are the most unique places to have a party, nearby farms to buy picked-that-day produce? Is there a psychic in town, an art glass restorer, a golden-fingered expert to repaint your BMW? What extras are provided by museums and performing arts ensembles? Who do you call when the pothole in your street grows to the size of a crater or when you feel all alone in the middle of the night?

Living Better in Cincinnati uncovers all of these city secrets. It locates caring people, stalks auctions and secondhand shops, steers you to stores that sell the finest bedding, toys, jewels, and tools. It's a gourmet underground guide to where you can get the most for your money.

All of the observations in this book are purely personal and are based on what I saw when I visited each place. I also talked to hundreds of people on the phone and sometimes relied on experts who knew the fields I was researching to gather additional information.

Be sure to phone out-of-the-way-to-you stores mentioned in the book before you visit. Businesses do move or sadly bite the dust. Merchandise changes with the seasons, too, but goods similar to those I mention should be available.

Note that the Kenwood-Montgomery area is exploding. Hundreds of shops are slated for that part of town but were still on the drawing board when this book went to press. I'll keep you posted in future *Living Better* editions.

However, if you know of unique places not mentioned in this book or discover new ones, please share them by filling out the coupon on page 166 and sending it to me. Keeping in touch with innovative people, those who have their fingers on the excitement of the city, is one of the greatest rewards in writing this book. I'd call that *Living Better in Cincinnati.*

Edibles

Though you may not be able to live by bread alone, it sure makes life finer to know where to pick up the best kinds. In fact, food is one of the most important ingredients in living well in any city. If you're new to Cincinnati, being able to buy what you've been used to makes a new place feel less strange. Even if you're a lifelong resident, clipping a recipe you'd like to try and not being able to buy some of the ingredients is infuriating. So, read on for a bite of some of the tastiest places in town—those that sell all sorts of specialties, except sweets. That chapter follows since candy, desserts, and ice cream certainly deserve a niche of their own. So do glorious fresh-picked fruits and vegetables. Look in "Fresh Picked and Pick-Your-Own," pages 44-49, for these.

Bread

Servatii's is an all-round top-quality bakery that makes crusty French bread, nice rye, good, hearty dense grain breads. Their muffins are tasty and they make a world of coffee cakes, tortes, and tarts. Ask about bread baskets you can custom order, which are lovely as centerpieces, as well as cakes, tarts, all sorts of special dessert items. Check your phone book for their many locations.

Buchheim makes wonderful egg bread—square loaves or twists. They'll bake especially long loaves of challa if you need it for a crowd. Pick up delicious hamantaschen (triangles filled with fruit or poppyseeds) at Purim as well as other delectable specialties at holidays throughout the year.
Buchheim Bakery
2200 Losantiville (Golf Manor)
631-4550

Camargo Bakery draws raves for the hard rolls they turn out on Saturday mornings, as well as the tiny buns, breads, and cakes they make daily.
Camargo Bakery
6927 Miami Ave. (Madeira)
561-5673

The Wyoming Pastry Shop bakes Bacher rye on Tuesdays, Fridays, and Saturdays—round and square loaves of this old Cincinnati recipe that yields bread that has a good texture and an even better aroma.
Wyoming Pastry Shop
505 Wyoming Ave. (Wyoming)
821-0742

You can find some varieties of Mainstay bread—wholesome loaves made with natural ingredients—at many supermarkets and specialty stores. But Stan Kingman, Mainstay's owner, says he bakes about thirty varieties, so if you'd like a particular loaf you can't find at your local supermarket, or if you like your bread unsliced, phone the Mainstay Bakery and Trading Co. to see if they have it in stock or to place a special order.
Mainstay Baking & Trading Co.
3919-25 Montgomery Rd. (Norwood)
631-3393

Many people make the trip to Bigg's just to buy their bakery products. The French bread and hard rolls seem to be everyone's first choice, with muffins and other breakfast rolls next in popularity. Check "Off-Price," page 103, for Bigg's address.

Kroger's has started baking! These stores are closer and more convenient for many people than Bigg's, and Kroger's is doing just fine in the bread department. Though many of their cakes and pies look too sticky-sweet to eat, their baguettes are downright satisfying. So are their big round dinner rolls, and some of their round breads. What a handy surprise! Check your phone directory for the Kroger's closest to you.

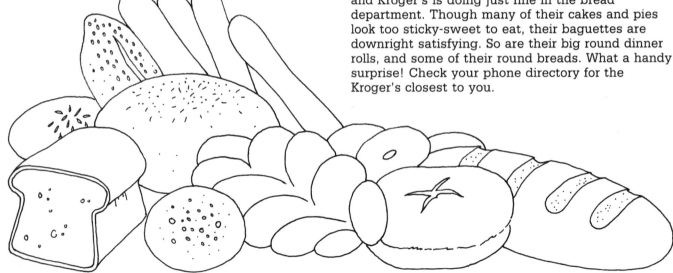

John Marx of Hot Bagels makes thirty kinds of water bagels from plain and poppyseed classics to eight-grain, date, blueberry, even banana nut. John turns out mini bagels in the same varieties, bagel thins, which are an alternative to melba toast, and giant bagels (hang them on a door like wreaths or fill the centers with a cream cheese spread for a crowd) and bagels in the shape of stars. You must special order these large ones as well as bagels in bright colors: Bengal bagels in orange and black, red at Valentine's Day, green at St. Patrick's Day. John is creative.

Hot Bagels
Valley Center (Roselawn)
821-0103
477 E. Kemper Rd. (Tri-County)
671-0278
Look for a third location in the Blue Ash area soon.

You can buy Old World Pita Bread in many supermarkets, but find different sizes and shapes than you're used to seeing around town at the bakery. There are large rounds the size of burritos, ovals, others that are made especially for certain restaurants. Old World also bakes hard rolls, kaiser rolls, specialty breads, and bagels. Phone the bakery to see what they have in stock.

Old World Bakery
1933 W. Galbraith Rd. (North College Hill)
931-1411

If you love monumental double-thick English muffins the size of tuna cans, you'll love Wolferman's. These Kansas City specialties have been around for years, but are just now being introduced in stores in Cincinnati. Bilker's (see below) has them for sure. Scout others. Varieties include whole wheat raisin, cinnamon, cheddar cheese, light wheat, and plain. If you have trouble locating what you want locally, phone Wolferman's toll-free number. They ship boxes of muffins all over the country.

Wolferman's
1-800-255-0169

Chemical-free whole grain breads that are delicious and dense can be ordered from Natural Ovens Direct in Milwaukee. There is a coterie of Cincinnatians who are sunny millet bread fanatics. This recipe contains oatmeal, sunflower and sesame seeds, millet, whole wheat flour, and barley malt—nutritious to say the least. Natural Ovens makes rye, cracked wheat, many other varieties. Write or phone for a catalogue. Orders are speedily shipped to Cincinnati.

Natural Ovens Direct
P.O. Box 17021
6125 W. Douglas Ave.
Milwaukee, WI 53218
414-464-2322

Meat and Poultry

Avril's, Wassler's, Huber's, and Clifton Meat Market are four old Cincinnati firms that stand out as meat sellers—they could probably come up with any cut of meat you need. Check out their poultry and fish as well. Note that Avril's is best known for its thirty varieties of homemade sausage and hams; Clifton and Wassler's deliver.

Avril & Son
33 E. Court St. (downtown)
241-2433

Wassler's Meat Market
4300 Harrison Ave. (Bridgetown)
574-9033

Findlay Market (Over-the-Rhine)
721-0057

Huber's on the Square
2719 Erie Ave. (Hyde Park)
871-4272

Clifton Meat Market
324 Ludlow Ave. (Clifton)
861-4215

Edibles

4 Fish

Since Ohio is a far cry from coastal waters, fish can taste decidedly tired by the time it hits town. If you're used to eating fish fresh from the dock, you'll be disappointed in Cincinnati's catch. Still, Kroger's brings in a large variety several times a week and some of the fish tastes pretty snappy. Check out the seafood counter at the store nearest you.

Cape Cod Fisheries has cases of seafood: all varieties of ocean fish, shrimp, crabmeat, lobsters, and oysters are regulars. However, the variety depends on the season and where the fish is coming from. The store also stocks a large variety of poultry. Cape Cod delivers in some of the eastern parts of the city as well as downtown if you place a $10 minimum order.
Cape Cod Fisheries
118 W. 6th St. (downtown)
241-5878

Coastal Seafood has a loyal following of seafood lovers. If you live in the Madeira area, your supply will be close by.
Coastal Seafood
6928 Miami Ave. (Madeira)
561-4487

Specialties

The Fourth St. Market at L.S. Ayres' downtown store has a good selection of imported cookies, biscuits, jams, spices, canned fruits, mustards, sauces, vinegars, and cheese. It's a nice shop to stock up on specialties for yourself, a great place to pick up edible gifts.
Fourth St. Market/L.S. Ayres
4th & Race (downtown)
352-5399

The gourmet section of Lazarus' downtown store has fine imported cheeses and candies, all sorts of special sauces, spices, mustards, honey, jams, many teas.
Lazarus
7th & Race (downtown)
369-6121

The Busy Bee Food Shop has imported canned soups, an ever-changing array of interesting snacks and biscuits, tangy vinegars, an assortment of pasta and coffee, wild rice and chocolate in bulk, and best of all, owners Joe and Jean Sumner, who will spend time telling you what's new, what you'll like, how to prepare it, then advise you what's the nicest wine to serve with your meal. Their wine department sports a varied and discriminating selection.
Busy Bee Food Shop
2707 Erie Ave. (Hyde Park Square)
871-2898

Maller's Cheese Shop offers a fine array of imported cheeses—superb Brie and Camembert, goat cheese, and some varieties of cheese that are low in cholesterol and salt. Besides wine, crackers, jams, teas, vinegars and olive oils, Maller's can special order six kinds of fresh caviar from New York and have it shipped in overnight. They will also special order leg of lamb, lamb chops, shoulders, and shanks from a farm in Pennsylvania that raises these animals on feed without additives and preservatives. Some of this meat is kept frozen in stock. Capons that were free-running and fed good-quality grains are also sold frozen. Ask about frozen crab cakes and fresh oysters from Maryland, the cheese and paté trays the store will make to order, custom gift baskets they will deliver anywhere in the city.
Maller's Cheese Shop
7754 Camargo Rd. (Madeira)
561-6956

Bilker Food Market has a world of imported foods—there's an entire counter filled just with luscious candy. There are jars of vegetables from Greece, Russian specialties that refugees drive from all over the Tri-State to buy, the best kosher dill pickles in town (watch out when you open the jar, the bubbling aroma can knock you out), a deli case packed with lox, smoked fish, herring, corned beef, tongue, and other specialties. If you're an Empire kosher chicken fan, and maybe you should be if you like top-quality poultry, Bilker's has a huge selection—from frozen whole chickens and Cornish hens to packages of parts. Notice the variety of frozen entrees. These ethnic answers to Lean Cuisine include bow-tie noodles and kasha, barley and mushrooms, all kinds of blintzes and knishes. At Passover, Bilker's has the most extensive selection of holiday food in the city. Take time to explore this supermarket of global treats—the stock will definitely widen your horizons.

Bilker Food Market
7648 Reading Rd. (Roselawn)
761-6280

The Big Melon has imported vinegars, jams, biscuits, cheeses, bottled waters, a nice wine section, a deli counter stocked with meats and salads, a fruit department that can fill many gift baskets.

Big Melon
8424 Vine (Hartwell)
821-7440

Gourmet has displays of jams, vinegars, crackers, oils, many ethnic specialties, a wine and bakery department, a deli case nicely furnished with already prepared salads and entrees as well as cheeses and cold meats.

Gourmet
Hyde Park Plaza
321-8100

The Culinary Emporium (see "From the Frying Pan . . . ," page 36, for information on their cookware collection) has a superb selection of coffee beans and teas, imported jams, mustards, sauces, candies. This store has all you need in specialty food and the pots and pans to prepare it.

The Culinary Emporium
Kenwood Towne Centre
793-2783
11439 Princeton Pk. (Tricentre)
772-1510

LaRosa's Food & Wine Shop features a large assortment of cheese and wine, pasta and ravioli made daily, homemade bread and pastries, bins of beans and spaghetti, dried fruit and spices, all sorts of seafood, Greek, and pasta salads.

LaRosa's Food & Wine Shop
2411 Boudinot (Westwood)
451-1520

The Pasta Market, a gourmet take-out store, sells a good variety of pasta made on the premises, homemade sauces from marinara to carbonara, as well as all sorts of pasta salads, ready-to-go lasagna, eggplant parmesan, and other entrees. All are freshly made and delicious. Notice about thirty types of cheese, many patés, prosciutto, smoked Scotch salmon, vinegars, chocolates, mustards, cookies, and cakes. Steve Shifman, Pasta Market's owner, sells only top-of-the-line merchandise. See "Home Entertainment," page 87, for his catering service.

The Pasta Market
8110 Montgomery Rd. (Kenwood)
745-9022

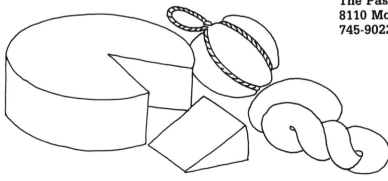

Edibles

6 The Cutting Board carries imported and domestic cheeses, jellies, preserves, condiments, bread, pastries, mustards. The store will make cold trays to take out: smoked salmon or paté with French bread slices, veggie and fruit trays, lobster and crab molds in the shape of, well, crabs and lobsters.
The Cutting Board
654 Highland Ave. (Ft. Thomas)
781-4299

The Coffee Emporium carries dozens of varieties of coffee beans that they roast and flavor themselves and a wonderful assortment of loose teas and tea bags. Pick up cakes and cookies in tins to nibble with your aromatic brew, or a handful of candy. Coffee pots? This store sells every kind of coffee maker imaginable.
The Coffee Emporium
3316 Erie Ave. (Hyde Park)
321-5943

J.R. Higgins has twenty-five to thirty kinds of coffee beans they roast fresh daily plus a passel of other epicurean delights. Phone the store and they'll deliver coffee to you for a small fee. Mine was UPSed to me the next day and the price of the Kenyan coffee I ordered was so low it offset the delivery cost.
J.R. Higgins
11561 Chester Rd. (Sharonville)
771-5020

Murray Bros. is the place to pick up bulk spices, beautiful dried fruit and nuts, a world of old-time candies, flour, corn meal, all sorts of cooking sundries. Murray Bros. has two downtown locations and stores in many malls. Consult your phone directory.

Soya Food Products, a wholesale and retail store owned by Ben and Nita Yamaguchi, manufactures and sells tofu, carries all sorts of Chinese and Japanese food products. There is frozen fish, fresh and canned vegetables, many varieties of soy sauce and rice vinegar, rice, beans, grains, noodles, seasonings, kitchen utensils including chopsticks and bamboo skewers. Ask for a catalogue; it reads like a trip to the Orient. All food you order will be sent to you via UPS.
Soya Food Products Co.
2356 Wyoming Ave. (Fairmount)
661-2250

The Saigon Market specializes in Vietnamese, Korean, and Chinese food: canned fruits and vegetables, fresh vegetables including greens and sprouts, bags of spices, noodles, dried mushrooms, and rice. This small, busy shop located in the Findlay Market area is full of pungent smells and unusual delicacies.
The Saigon Market
119 W. Elder St. (Over-the-Rhine)
721-8053

The Oriental Center sells Chinese products: canned foods, grains, noodles, rice, sauces, and spices.
The Oriental Center
209 W. McMillan (Clifton Heights)
241-1171

India Quality Foods carries a full line of Indian spices and teas plus all sorts of canned goods, beans, rice, and noodles.
India Quality Foods
268 Ludlow Ave. (Clifton)
961-4184

If you're cooking a Caribbean recipe and haven't been able to find the ingredients, try Madera's Latin American Market. This store carries fresh, frozen, and canned food from Mexico, Puerto Rico, Cuba, Venezuela, Jamaica, many Caribbean countries. Look for specialties such as Masaharina flour used to make tortillas, all kinds of dried and fresh peppers, mangoes, plantains, Mexican sausages—that country's version of salami.
Madera's Latin American Market
4314 Montgomery Rd. (Norwood)
531-5291

Patel Bros. is a Pakistani and Indian grocery store featuring many spices, condiments, chutneys, teas, oils, flour, rice, nuts, raisins, vegetables, much canned goods and cooking implements.
Patel Bros.
Valley Center (Roselawn)
821-0304

Barresi's Deli sells pasta, cheeses, salami, prosciutto, olive oils, capers, red peppers—all sorts of Italian items. It's located next door to the restaurant.
Barresi's Deli
4111 Webster Ave. (Deer Park)
793-2540

Fruit cakes and cheese made by the Trappist monks at Gethsemani Farms in Kentucky are popular gift items at Christmas. While the Monterey Jack, Colby, and cheddar cheese are as good as the fruitcake, better yet, all food products are boxed in keepsake-quality wooden containers. Write for a catalogue. Food items are available year-round.
Gethsemani Farms
Trappist, KY 40051
502-549-3117

Custom gourmet baskets designed for a housewarming gift, a new baby, to say "thank you"—you tell Patty Wise and Rita House what food items you want to send, they'll put the basket together, wrap it to suit the occasion, and deliver it. No perishables are included, but you can choose all sorts of candy, crackers, nuts, popcorn, jams, pasta—ask.
PR Baskets
Daytime: A.B. Wise Co.
874-9642
Evenings:
Patty Wise
489-4568
Rita House
530-5656

To Market, To Market

Findlay Market, the Cincinnati version of a European open-air market, is where you can pass a few hours filling a shopping bag with your week's groceries or filling your soul with the Old World atmosphere. On market days, which are Wednesday, Friday, and Saturday, stands, shops, and cubbies sell fruit and vegetables, eggs and oysters, pig's feet and sauerkraut, olives, oysters, spices, and cheese. There are dozens of meat, fish, poultry, and pastry sellers inside the enclosed building. Fruits and vegetables are generally sold outside. Come early in the day if you want the pick of the crop. Arrive late on the scene if you're looking for bargains. That's when proprietors drop prices because they are anxious to get rid of merchandise and go home. For browsing, for buying, for smelling and strolling—Findlay Market.
Findlay Market
1800 Elm (Over-the-Rhine)
352-3419

Court Street Market appears on Tuesdays and Thursdays. In fact, some of the same fruit and vegetable stands that are at Findlay Market set up on Court Street on alternate days. Though Court Street Market is smaller, it has the same ambience as Findlay Market. Many people who work in the vicinity eat a walking lunch here, picked from the stands.
Court Street Market
Court St. between Main & Vine Sts. (downtown)

Direct from the Factory

The fragrance of freshly ground flour that engulfs you at H. Nagel & Son is guaranteed to put you in the baking mood—you are buying flour directly from the mill. Notice the huge Keebler trucks in the parking lot when you pull in here. That's the kind of companies the mill supplies. Still, Nagel will sell to retail customers who want three- to 100-pound quantities of flour such as unbleached cake, graham, buckwheat, cracked wheat, farina, wheat germ, white and yellow corn meal. The store is in back of the mill. Enter from the rear.
H. Nagel & Son
2641 Spring Grove Ave. (Camp Washington)
681-2550

Edibles

8   VIP Products makes pizza shells and hoagie buns for many independent pizza stores in the city and sells all sorts of pizza fixings at the factory for those who want to make pizzas at home. In addition to shells and buns, you can buy frozen balls of dough, pizza kits that contain enough shells, sauce, cheese, and topping for four pizzas, French bread in all sizes, large loaves of assorted cheeses, half-gallon containers of salad dressings, five-gallon jars of pickles, and other food items.
VIP Products, Inc.
1400 State Ave. (Price Hill)
921-6600

At Beppo's, which also supplies independent retailers in the city with pizza products, you can buy packs of ten precooked shells in a variety of sizes, sauce by the gallon, shredded cheese, pepperoni—whatever you need for your own pizza creations.
Beppo Pizza Crust
2071 Harrison Ave. (Fairmount)
661-6804

Wholesale

If you want to buy bakery supplies in large quantities, see what Karp's Cincinnati Bakers' Supply has to offer. Flour comes in 100-pound bags, sugar in fifty-pound bags. You can buy thirty pounds of nuts, raisins, and dried fruit, vanilla and spices in quarts and gallons, chocolate in ten-pound blocks, all sorts of bakery mixes such as donut, cake, and cookie in fifty-pound bags. Planning a bake sale? Shop here.
Karp's Cincinnati Bakers' Supply
7736 Reinhold Dr. (Roselawn)
821-1855

You want smoked fish and lox—lots of it for a brunch. Cincinnati Food Distributors, Inc. can help you out. You can buy lox in three-pound tubs, smoked fish such as chubs and sable in five-pound quantities, whole sides of smoked salmon. All the fish is frozen except the herring in cream or wine sauce, which is in half-gallon jars. Relishes and salad dressings are also available in gallon jars, cheeses in five- to seven-pound loaves, boxes of 100 frozen hors d'oeuvres, boxes of twelve chicken breasts Florentine.
Cincinnati Food Distributors, Inc.
6262 Wiehe Rd. (Golf Manor)
731-6200

Food wholesalers that supply institutions and restaurants are also places where you can buy in quantity—if you can use the quantity. Some sell cans of fruit and vegetables that weigh six pounds apiece. Some have cases of smaller cans, but you must buy by the case. Ask about boxes of hamburger patties, six-pound trays of lasagna (handy for a party), boxes of chicken breasts prepared for restaurant entrees—ready for you to heat and serve—boxes of frozen fish, bags of shrimp, all sorts of desserts. You may want to call the following places to see if what you want is available, or stop in and look at their voluminous food lists.

Ellenbee-Leggett Co.
1999 Section Rd. (Roselawn)
531-5544

C. Eberle Sons, Co.
3222 Beekman (Cumminsville)
542-7200

L & B Distributors
3110 Spring Grove Ave. (Camp Washington)
542-0575

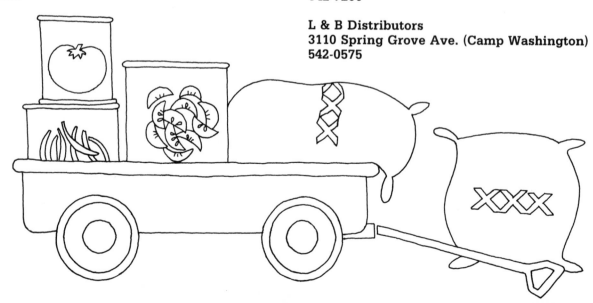

The fruit and vegetable wholesalers along Pete Rose Way (formerly Second Street), downtown, will sell you fresh produce if you buy by the case. Just don't make the mistake of asking for that nice red apple over there. These people are busy, so choose what you need and get out of the way of the trucks. If you're making fruit baskets at Christmas, these are good places to stock up. Degaro, one of the wholesalers, sells gift baskets by the dozen at Christmas. Fries Bros. sells bedding plants in the spring, poinsettias, Christmas trees, and pine roping at Christmas. Caruso-Ciresi also has Christmas trees and pine roping in season. Shop early at all produce wholesalers. They're open around 3:00 A.M., when retail store trucks pull up for the day's supplies; everything is closed tight by noon. Drive down Pete Rose Way and the surrounding area—you can pull up at any of the wholesale operations to see what you can buy. However, these are some of the outfits I've found accommodating to the retail trade.

Fries Bros. Inc.
221 W. Pete Rose Way
621-6978

M. Degaro Co.
225 W. Pete Rose Way
241-7870

Benny Mandell Produce Inc.
Mehring Way & Plum
381-5411

Caruso-Ciresi
305 W. Pete Rose Way
721-1073

Off-Price

See "Off-Price," page 103, for full descriptions of what Makro and Bigg's have to offer. If you aim to cut corners on your grocery budget, these are fine places to put on your shopping list.

So is Squeri's Cash & Carry Grocery. This retail store in the wholesale district offers deals of the week on such items as five-pound packs of American cheese slices, five-pound bags of chicken nuggets, five-pound presliced cheesecakes, liters of Coca-Cola. Squeri's is operated by the same family who owns the restaurant and institutional food supply business, so this store is an outgrowth of the wholesale operation. Therefore, quantity buys are broken down so that retail customers don't have to buy by the box, but can still save money on industrial sizes, which most supermarkets do not stock.

Look for gallon jars of pickles and other condiments, canned fruits and vegetables, large tins of spices, many types of frozen fish and prepared entrees, loaves of cheese, large packages of muffins, rolls, dessert items, a large selection of paper products. Squeri's has carved out a unique niche for itself in the grocery trade in the city.
Squeri's Cash & Carry
49 Central Ave. (downtown)
579-0044

Health Food

Health food is hot. People who never shopped health food stores before are now regulars as the search for whole grains and organic products intensifies. There are many health food stores in the city. Here are a few favorites you might like to check out.

New World Food Shop & Restaurant has a good variety of packaged and canned food, sells whole grains and beans in bulk, low-sodium products, local cheeses and honey, dried fruit and nuts, macrobiotic foods. Lunch and dinner is served in the restaurant in the rear of the store. This place is also a great information center.
New World Food Shop & Restaurant
347 Ludlow (Clifton)
861-1101

Edibles

Natural Life has nice canned goods, assorted bottled waters, organic fruits and vegetables, frozen foods, a good selection of yogurt and vitamins, offers freshly squeezed veggie juices. The Hyde Park store I visited is light and airy. All the food looked fresh and appetizing.

Natural Life Health Foods
2946 Wasson Rd. (Hyde Park)
631-0300
5073 Glenway Ave. (Price Hill)
251-2901
8182 Beechmont Ave. (Beechmont)
474-4990

Mainstay Baking & Trading Co., besides selling the full line of Mainstay Bread, is a complete health food grocery store. There is a counter of organic fruits and vegetables, much canned goods, a supply of organic eggs, macrobiotic foods, a lot of interesting stock to choose from. The store offers 10% discounts if you join their buying club, offers 15% over wholesale prices for case and large-quantity purchases over $35. See Mainstay's previous listing in this chapter under "Bread" for the address.

Spatz's has a juice bar where you can buy freshly squeezed carrot, celery, orange, and grapefruit juice. If that's your lunch, you can also buy some yogurt, nuts, or raisins to round out your meal. The store has a large selection of vitamins, shelves of interesting canned and packaged food, and staff who are willing to offer good advice.

Spatz Health Foods
607 Main St. (downtown)
621-0347

Cincinnati Natural Foods and Cincinnati Food Emporium (under the same management) carry a complete health food line: yogurt and cheeses, herbs, teas, honey, juices, canned and bulk foods, fresh produce, organic beef and chicken, food to accommodate special diets such as those with no salt and for people with specific allergies.

Cincinnati Natural Foods
7754 Camargo Rd. (Madeira)
271-6766
Cincinnati Food Emporium
9268 Colerain (Northgate)
385-9622

An organic produce market is open on Wednesdays at Wooden Shoe Gardens. See "Fresh Picked and Pick-Your-Own," page 47, for all the particulars.

Americans For Safe Food, a coalition of consumers, environmental and farm groups dedicated to eliminating potentially dangerous pesticides, fumigants, growth promotants, antibiotics, hormones, and additives from American food products, have put together a list of companies and farms from whom you can buy untainted food by mail. So if you want direct-to-you foods: produce, wine, pancake and waffle mixes, lamb, veal, beef, nitrate-free bacon, baked goods, cereal, fruit conserves, dill pickles—a cornucopia of healthy products—write for their catalogue listing food sources, and enclose a stamped, self-addressed, business-size envelope.

Organic Mail Order
Americans For Safe Food
P.O. Box 66300
Washington, DC 20035

Water! Water!

As an alternative to Cincinnati's sometimes controversial and pungent water supply, bottled waters flourish on supermarket and health food store shelves. However, if you want home delivery instead of having to lug containers from the store, these three companies can tend your water supply. Ask about minimum orders, prices, and delivery schedules.

Mountain Valley Water
241-3925

Talawanda Springs
271-1790

New Life Pure Water
734-1177

Sweets

You have a sweet tooth. Well, you're not alone. The city's craving for sugar-spun treats has spawned dozens of dessert bakers and chocolate makers who turn out mouth-watering delicacies daily. From tortes to truffles, double chocolate chip ice cream to homemade caramel-covered popcorn, you'll find all of these specialty sweet makers in this chapter.

This Takes The Cake

Avi Bear, pastry chef and owner of the Truffle Cake, has built an enviable reputation because of the quality of the pastries and cakes he supplies to restaurants and country clubs. These include cakes such as amaretto truffle, pistachio, white chocolate cream, napoleon, and Sacher tortes. Pastries? How about chocolate eclairs, petit fours, lemon squares, apple flans, all sorts of tarts? His confections also include truffles: dark chocolate shells filled with dark chocolate, Grand Marnier flavored ganache coated with dark chocolate; even white chocolate and milk chocolate versions. Cake slices, tarts, and truffles are always available in Avi's store. You can pick them up anytime. However, if you want to order a whole cake, a special birthday cake, or one of Avi's elegant wedding cakes, you must order ahead.

The Truffle Cake
2342 Robertson Ave. (Norwood)
631-4393

At Mullane's in Clifton you can eat slices of their great-looking tortes, tarts, fruit pies, and cakes on the premises, take them home, or order whole pies and cakes ahead. Specialties include a pie with pecans on the bottom, a layer of toffee mocha whipped cream on top just like the kind you used to eat at Mecklenburg's in the good old days. Mullane's makes a great-tasting carrot cake and a dense chocolate cheesecake—wall-to-wall chocolate.

Mullane's in Clifton
308 Ludlow (Clifton)
861-4777

The Bonbonerie supplies a long and luscious list of desserts to restaurants throughout the city, but will accommodate individual orders if customers phone ahead. Chocolate specialties include a chocolate truffle cake containing more than a pound of chocolate, a Toll House torte filled with coffee butter cream, an apricot chocolate torte, dobos torte, and Mississippi Mud—a dark chocolate and coffee flavored confection. In their nonchocoholic category, you can ask for an English lemon cake, a hazelnut torte, a walnut spice cake, five kinds of cheesecake, and multiple miniature pastries, from poppyseed hearts and coconut walnut bars to double-rich brownies and triple meringues.

The Bonbonerie also makes truffles, will whip up just the size cake you specify, can create spectacular wedding cakes. They do not accept drop-in business and there is no retail store, so phone to ask that their dessert list be mailed to you or to place orders. All cakes must be picked up at their Walnut Hills commissary.

The Bonbonerie
1349 E. McMillan (East Walnut Hills)
281-7555

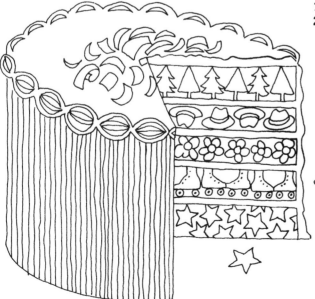

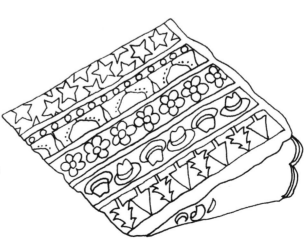

Sweets

12 Besides selling candy- and cake-making supplies, The Party Cake Shop makes wedding cakes that are in great demand. Since the shop will only turn out three cakes per week, when I called the owner in February, he told me the months of June, July, and September were already sold out, though there were a few weeks in August still open. When you go to Party Cake, you select your wedding cake from eighty slides and six display cakes. Bridges, fountains, any fantasy can be constructed. Just make your plans and your reservations well in advance.

The Party Cake Shop
1785 E. Galbraith Rd. (Reading)
821-6161

Cheesecake Please wholesales its creamy cheesecakes to about seventy-five area restaurants, but keeps some in stock in the store for retail customers. Or you can order them ahead. Owners Katie Zipf and Julie Brougher make twenty varieties, from classic to banana split, in five-, seven-, or ten-inch sizes. You can also buy one slice of cheesecake, several, or fill a round cake plate with an assortment—you build your own variety cake. Cheesecake Please makes seasonal cheesecakes—pumpkin in the fall, mint at Christmas—introduces new flavors every month, even makes giant cheesecake wedding cakes, French pastries, and a chocolate mousse pie. The shop will ship its cheesecakes anywhere in the continental U.S.A.

Cheesecake Please
9730 Montgomery Rd. (Montgomery)
791-6105

Susan Hunter of Cheesecake Cheesecake bakes primarily classic ten-inch cheesecakes, as well as chocolate marble, praline, amaretto, and raspberry swirl. If you want a cake in a hurry, she generally has them on hand in the freezer, or phone a week ahead for special orders. She's happy to come up with made-to-order concoctions, will work with groups who want to sell her cakes as a fund-raiser. Phone for details.

Cheesecake Cheesecake
861-CAKE

Blue Chip Cookies whips up thirteen varieties of their popular cookies from chocolate chip and oatmeal raisin to their most popular white chocolate chip macadamia nut. Only natural ingredients are used and no preservatives. Though there are four Blue Chip locations at the present time (check your phone directory for the downtown and mall stores), look for more to open in the future.

Sending telegrams is old hat when you can phone TeleCake's toll-free number and arrange to have a cake delivered anywhere in the country. Birthdays account for the company's biggest volume, but anniversaries, Mother's, Father's, and Valentine's Day are close runners-up. You specify the kind of cake you want, the message, and what the accompanying card should say. They do the rest.

TeleCake
1-800-225-3872

Ice Cream 'n' Candy

Some people say Aglamesis' ices are better than Graeter's, while Graeter's diehards would defend the firm's Grade A ice cream and sherbet status to the end. There's no doubt about it, Graeter's and Aglamesis are firmly entrenched as Cincinnati traditions. And rightly so. They both make fine ice cream and ices with old-world care and pure ingredients. Both Aglamesis and Graeter's make candies as well, so eating your way through their confectionary cases to decide whose chocolates are richer is not such a bad thought. Whoever winds up champion in your book—well, the decision making is the very best part.

Aglamesis Bros.
3046 Madison Rd. (Oakley)
531-5196
9887 Montgomery Rd. (Montgomery)
791-7082

Graeter's
Office and information: 2145 Reading Rd.
(Mt. Auburn)
721-3323
There are a dozen luscious suburban locations. Check your phone directory for the one closest to you.

You love rich, wonderful ice cream and your cholesterol level shows it. An alternative that may satisfy your craving and accommodate your diet is a trip to one of the ''TCBY'' yogurt stores. Known as The Country's Best Yogurt, the product has 96% of the fat removed so sweet lovers can indulge without guilt. There are many flavors, all sorts of specialty items like banana splits, yogwiches (a yogurt and cookie sandwich), yogurt crepes, frozen yogurt pies. For those who must have lactose- and cholesterol-free treats, go for the frozen tofu.

''TCBY'' franchises are opening fast—there will probably be well over a dozen in the Cincinnati area. Check your phone book and look for announcements of new locations.

Bob Schneider worked for the Bissinger Candy Co. for many years before he purchased the business two years ago. In addition, he opened two candy stores he named The Sweet Tooth. Bob makes wonderful, rich chocolates and ice cream he says contain 15% butterfat. His ice cream sauces are homemade, too, but you haven't tasted anything until you've tried one of the chocolates he calls French Nothings. They are definitely something. These cream-filled dark or light chocolate pieces are addictive. But so are his truffles and opera creams and nutballs. Look for specialty chocolate items on all the holidays.

The Sweet Tooth
125 W. 11th (Newport)
581-6763
2929 Dixie Hwy. (Crestview Hills, KY)
331-0883

Bissinger's has been around since 1863 and their reputation for opera creams and nutballs is hard to beat. Since Bob Schneider purchased the company, chocolate quality remains superior. Call the factory at 581-4663 to ask for a catalogue of all Bissinger's confections and to place mail orders. The company's mail-order business is large and they ship candy anywhere in the country. Or just stop in at their retail store in the Carew Tower Arcade.

Bissinger's Candy
Carew Tower Arcade (downtown)
241-0600

Sweets

14 Schneider's Sweet Shop has been making chocolates and ice cream since 1939. Recently, Jack Schneider has taken over the business from his father, but says that opera creams are still their most popular item. Caramels and fudge are close seconds, while sugared jelly candies take over first place in the summer. Ice cream? There are nine homemade flavors.
Schneider's Sweet Shop
420 Fairfield Ave. (Bellevue)
431-3545

Esther Price Candies, rich beyond belief, are made by hand with all natural ingredients and no preservatives. There are twenty dark and light chocolate varieties, hard candies, caramels, even bubble-gum balls. You can buy boxes of assorted chocolate creams at specialty stores and supermarkets throughout Greater Cincinnati, but to get a glimpse of the entire Esther Price line you must visit the store.
Esther Price Candies
7501 Montgomery Rd. (Kenwood)
791-1833

Ethel Brower and her son, Robert, are the duo behind Brower Chocolatier. Their hand-dipped dark and milk chocolates come in two dozen varieties: creams, chocolate-covered fruits and nuts, all sorts of miniatures. Ethel Brower is happy to accommodate special orders for all occasions. She can make chocolate party trays, decorate chocolates with names or flowers, make molded chocolates— bunnies, hearts, tennis racquets, golf balls and clubs, whatever you specify. That these good-tasting and great-looking chocolates are also certified kosher is an added plus if you observe those dietary laws. If you desire, candy can be shipped anywhere in the country. There is free gift wrap and delivery in Greater Cincinnati.
Brower Chocolatier
531-5100

Galerie Au Chocolate stocks handmade French candy well known in Europe and the United States: many varieties of chocolate creams, chocolate-covered nuts, white chocolate, marzipan, seventy-two flavors of jelly beans. Look for specialty items on holidays, from chocolate Valentines to chocolate-filled Christmas ornaments. There are great gift items for chocoholics at this store.
Galerie Au Chocolate
Westin Hotel (downtown)
421-4466

Want a molded chocolate basket filled with candy, or a chocolate plate on which you can arrange a chocolate candy assortment? Eat the chocolate pieces, then the container. Sounds good to me. The Confection Connection specializes in these kinds of candy creations. Names in chocolate, numbers, flowers, a foot-long tennis racquet—they'll make whatever you desire. This candy is kosher and parve.
The Confection Connection
Sheila Gelfand
791-2255
Jo Ann Singer
931-7279

Executive Sweets has eighty to one hundred chocolate figures to choose from, will even make corporate logos in chocolate. Other specialties include homemade peanut brittle, coconut brittle, fudge, and Oreo bark.
Executive Sweets
119 W. Convention Way (Skywalk)
621-5026

I Can Get It For You Wholesale

Just imagine wall-to-wall, floor-to-ceiling boxes of Hershey bars, Mounds bars, Chuckles, Reese's Cups, Good and Plentys, Charleston Chews. Stop drooling. Head for a candy wholesaler, a business that supplies concession stands and small independent dealers but who will also sell to you as long as you buy by the box (some contain thirty-six or twenty-four bars). You can also buy gum at candy wholesalers, as well as boxes of football and baseball cards, cough drops, mints, and in some places, jars of cocktail cherries, flavorings, syrups, peanuts, and cans of fruit juice. At some warehouses you'll find old-fashioned candy you haven't seen in years, like candy dots on paper strips, wax lips and moustaches, Mary Janes. Look for bags of penny candies and little novelty items. Definitely keep these wholesalers in mind at Halloween or when you need party favors, even birthday gifts. You can save money at these places if you can use the quantity. The following three wholesalers happily sell to retail customers.

George Hengehold & Son
1239 Ellis (Northside)
541-8831

Hussel Candies
4714 Vine St. (St. Bernard)
641-3333

Peter Minges & Son
138 W. Court St. (downtown)
241-7376

Popcorn! Peanuts!

Peanuts, pecans, cashews, blanched and unblanched almonds, filberts—find a case of good-looking nuts and nut mixes at the Jansen Nut Co. You can buy salted and unsalted varieties, beautiful dried fruit. Close your eyes when you walk past the fudge, peanut brittle, and other sugary goodies.

Jansen Nut Co.
608 Main St. (downtown)
421-3453

Follow the popcorn aroma down Walnut St. to Walnut St. Popcorn & Sweets. Adele Gutterman and her son Hiram pop fresh corn constantly to fill the cases with all varieties of homemade popcorn such as cheese popcorn smothered with real cheese, not a synthetic powder, and caramel popcorn covered with a creamy essence. Buy a bag of caramel and cheese corn tossed together. It's a sweet and salty specialty Adele says is the rage in Chicago. In fact, popcorn stores are extremely popular in Chicago, and she hopes the idea of a specialty store of this kind will become a staple in Cincinnati. There are all sorts of popcorn varieties at Walnut St. Popcorn & Sweets, even healthiest air-popped corn that contains no oil or salt. You can't miss the homemade fudge and peanut brittle—it's on the shelf right below the cash register. Ask Adele about the caramel apples she makes to order. Choose a cute gift container in the shop and have it filled with any kind of popcorn. Adele will deliver it anywhere in the city or ship it anywhere in the country. She makes many popcorn gift runs to hospitals these days, and business soars around Super Bowl time.

Walnut St. Popcorn & Sweets
637 Walnut St. (downtown)
651-0707

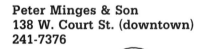

Sweets

16 Why do you see flight attendants and airline pilots rush off planes when they make a stop in Cincinnati? Why do you see them get back on board carrying bags of freshly popped corn or containers of kernels? The Queen City Country Stores, in the three Greater Cincinnati Airport terminals, are the reason. Word is out about the superior fluffy quality of the popcorn they sell. Travelers make it a point to visit the shops. People picking up arriving guests often pick up popcorn as well. Now you can, too.

The Queen City Country Store
Greater Cincinnati International Airport
283-3188

You like to pop your own corn, so much of it you want to purchase it in quantity. Go to Gold Medal Products. This manufacturer of popcorn machines also sells popcorn-making supplies. The smallest size bag of kernels you can buy is a twelve-and-a-half-pound bag or a case containing thirty-six six-ounce preportioned packs. This is good-quality popping corn priced much lower than what you'll find at the supermarkets. Gold Medal also manufactures Flavacol, a yellow-colored butter-flavored salt that you may want to sprinkle on your popcorn. But if you just like to eat popcorn, not bother with popping it, buy a giant bag of already popped corn at Gold Medal. This twenty-two-ounce quantity should serve twenty-two people, and the cost is only $1.50.

Gold Medal's popcorn machines come in all sizes. Some are the size used at Riverfront Stadium. But a superior small model many people are now purchasing for home and office use is the P60—ask for Gold Medal's catalogue. It's 16 x 18 x 28 inches in size, pops six ounces of popcorn every three minutes, and has a warming cabinet to keep popcorn fresh until the next day. This dandy machine costs $439.

Gold Medal Products
2001 Dalton (Queensgate)
381-1313

Concession Specialties' main business is supplying concessions at fairs and schools, but party givers can get a good price break on bulk purchases here. You can buy already popped popcorn in ten-ounce to two-pound bags or order it ahead in any quantity you wish—plain, buttered, cheese-flavored, or caramel. Buy popcorn kernels in four- or ten-and-a-half-pound tubs as well as snow cone syrups, drink bases, concession paper products.

Concession Specialties
9799 Princeton Pk. (north of Tri-County)
874-4360

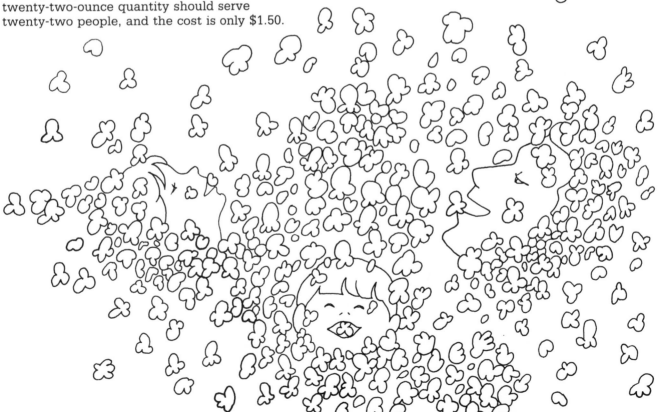

Wearables

Whether you dress for success, for "today's look," for casual comfort, or just for fun, I couldn't attempt to chip away at the long list of clothing stores in the city. But if your taste runs to classic styles, you're probably a dyed-in-the-wool Brooks Brothers-Jos. A. Bank shopper already. You pick up Shetland sweaters, oxford-cloth button-down collar shirts, poplin slacks at the stores lining Hyde Park Square and on the streets that surround it. If you're a big-time spender, you may be a Gidding-Jenny fan. You shop at Saks, Henry Harris, have favorite departments at L.S. Ayres, Lazarus, McAlpin's, and suburban specialty shops. You know about these! So what I've done is pull some clothes alternatives out of the closet: where to have clothes custom made, the best vintage shops, where to buy work clothes and novel accessories; I've investigated consignment shops, off-price markets, clothes for small fry—so you can add all of these to your wardrobe know-how.

Off-Price

There are half a dozen or so off-price clothes stores that fashion-conscious men and women depend on. These are the places that stock great designer names on an everyday basis and are the ones I've included in this section.

Who shops at Loehmann's? Women who love good clothes at bargain prices. Just look around at what the customers in the store are wearing and you'll see how they put together such great outfits. They shop other stores first so they can recognize Loehmann's label-less gems, often band together in the aisles asking each other, "Whose jacket do you think this is?" or "That's a Ralph Lauren—I saw it at Saks." Loehmann's breeds camaraderie, especially in its communal dressing rooms. This place is not for the meek or the modest. And having fashion imagination is a decided plus. Sometimes you can find whole outfits; often bits and pieces are strung out on several racks. Maybe you'll have to wait until your next trip to find a sweater to match your slacks. Still, Loehmann's is addictive. Stalking Trigeres, the Kleins—Anne and Calvin—Escada, Dior at the Tiffany's of discounters can be habit forming. Oh yes, bring cash or checks when you go shopping. No credit cards are accepted at Loehmann's, nor are returns allowed.
Loehmann's
11974 Lebanon Rd. (Sharonville)
563-4111
Union Terminal
579-9900
This location may change in 1988.

Value City Department Stores buy clothes from manufacturers and department stores that are clearing out merchandise or are having financial trouble, announce the big buy-outs in the newspapers, and expect customers to jam the store. The owners are never disappointed. I've seen people try on clothes in the aisles when free dressing rooms became scarce. On the other hand, on some occasions when you shop Value City, you may find little that entices you. Still, always look for big-name clothes and shoes for men, women, and children. Remember the day you came upon a table piled high with cashmere sweaters priced just right? That alone will bring you back for more. Check your phone directory for locations.

T.J. Maxx has tables loaded with great-looking socks and underwear. These stores are among the best places in town to buy blouses, skirts, T-shirts, and sweaters for men, women, and children at terrific prices. Don't overlook the racks of robes, slacks, and jeans either. There are always designer names at small prices in these sections. Check your phone book for the store nearest you.

Wearables

The Burlington Coat Factory Outlet has such an extensive selection of coats—moderate-priced labels to snob-appeal designer fashions—that many people shop here first when they need anything in outerwear. Besides coats for men, women, and children, Burlington has a large selection of clothing: undergarments, separates, dressy clothes, sports jackets, shirts, sweaters, shoes, ties, and purses. The day the Fendi bags arrived, there was a stampede.

Burlington Coat Factory Outlet
485 E. Kemper Rd. (Springdale)
671-3111

Hit or Miss has women's clothes: jeans, slacks, sweaters, blouses, dresses, and coats. Expect brands such as Guess?, Liz Claiborne, sometimes Tahari and Christian Dior as well as many others. Look in the phone book for their downtown and suburban mall locations.

The Gentry Shops buy out top-label designer menswear—conservative and more fashionable styles. This is the place many young men fresh out of college come to suit up for their first jobs. There is always a good selection of shirts, ties, sweaters, blazers, sports jackets, suits, topcoats, and all sorts of accessories. The huge inventory changes constantly.

Gentry Shops
11489 Princeton Rd. (Tricentre)
772-3000
6485 E. Galbraith Rd. (Kenwood)
791-9800

The Mill Outlet is the factory outlet for Palm Beach clothes but also sells Austin Hill, Evan Picone, and other brands for men, women, and young boys. Belts, shoes, shirts, sweaters, and many other accessories are generally in stock. Plans are for this popular operation to move to 6th and Washington Streets in Newport by March of 1988. Other factory outlet stores will be located in the same complex. Watch for details.

The Mill Outlet
5th & Washington (Newport)
581-7666

The Men's Clothing Outlet buys first-quality overruns from manufacturers of men's suits, slacks, and sports coats. It's no coincidence the outlet is located in the Dixie Terminal Building right in the midst of so many high-quality men's retail stores. Shop the outlet and you'll see a striking resemblance to store fashions at about half the price.

Men's Clothing Outlet, Inc.
4th & Walnut (Dixie Terminal Bldg., downtown)
579-0033

Best Buys owner Eileen Magenheim buys women's brands such as Skyr, Harvé Benard, and many others, then discounts them 30% to 40%. She has suits, blazers, sweaters, skirts, slacks, many knits—all current merchandise. If you need contemporary sportswear or office clothes at a good price, see Eileen. She gives much personal service, always tries to help you find what you need.

Best Buys
2221 Losantiville Rd. (Golf Manor)
631-6122

The only Gap outlet in the country is located at the company's major distribution center in Erlanger, Kentucky. It's full of men's, women's, and children's irregular clothing, damaged and returned merchandise that flows into the store daily. Some merchandise is off season, but a good part of it is current. So if you love the Gap sportswear look, find it at half price at the outlet, but note, clothes disappear as fast as the store is replenished.

Gap Distribution Center
3434 Mineola Pk. (Erlanger)
283-1100

Hot Stuff

Soft leather slacks and jackets, creamy cashmere sweat suits, flouncy silk dresses, the latest skinny French jeans, European-style suits, supple shoes—find one of the best selections of up-to-the-minute men's and women's clothing at Rags 2 Riches. If you want a sensational dress for a party or nifty daytime casual clothes, these shops have it. Owner Jerry Lauch has a great eye for fashion and stocks his stores with a fine collection. Besides, he and his staff offer good personal service. If you've gone to New York to buy clothes in the past because Cincinnati shops "just don't have what you like," stop off at Rags before you buy a plane ticket to Manhattan.

Rags 2 Riches
Kenwood Towne Centre
793-8060
2728 Vine St. (Corryville)
861-8067

The Looking Glass recently opened a few doors away from Rags 2 Riches in Corryville—and is it welcome! The store has dresses with style, snappy slacks, tops, and shirts, sweaters, blouses, good-quality clothes with flair. There are leather belts with artsy buckles, all sorts of unusual earrings and scarves, small purses and industrial-strength carryalls.

The Looking Glass
2722 Vine St. (Corryville)
861-7333

Walk down Vine St. a little further and pop into Diamond Lil's. You can pick up a rainbow variety of T-shirts at nice prices, pants to match, some knit dresses, fun cotton play clothes, interesting earrings. This is a nice store to check out.

Diamond Lil's
2702 Vine St. (Corryville)
861-4040

Keep walking down Vine. You can't miss Scentiments. This store is the princess of punk and funk. T-shirts sport monster faces, rock groups—whatever or whoever is "in." You can buy pink, yellow, or red pointy-toed high-top gym shoes, turquoise loafers, sunglasses shaped like cats' eyes, yellow, purple, gold, or orange mascara. This store always stocks ahead-of-the-trend stuff, at least it's ahead of the trend in Cincinnati.

Scentiments
2614 Vine St. (Corryville)
281-1667

Alyson Warner's two shops have clothes women look good in and feel comfortable wearing. From cashmere two-piece outfits (skirts and tops, slacks and tops), 100% cotton knit sportswear, all sorts of jackets, T-shirts, and belts—you can put together an entire easy-to-wear wardrobe. Alyson's clothes make fine travel partners. They do not rumple on the plane, you can work in them all day, and by evening you still look fresh. Ask Alyson what's new in the store. She or one of her managers will start pulling pieces off the racks to get you together. "Tuck it in." "Wear this pulled out." "Take it off—that doesn't look right." These days, it's nice to shop where people still take time to care.

Alyson's: Comfort and Style in Clothing
2727 Erie Ave. (Hyde Park Square)
321-7767
9416 Montgomery Rd. (Montgomery)
891-7767

Benetton means sweaters, slacks, T-shirts, and dresses—every color under the sun for men and women. Benetton clothes are hot, and this Italian-based operation's franchised stores have swept the country. Presently, there are three in Cincinnati.

Benetton
39 W. 5th St. (downtown)
421-0899
Tri-County Mall
671-6553
Kenwood Towne Centre
793-7114

The Limited stores are as upbeat as the music that blasts through these busy places. Designers like Kenzo and Krizia who create lines especially for The Limited chain have set the "current fashion at moderate price" tone that women applaud. Always check the bulging sale racks; prices are constantly reduced. Consult the phone directory for The Limited's downtown and many mall locations.

Men who want sizzling stuff shop at Dino's. European tailoring, imported fabrics—these clothes make a fashion statement.

Dino's For Men
6th & Race (downtown)
421-5692
Tri-County Mall
671-1800

Wearables

20 **Custom Creations**

You want classic suits and shirts custom tailored especially for you. You want to pick the fabric, the style, and you don't mind paying the price for good-quality garments. The following establishments can accommodate your taste. Some will even accommodate your busy schedule. Staff will bring fabric swatches, take measurements at your home or office. Finished garments are delivered a few weeks later. Nice touch!

Fittings
105 E. 4th St. (downtown)
421-2929

Mike Trotta Tailors
406 Walnut St. (downtown)
621-2930

Brooks Brothers
100 E. 4th St. (downtown)
651-1800

Burkhardt's
8 E. 4th St. (downtown)
421-7100

Custom Shop Shirtmakers
43 E. 4th St. (downtown)
621-4052

DiPilla Custom Tailors
37 E. 7th St. (downtown)
721-3601

Frank Stavale
27 E. Court St. (downtown)
421-2061

Arslan Custom Tailoring
809 Sycamore (downtown)
621-8136

Santoro Aldo Tailoring Shop
3438 Edwards Rd. (Hyde Park)
871-3160

The following master craftswomen stitch up more individual feminine looks.

Mei Chi creates her own designs, can copy anything you bring in, can make whatever you fancy from her stock of beautiful imported natural-fiber fabrics, and also does alterations. She makes wedding dresses, but call far in advance for an occasion this important.
Mei Chi's Creations
7690 Camargo Rd. (Madeira)
561-8200

Ute Ingmann designs and hand knits one-of-a-kind Missoni-quality sweaters. You look through her books of designs or describe what you want and she'll make a pattern. Pick yarn from her imported samples or Ute will buy yarn for you when she goes to Europe.
Ute Ingmann
779-2371

Mary Fisher (see "Handiest People in Town," page 55, for her antique dress restoration abilities) can make beautiful antique-looking clothes: simple daytime cotton dresses, intricate dresses for vintage dances, all sorts of street clothes, wedding dresses, children's clothing that looks like it's straight from the pages of Mother Goose. Give Mary an idea; she'll design the dress. But listen to her ideas— they're wonderful.
Mary Fisher
491-6746

Jennifer Gleason (see "Handiest People in Town," page 55, for information on her antique garment restoration) makes all sorts of interesting apparel. If a bride decides to wear an antique wedding gown, Jennifer can make camisoles, petticoats, headwear to fit the period of the dress. She can design and make bridesmaids' dresses that are simpatico companions. One of Jennifer's specialties is making reproduction antique dresses, but she can stitch coats, evening wear, any kind of daytime clothes. She's a talented artist.
Jennifer Gleason
431-1974

The Custom Clothes Collection is sold through two private home showings per year by company representatives. You go to the showing, look at sample garments—mostly conservative-looking mix-and-match separates—and then pick out the 100% cotton fabrics you'd like the clothes made in according to your measurements. Phone any of these area representatives and ask to be placed on their mailing list so you will be notified when showings are scheduled.

Custom Clothes Collection
Sherre Johnson (Montgomery)
984-3446
Sue Newman (Hyde Park)
321-2142
Suzanne Lakamp (Terrace Park)
831-6111

Vintage Clothes

You can find a rack or two of antique clothes in many shops in town, but the following stores are the core group with the largest selection. Note, if you love vintage wearables, be glad you're buying them in Middle America. Compare Cincinnati prices to those on the east and west coasts and you'll consider yourself lucky. That's why out-of-town dealers shop here regularly.

Down Town Nostalgic carries men's and women's clothes from the 1920s to the funky '50s. Look for suits, jackets (dig the tweeds with the big shoulders), overcoats, all colors of gloves in leather, lace, and cloth, socks, anklets, purses (beaded evening bags to clutches), shirts (Hawaiian to tuxedo), vests, hats (fedoras to sweet little pillboxes with veils), nightgowns, evening dresses, super costume jewelry, and shoes. The store is always filled with wonderful wearables.

Down Town Nostalgic
119 Calhoun (Clifton)
861-9336

I am impressed with Garbo's selection. In the men's section, I spotted '30s cashmere and alpaca overcoats, wonderfully tailored suits and jackets. Women's clothes run the gamut from slinky '20s gowns to Joan Crawford-style '40s suits. This store is packed with merchandise at especially fair prices. Their collection of costume jewelry is outstanding, and the word is out about the rhinestone numbers—dealers regularly sweep through the store. Notice Garbo's purses, accessories, undergarments, too. People who are serious about vintagewear always check out this store.

Note: Garbo's collection of beautiful old Victorian whites, lawn dresses, nightgowns, pillow shams, all sorts of lace and linens—everything that looks perfect with white wicker furniture, has moved to a special shop called Pavlova's Lace a few doors down the street. Don't miss it.

Garbo's
641 Main St. (Covington)
291-9023

Pavlova's Lace
520 Main St. (Covington)
291-9023

Sandy Clo of Wearable Heirlooms has a superb selection of Victorian, Edwardian, and '20s clothing and linens. She does a big wedding business with customers who want to wear garden-party dresses instead of contemporary wedding gowns. Sandy has lovely table and bed linens, quilts, lace curtains, silver dresser sets, boudoir items, accessories such as hats, shoes, purses, and gloves. Her stock is mint condition, and top quality.

Wearable Heirlooms
1006 Delta Ave. (Mt. Lookout)
871-3544

The Way We Were has nearly new and vintage clothes: '40s suits, blouses, skirts, dresses, slacks, bunches of hats and shoes, lots of old bow ties men can wear with their suits but women snap up to tie in their hair.

The Way We Were
3540 Columbia Pkwy. (Tusculum)
871-9068

Wearables

22   Government Surplus and Work Clothes

Many companies rent work clothes and uniforms for their employees: pants and shirts, lab coats, supermarket checkers' smocks, gas station attendant jackets, even blazers and dress shirts. When these clothes are retired, the rental company sells them to retailers who grade the garments and price them according to their category and condition. There are several stores in Cincinnati where you can buy these handy, bottom-priced clothes, which are perfect to wear when you're doing messy chores around the house. Some clothes have patches and stains, others are in fine shape. Some must be bought in bundles, others can be purchased singly. Besides shirts and pants, look for all sorts of work gloves, coveralls, cooks' white pants, already broken-in blue jeans. Send these clothes to camp with your kids. High school and college students love the look of garage-mechanic chic. Maybe you will, too.

Surplus Work Clothes
4553 Montgomery Rd. (Norwood)
631-2746

Three L Sales
9004 Blue Ash Rd. (Blue Ash)
984-5185

Work Clothes Discount Center
4034 Hamilton Ave. (Northside)
541-8700

Fechheimer Bros. Co. is a uniform manufacturer. Customers include the U.S. Postal Service, bus companies, police and sheriff's departments, and many others. Their factory outlet store, in a corner of the manufacturing plant, is where you can pick up seconds, overruns, and discontinued styles: jackets made to keep Forest Service employees warm, police officer's heavy-duty jackets, blue post-office sweaters, sheriff's blazers and slacks, baseball-style caps favored by some police departments, quilted jacket liners, work shoes—racks of well-made, heavy-duty clothes at great prices.

Fechheimer Bros. Co.
4545 Malsbary Rd. (Blue Ash)
793-5400

The Government Surplus Depot has one of the best selections of military clothes and bags I've seen in any store of this kind. Owners Gerald and Beverly Tonkens have a knack for turning armed forces gear into high-fashion apparel, and they buy surplus from every army in the world. Look for beautiful English sweaters, khaki drill pants with a multitude of pockets (see them copied in all the preppy catalogues), pea jackets, leather flight jackets, all sorts of handsome bags that can be used as flight bags, carryalls, or purses. Stock always changes, so if you are searching for a place to buy well-made, heavy-duty clothes that are also chic, make periodic stops here.

Government Surplus Depot
4031 Hamilton Ave. (Northside)
541-8700

GIJ Surplus has military clothes, from navy bell bottoms and pea coats to army shirts and bush jackets. They stock all sorts of boots, hammocks, backpacks, sleeping bags, and army cots you might find handy when all your relatives come to visit. Look for trunks (convenient for sending a kid off to camp or college with) that can double as a coffee or end table in a dorm room or sparsely furnished apartment.

GIJ Surplus
1200 Race St. (downtown)
621-5043

The Army Store in Fairfield sells military gear—coats, jackets, hats, pants, shirts, rain suits, trunks, hammocks, canteens—as well as nonmilitary merchandise such as gym and soccer shoes.

Army Store
4838 Factory Dr. (Fairfield)
829-7888

The Army Store in Covington sells American and foreign military clothing as well as trunks, hammocks, sleeping bags, and backpacks. Work boots and shoes are a specialty—military and civilian.

Army Store
508 Madison Ave. (Covington)
261-0184

Accessories and Glitz

Does wearing dressed-up sweats on a Saturday night sound like your style? Well, phone Terry Hiett of Sweet Sweats to have some custom designed. Terry transforms plain sweats into one-of-a-kinds with paint, glitter, and lamé appliqués. She'll cut off the sleeves and add studs, make dolman sleeves or cowl necks. Terry takes on denim, too. She'll stud pants and tops any way you like, will even apply sequins, lace, rhinestones, and pearls to white tennis shoes. That's really stepping out. Phone her to see samples and to discuss your special order.

Sweet Sweats
891-7226

Sweats is what Beth Kerstein sells at Beth's Body Shop—those decorated with silver lamé, studded with stones, hand printed with silver designs. Beth sells T-shirts, sweaters, skirts, hair accessories like the ones you see at Bendel's in New York and earrings like the playful kind at the Ylang Ylang stores. Phone Beth for an appointment to see her stock.

Beth's Body Shop
489-6665

Get in touch with Eileen Chalfie and Nancy Wolf of Trends if you're looking for hair accessories. They have deco-looking barrettes and combs, some decorated with semiprecious stones, some handsome plain ones. They have one-of-a-kind belts, scarves that can double as belts, especially the woven ones, a variety of handbags. All merchandise is priced 20% to 35% lower than the retail stores (Bloomingdale's, Bergdorf's) that carry the same stock.

Talk to Eileen and Nancy about bringing their merchandise to your home if you organize a group or make an appointment to see the accessories on your own. They'll also do benefits for charitable organizations.

Trends
Eileen Chalfie
522-7272
Nancy Wolf
531-3443

High-fashion handbags at a 20% discount: metallics, pastels, some made of denim, some decorated with fringe, big shoulder purses, small cocktail clutches—phone Patsy Kohn and Harriet Adams of Accessories Plus to see their collection.

Accessories Plus
Patsy Kohn
891-8856
Harriet Adams
793-8877

Try finding a swimsuit out of season and you'll weave your way through most shops in town and wind up empty-handed. A good place to know about is the One Stop Bra and Swim Shoppe. Women's swimwear (sizes 6 to 46), beach cover-ups, and every hard-to-find undergarment imaginable (bra sizes go up to 52DD) are stocked all year long. Breast prostheses and mastectomy bras are a specialty here, as well as largest-size heavy-duty corsets—the old-fashioned lace-up, hook-up ones and a wide range of less restricting types. One of the best features of this store is the care and privacy in which garments are fitted. You may even ask for alterations and place special orders.

One Stop Bra and Swim Shoppe
9217 Reading Rd. (Reading)
769-6020

Wearables

Men's hats—conservative executive types, wide brims, narrow brims, cowboy hats, wool caps, leather caps—headwear to suit any man's taste is stocked at Batsakes. You pick a likely candidate and the salesperson will make sure it fits. If it doesn't, he'll make adjustments, block it, and put your initials inside—free and while you wait. Maybe you'll want to hop up on one of the chairs along the wall and have your shoes shined till your hat's ready. Batsakes is also the place to bring your hat to be cleaned should a bird decide to use it for target practice. They'll restore it so that it will be as good as new.

J&G Batsakes
605 Walnut St. (downtown)
721-4030

For more accessories—socks, purses, wallets, scarves, belts—be sure to check out Value City, T.J. Maxx, Loehmann's, and Burlington.

Shoes

If you want a few alternatives to your favorite shoe stores, try your luck at these discount shoe supermarkets.

Foot Wear House, located in a former Thriftway store, is operated by the same company that leases the shoe departments in all the Value City stores, so you know what kind of merchandise to expect if you go there. If you're a Value City fan, you'll love Foot Wear House. The store has voluminous quantity—many buy-outs from department stores with labels still attached, buy-outs from manufacturers, much imported merchandise—a good percentage of which is from Brazil. Brands run the gamut from modest to high-priced. When cases of new shoes arrive each week, some store merchandise is piled on tables and reduced. That's when you'll see the $7 specials.

Foot Wear House
7990 Reading Rd. (Roselawn)
821-3388

The Shoe Market stores are outlets for U.S. Shoe merchandise plus buy-outs from other manufacturers. You'll see brands such as Pappagallo, Selby, Aigner, Bandolino, 9 West, LJ Simone, many others. Some merchandise is current, some from last season. To figure out prices, look for the color of the dot on the bottom of the pair of shoes you are considering and match it to the price chart on the wall.

The Shoe Market
Valley Center (Roselawn)
761-7644
11439 Princeton Rd. (Tricentre)
772-6757

People who have liberated their feet from constricting styles have worn Birkenstock sandals for years. These are made of elastic cork molded to simulate the contour of a footprint, and the surface not only supports your arch, but also gives your toes the room to grip downward with every step. I've found these shoes at two stores in Cincinnati: New World Bookshop, which sells Birkenstocks along with their books, and The Natural Shoe Store, which sells all varieties of comfortable shoes for daily wear and for heavy-duty walking.

New World Bookshop
336 Ludlow (Clifton)
861-6100

The Natural Shoe Store
2610 Vine St. (Corryville)
281-6464

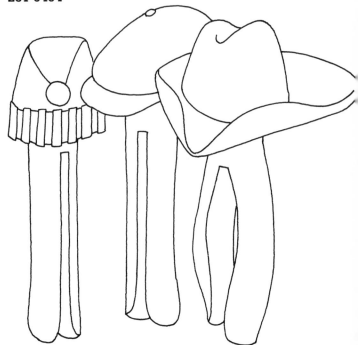

Where do Ground Grippers come from—sensible, low-heeled, lace-up shoes in a variety of styles and sizes that are favorites with men and women with hard-to-fit feet? Try Holzman's Shoe Store.

Holzman's Ground Gripper-Cantilever Shoe Store
4th & Walnut (Dixie Terminal Bldg., downtown)
621-0185

What do you do if you're a woman who needs a size 13AAAA shoe? You shop at Extremes, which thankfully stocks high-fashion brands such as Vanderbilt, Golo, Sebago, and others. All the salespeople at this shop wear at least a size 9 or above, so they understand what women go through to buy large-size shoes.

Extremes
435 Elm St. (Convention Place Mall)
241-4646

Second Time Around

Consignment shops are great places to recycle your clothing, especially children's expensive overcoats and party clothes that are barely worn before they're outgrown. Take garments you want to clear from your closets to the shops listed below, but ask what the consignor/consignee split will be, how long clothes will be kept on the floor, what kind of clothes they especially want, and in what condition they must be. These questions will save you time and maybe a fruitless trip. Check out the clothes for sale at these places, too. You may come away with more than you brought.

Snooty Fox operates the leading consignment shops in the city—they accept only top-quality men's, women's, and children's merchandise. You'll find labels from all the big designers and best-quality stores. Snooty Fox now has five locations. Check the phone book for the one nearest you.

Act II Boutique takes women's and children's clothing and accessories: hats, purses, scarves, gloves, and shoes. Name brands and more modest ones stock this shop.

Act II Boutique
104 Main St. (Milford)
831-2445
9303 Cincinnati-Columbus Rd. (West Chester)
779-9520

Secondhand Rose accepts men's, women's, and children's contemporary clothing and accessories as well as vintage garments. See "Dress-Ups," page 153, for addresses and phone numbers.

Strike Two will accept women's clothes that are less than two years old as well as jewelry, belts, robes, shoes, and other accessories.

Strike Two
9429 Montgomery Rd. (Montgomery)
984-0470
309 E. Sharon Rd. (Glendale)
771-3982

Second Avenue is upstairs from Strike Two. It is a children's and maternity clothes consignment shop that also accepts toys, shoes, car seats, and crib sheets. You can find basic brands to designer lines.

Second Avenue
9429 Montgomery Rd. (Montgomery)
791-8055

Peacock accepts high-quality men's, women's, and children's clothing—casual to dressy styles—shoes, jewelry, scarves, and other accessories.

Peacock
3048 Madison Rd. (Oakley)
396-6464

Designer Dress Days, a spectacular once-a-year dress sale sponsored by the National Council of Jewish Women, is a two-day event held in late October or early November at locations that can change yearly. Thousands of gently worn, nearly new men's, women's, and children's clothes—coats, evening gowns, suits, sweaters, slacks, shoes, furs, all sorts of wonders—are sold for one third to one half off their original prices. This sale draws loyal crowds who wait for this premier sale to fill their closets. Watch the newspapers for Designer Dress Days announcements or phone the Council office for information.

Designer Dress Days
National Council of Jewish Women
631-2537

Wearables

When Mr. Tuxedo retires his rental tuxes, the shop has a sale usually held at the end of June or beginning of July. That's when men and boys can pick up classic black tuxes for about $135, shirts for $15 to $18, and ties for $5 to $8. Band members, bartenders, caterers, anyone who needs formal attire for work or play looks forward to this sale, which is never advertised. Call to find out when it is scheduled.

Mr. Tuxedo
109 W. McMillan St. (Clifton)
281-2400

The Seven Hills Clothing Exchange has a full line of furniture (see "Then and Again," page 111) but is one of the best places to pick up barely worn preppy clothing. Many are retired Brooks Brothers numbers: suits, ties, shirts, cashmere sweaters. There are evening gowns, daytime dresses, separates, all sorts of shoes and accessories. This place has blue-chip stock.

The Seven Hills Clothing Exchange
5466 Red Bank Rd. (Madisonville)
271-7977

Kidswear

Castle House is one of the best children's clothing shops in the city. From infants' to preteen sizes, this shop carries the finest lines of classic and contemporary-look clothes. Whether you need a traditional Eton suit or want Guess? jeans for your baby, Castle House has them. The shop has a Goofy Sale twice a year when merchandise is priced 25% to 75% off and the place is packed. Get on the mailing list for advance sale notification.

Castle House
3435 Edwards Rd. (Hyde Park)
871-2458

Chatterlings is as popular with mothers as Castle House. Traditional to trendy looks, this department store for kids can outfit children from head to toe. All the bright star brands are here. Chatterlings' twice-a-year sales, when merchandise is half price, are popular events.

Chatterlings
9420 Montgomery Rd. (Montgomery)
984-2520

French Frogs was located on 4th St., downtown, may open another retail shop in the future, but for now is a mail-order business selling darling 100% French cotton clothing with a classic European look. There are twenty-seven colors of one-piece stretch suits for infants up to size 4, twenty-seven different colors of turtlenecks and jogging pants. French Frogs also sells dresses, playwear, and accessories. Write or phone owner Elizabeth Bieser for her complete catalogue.

French Frogs
719 Park Ave.
Cincinnati, OH 45174
248-1318

The Lilac Bush clothing has a traditional look, much of which is decorated with appliqués and monograms. Play to party clothes, there's a good selection for infants through children's size 14.

The Lilac Bush
9901 Montgomery Rd. (Montgomery)
791-4555

Kiddieland carries high-fashion, trendy-look play and dressy clothes, coats, underwear, and sleepwear. Notice all the pictures of celebrities who shop here on the wall.

Kiddieland
9 W. 6th St. (downtown)
721-1662

Margie Meyer and Meryl Juran, the owners of M & M's, sell their French and Italian lines of "adult clothes for children" through five hotel sales a year, and by appointment. Kids wearing these outfits look just as sizzling as Mom and Dad. M & M's prices are generally half of retail, but are marked down to 70% off at the end of each season. Phone M & M's to see when the next sale is scheduled or to set up a date to see the lines on your own.

M & M's
Margie Meyer
984-2345
Meryl Juran
489-3532

Fantasia has traditional and contemporary-look clothes, moderate to high-quality lines.
Fantasia
2115 Beechmont Ave. (Mt. Washington)
231-7178

The Parisian stocks a complete line of boys' clothing with an especially good supply of husky sizes. The shop also specializes in fitting clothes for handicapped boys. For example, they will remove the buttons on a coat and put on Velcro closings, pad one hip to make it the same size as the other, shorten one sleeve of a shirt or one leg of a pair of pants. Good to know about!
The Parisian
40 Pike St. (Covington)
291-6191

At Littles you can find play and dressy clothes—infants' to girls' and boys' size 14. Store personnel say their markup is less than other retail stores—check it out. Also look at their great selection of accessories: hair bands and bows, jewelry, belts, purses, hats, socks, watches. These make terrific stocking stuffers at Christmas.
Littles
Bigg's Place Mall
752-0042

The Children's Outlet has a large stock of children's wear, from infants' sizes to bigger kids' clothes. I saw lots of Health-Tex and Oshkosh—compare prices to other stores to see what you're saving.
The Children's Outlet
Outlets, Ltd. (Kings Island)
398-0566

Polly Flinders manufactures hand-smocked dresses, tiny to girls' sizes, which are sold in retail stores throughout the country, and at their two local factory outlet stores. Besides racks filled with dresses, you'll find robes, sweaters, underwear, leotards, baby shoes, a table piled with dress fabric—prints, flowers, plaids, lace, and eyelet.
Polly Flinders Factory Outlet
234 E. 8th St. (downtown)
621-3222
2430 E. Kemper Rd. (Shapely Outlet Center)
771-7414

Kid's Mart has two huge stores filled with well-priced children's clothes—brands such as Health-Tex, Billy the Kid, their own house brand.
Kid's Mart
Hyde Park Plaza
321-8311
6180 Glenway Ave. (Westwood)
481-6565

Don't forget Value City, T.J. Maxx, and Burlington for kids' clothes. Check your phone book for addresses and phone numbers.

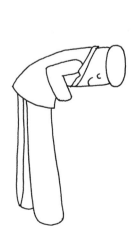

Furniture and Accessories

Everyone has his own special taste in furniture, and luckily there are many stores where you can find just the styles you like. From Contemporary Galleries' high-quality contemporary lines to Closson's blue-ribbon wide variety, these are the stores you already know about (or will soon discover if you're a newcomer) without any prompting from me. So I've tried to come up with places you may not find in your everyday travels that are chock-full of interesting bits and pieces to feather your nest.

Previously Rented

Americans are mobile. And because many companies transfer employees from one city to another after a short period of time, people are often forced to pare down acquisitions. One way is to rent furniture rather than bear the expense and burden of hauling it from place to place. Companies that rent furniture to people take it back when the rental period is over and sell it for less than half its original retail price. Most often the furniture is traditional contemporary brands—standard styles—for it must be plain enough to appeal to a variety of tastes. But if you're looking for a couch, upholstered chairs, coffee tables, lamps, desks, breakfast tables and chairs—warehouses selling previously rented furniture are great places to buy staples.

Don't let office-furniture rental companies escape your eagle eye either. Many have all sorts of desks, upholstered chairs, couches, tables, lamps, and other accessories that might be perfect for your home. Some also sell new "scratch-and-dent" furniture, which may have been slightly damaged in transit but is always a great buy.

Cort Furniture Rental Warehouse Clearance Center
7400 Squire Ct. (West Chester)
777-6104

Globe Furniture Rentals
1925 Greenwood Ave. (Sharonville)
771-4242

Alexander-Patterson-Groneck, Inc.
332 E. 8th St. (downtown)
621-9111

The Quality Office Furniture That's Sensibly Priced Store
435 E. Galbraith Rd. (Arlington Heights)
761-9674

Polinsky Office Furniture
210 E. 9th St. (downtown)
241-1111
The secret here is the third floor—final resting place for oak tables, chairs, and desks—some fifty years old. You may find an occasional hat tree, a storage cabinet or bookcase with a glass front. And be sure to inspect Polinsky's collection of old safes. You are likely to spot one that is circa 1900 with a marble top and hand-painted flowers inside the door.

Futons

You or a guest can sleep on it at night, then roll it up in the morning and store it in a closet. If you're short on furniture, fold it into an S-shape, prop it against a wall, and use it during the day as a couch. "It" is a futon—traditional bedding in Japan—made of layered cotton batting with a muslin cover. And it is gaining popularity in this country because of its wondrous versatility.

At Family Futon, you can order custom futons of any size and have covers made out of a variety of lovely fabrics. Then, if you buy a bed frame or a convertible sofa frame for your futon (available here in a variety of hardwoods), you have a multiple-use piece of furniture. Family Futon also makes zabutons, Japanese foam cushions constructed similarly to futons, which are great to use for low

sitting areas; zafus, Japanese meditation cushions; bolsters, and throw pillows.

Family Futon has also added a stunning selection of Turkish kilims, 100% wool rugs in a variety of designs, and Isamu Noguchi lamps. These lamps have rice paper shades and are architectural wonders. They work beautifully with contemporary or traditional furniture, and Family Futon sells end tables and coffee tables that truly show them off in their best light.

The Family Futon
4621 N. Edgewood Ave. (Winton Place)
541-3767

The Futon Gallery, Etc. has futons galore at their two stores. You'll find all sizes, many covers and frames to choose from, as well as tatami mats (made of a greenish ropelike material), Japanese screens, bedside and coffee tables, nice-looking lamps.

Futon Gallery, Etc.
2628 Vine St. (Corryville)
751-4419
8110 Montgomery Rd. (Kenwood)
745-9946

Custom Plastics

If you want furniture and accessories fabricated from acrylic, from a tabletop and shelves to bookends and cutting boards, Cincinnati Plastics and Cadillac Plastics can build anything you desire from a plan or a picture. These two companies are also kind about selling their leftover cutoffs to do-it-yourselfers. For instance, Cadillac Plastics, which sells tubes and rods by the foot, puts its odds and ends in a barrel you can pick through. Look for all sorts of pieces you can buy by the pound—great if you're into crafts or can make frames on your own. Cincinnati Plastics sells scraps—all colors and sizes—for 75¢ a pound. There's a bin to poke through. They can also supply adhesives, drill bits—all sorts of equipment you'll need for build-it-yourself projects. Polyethylene film is available here by the box. Use it for floor and dust covers when you're painting the house.

Cincinnati Plastics
10731 Reading Rd. (Evendale)
563-9333

Cadillac Plastics and Chemical Co.
3818 Red Bank Rd. (Fairfax)
271-2780

Butcher-Block Furniture

You like natural hardwood furniture, butcher-block work tables and serving carts, maple Shaker-style dining tables and harvest tables, Windsor side chairs, solid-oak occasional tables, maple bunk beds—you've been admiring this good-quality furniture in contemporary furniture stores and cookware shops all over Cincinnati. The only thing you don't like about this furniture is the price. Good news. Drive to Dayton. That's where Taylor Woodcraft's showroom is located, and this prime manufacturer of hardwood furniture will sell you anything in their catalogue for 30% off suggested retail prices and give you even greater discounts the larger your purchase. Call for a brochure or write to them enclosing $3 for their complete catalogue. You can even phone them with the catalogue numbers of their furniture you spot in retail stores in this area. Taylor staff will quote you their discounted prices on the phone.

Taylor Woodcraft Home Furnishings Showroom
Plaza 5
20 Prestige Plaza Dr.
Miamisburg, OH 45342
1-434-9663

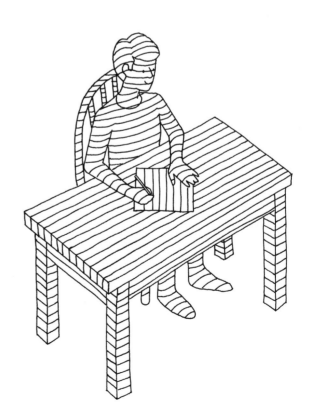

Furniture and Accessories

30 ## Kidstuff

Wonderful wooden Adirondack chairs are now available in a pint-size version called the "Addy." Helen Schereur, owner of Tink, Inc., has "Addys" made out of white painted solid wood, and will ship them anywhere in Greater Cincinnati or the country. The basic cost of the chair is $24. Now kids can sit on the front porch or lawn in style, just like their parents. These chairs would also be perfect in a child's room and would make terrific gifts.

Tink, Inc.
P.O. Box 118580
Cincinnati, OH 45211
481-7858

Custom Designs

If you'd like custom furniture—tables, chairs, cabinets, a few pieces or enough to fill your house—these three craftspeople are highly recommended.

Bob Flottemesch has one of the best reputations in the city, as did his father. (Bob's son is following in the family business, too.) He can build any kind of cabinet for home or office, construct library shelves, an entire kitchen—make anything of impeccable quality out of wood or laminates. He's in heavy demand.

A. Flottemesch & Son
8201 Camargo Rd. (Madeira)
561-1212

Heartwood is the partnership of Robert and Michael Toombs. They can construct anything according to your designs or design anything for you. Furniture, cabinets, libraries, wine racks, or an entire wine cellar, this firm turns out great-looking, good-quality work in traditional or contemporary styles. Ask about the executive boardroom table they've built for one of Cincinnati's largest companies. It may inspire you.

Heartwood Furniture Co., Inc.
4212 Airport Rd. (near Lunken Airport)
321-5790

I first wrote about Appletree Design Works in 1977, when Jim McMahon was building beautifully crafted hardwood furniture in his house. Now he has a 15,000-square-foot operation in Covington where he builds the same fine-quality pieces, only more of them, and he has the facilities to construct large pieces. Basically, he can build according to your designs or design for you: kitchen cabinets, a houseful of furniture, a single table or chair. Jim is highly recommended by some of Cincinnati's most particular builders.

Appletree Design Works
234 Scott St. (Covington)
261-7856

Chris Weidenbacher of Functional Furniture can custom build a desk or an entire office full of furniture, a reception area, kitchen cabinets—just bring him the drawings. Otherwise bring him your ideas and he'll come up with concrete plans.

Functional Furniture & Cabinets
2449 W. McMicken (lower Clifton)
621-2647

Accessories

Video- and audiophiles can find just the furniture they've been looking for at AudioVision Plus. This is where you can buy an entertainment environment—nice-looking, high-tech furniture for your electronic world.

AudioVision Plus
8110 Montgomery Rd. (Kenwood)
891-7444

Mirrors—a huge framed selection, mirrored screens, glass tables (you can ask for custom sizes), faux stone table bases—find all sorts of unusual accessories at Second Look Designer Mirrors.

Second Look Designer Mirrors
3275 Erie Ave. (Hyde Park)
321-5111

If you've had a hard time finding the hardware you need, whether it's a contemporary-looking light switch or a water faucet in the shape of a swan, go to these two places. Cabinet and door knobs, latches, soap dishes—whatever you can't find other places, you will probably uncover here.

Key Decorative Hardware
2727 Madison Rd. (Hyde Park)
321-0099

Bona Decorative Hardware
3073 Madison Rd. (Oakley)
321-7877

Home is where the hearth is, and if you need anything to dress up your fireplace, go to Bromwell's. Besides screens and andirons in many styles and materials, you'll find old-fashioned long-handled popcorn poppers, log carriers, fireplace gloves, brooms—a wondrous assortment.

The Bromwell Co.
117 W. 4th St. (downtown)
621-0620

Pat Nolan of Rug House will hand braid rugs to your specifications as well as weave classic American-style rugs of wool weft and linen warp. You pick the colors and tell Pat the size. She makes them for people all over the country.

The Rug House
871-0890

Page through "Handiest People in Town," pages 50 to 56. Many craftspeople mentioned in that chapter can fill your house in grand style.

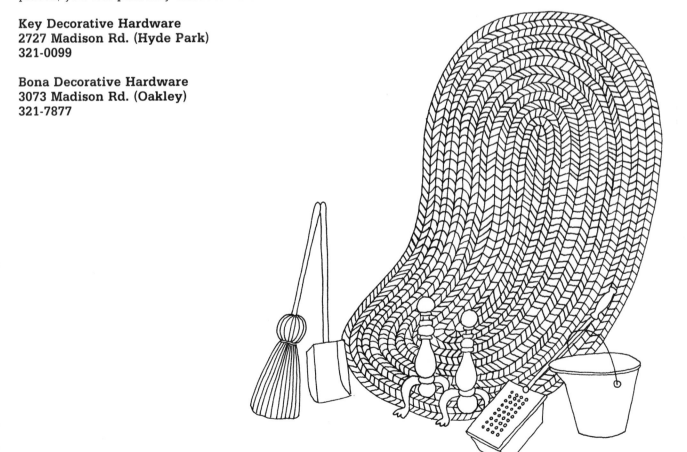

Bedding

Gattle's reminds me of my grandmother's linen closet. She, along with generations of Cincinnatians, lined her shelves with treasures from this store: bed linens, towels, delicate tablecloths and napkins, luxurious comforters, and made-to-order bedspreads that last a lifetime and then are passed along to the next generation.

Gattle's, Inc.
3456 Michigan Ave. (Hyde Park)
871-4050

The Down Lite International factory outlet is the retail store for the company that makes the gorgeous down comforters you see in catalogues like L.L. Bean, Neiman-Marcus, and Bloomingdale's. But you pay a whole lot less for them in Blue Ash. The shells of these comforters—in all sizes and patterns—are made of the finest Egyptian cotton in a multitude of colors. Down Lite will also make comforters to your specifications, along with duvet covers in coordinating hues to protect these goose-down beauties. Down Lite makes pillows, too—in a variety of combinations of feathers and down, depending on how firm you like your pillow. Comforters wearing thin on the corners can be repaired here as well as refluffed. Down can be added to limp pillows also. Look for down coats, vests, parkas, shirts, and sweaters in the factory store. New items are bought seasonally, so there are always fine surprises.

Down Lite International
7818 Palace Dr. (Blue Ash Commerce Center)
489-DOWN

The Down Connection also manufactures finest-quality down comforters. The shells are of 100% Egyptian cotton that the company imports from Germany and then fills with down on the premises. Pillows, of 100% white goose down, 50% down and 50% goose feathers, or 10% down and 90% feathers, are available, as well as magnificent duvet covers imported from Switzerland. (Comforters and pillows can be repaired and refluffed.) Rita Finer, the manager of the Down Connection, says she often works with interior designers to create "bedroom looks" and can have whatever you need made to order. Also look for down robes and booties at the store, as well as coats, vests, jackets, and some hand-knit sweaters from Uruguay. Rita is always on the lookout for new merchandise worldwide, and stock changes from season to season.

Down Connection
2525 Commodity Circle
(Sharonville Commerce Center)
772-3696

The Whiting Manufacturing Co., one of the largest manufacturers in the country of comforters, sheets, bedspreads, pillows, draperies, table linens, and slumber bags, has a factory store at the manufacturing plant (plus two other locations), where you can buy many of their products at terrific prices. You'll find first-quality overruns, close-outs, and seconds in great quantity and variety. Merchandise changes constantly according to what comes out of the factory. Whether you're dressing a whole bedroom or you just need a warm comforter to snuggle into on chilly nights, this place is definitely worth a stop.

Whiting Manufacturing Linen Outlet Stores
9999 Carver Rd. (Blue Ash)
791-8708
6975 Dixie Hwy. (Fairfield)
874-0550
6149 Glenway Ave. (Westwood)
661-9366

Linens, Etc. has two store locations and an overflowing selection of anything you could ever need for a kitchen, bedroom, or bathroom at discount prices. There are walls of comforters, sheets, all sorts of designer ensembles in current colors and patterns. Big names like Martex, Wamsutta, Dan River, Marimekko, Bill Blass are always in stock. From bath towels to kitchen towels, shower curtains to place mats, these stores are packed. There are closet accessories, stylish woven bathmats, and hundreds of knickknacks like hand brushes and sponges—all the things you never think you need until you walk into the store.

Linens, Etc.
11429 Princeton Rd. (Tricentre)
772-4193
7340 Kenwood Rd. (Kenwood)
791-4197

Linens 'n Things, a bed and bath supermarket, is always overflowing with good-looking merchandise—comforters, bath linens, and blankets.

You can coordinate a designer look here for less money than you'd pay in regular retail stores. Linens 'n Things has accessories galore: from hangers to hot mitts, there is a tasteful selection.

Linens 'n Things
Outlets, Ltd. (Kings Island)
398-4868

Bath and Bedspread World offers top-of-the-line brands such as the ones you'll find at Gattle's and Bloomingdale's but at a 25% discount on in-stock items. Owner Sam Evans is very accommodating about special orders, too. He'll go out of his way to locate what you need—in fact, all the staff here offer personalized decorating assistance—and still give you a 20% discount on special orders. Draperies, bedspreads, bath accessories, rugs— you'll find whatever you need for a luxurious "total look."

Bath and Bedspread World
9905 Montgomery Rd. (Montgomery)
984-2233

There are Cotton Mill Stores dotted all over Cincinnati (check your phone book for addresses). They are outlets for the Leshner Corporation, a manufacturer and distributor of sheets, towels, bedspreads, and all sorts of assorted linens. These stores are fun for bargain hunters who love to plow through tables piled with five-for-$10 packs of white bath towels, bundles of kitchen towels, mounds of washcloths, bathmats, and pillows. There is some high-quality merchandise; most is modest, but colorful and plentiful. If you're looking for anything linen-related, from chef's aprons to curtain sheers, these stores are great places to browse.

From the Frying Pan...

Cooking up something special? Here are all the ingredients you'll need: sturdy kitchenware, snazzy table settings, candles to add a little romance, and even basket centerpieces for ambience.

Restaurant Equipment

For good buys in kitchen supplies, from saucepans and stockpots to cutlery and gadgets, it's hard to beat the offerings at restaurant supply houses. Here's why. Restaurant equipment has to be top quality because it's designed for a life of heavy use. Sometimes it may cost more than what you'd pay in a retail store; sometimes less than at a gourmet cooking-equipment shop. And don't be intimidated by thinking you'll only find oversize items. There's an outstanding variety. You can buy stockpots and saucepans to make soup for a hundred or just for your family, plus cutlery, can openers, spatulas, muffin pans, baking trays, brushes, whisks, hot mitts, aprons, stainless flatware—all are sensible and durable.

There are glasses and dishes at restaurant supply houses, too. Drinking glasses, bar glasses, all sorts of dishes and mugs. Mothers with small children should check out china designed for hospitals, prisons, and other institutions. Believe me, it's unbreakable.

These are three restaurant suppliers happy to sell to off-the-street customers. All have staff who will knowledgeably advise you on the best equipment to buy.

Dunsky's Bar & Restaurant Supply
37 E. Court St. (downtown)
621-8041

Western Fixture Co.
219 W. 4th St. (downtown)
241-0576

The Weber Co.
1440 W. 8th St. (Queensgate)
852-6795

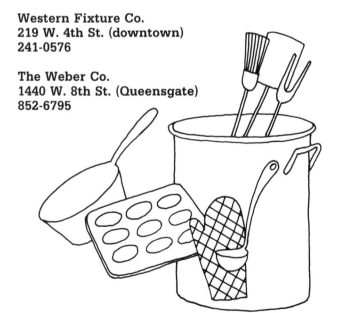

Off-Price Accessories

The Kitchen Collection, an outlet for Proctor-Silex and Wear-Ever products, has impressive stock and prices to match. A back wall is hung with all kinds of dented saucepans and stockpots (damage looked minimal to me) at a 70% savings. Other shelves are filled with lobster pots, vegetable and rice steamers, roasting pans, skillets and saucepans, kitchen gadgets—a terrific selection.

You can get great deals on small electric appliances here such as toaster ovens, food processors, blenders, can openers, irons, mixers, Crockpots, and woks. Anchor Hocking dinnerware is on display, too. You'll find solid colored plates, mugs, bowls—you can put together your own place settings. People who need to set up a first kitchen or who just need additional accessories should put this store on top of their shopping list.

Kitchen Collection
Outlets, Ltd. (Kings Island)
398-1031

Another gold mine of values is Factory Direct, an outlet for the Lancaster Colony Corporation, which owns Indiana Glass, Candle-lite, Marzetti Salad Dressing, Mountain Top Pies, and Pretty Products (interior car accessories). From this list of companies you can imagine what the stock of this store is like, and it is just as good as it sounds. You can buy any size candle here, in any color, in any fragrance. Specials such as a dozen candles for a dollar are common. Large 3x6 inch candles are priced at $1 here and they'd sell for as much as $3 or $4 in retail stores. Caterers and restaurant owners stock up on candles here as a matter of course.

Truckloads of Indiana Glass arrive often: beer mugs, compotes, tumblers, pitchers, sherbet dishes, shot glasses, punch bowls (restaurants buy them for their salad bars), any size glass plate that's made. Besides all this, there is a freezer full of Mountain Top Pies—every variety—shelves of Marzetti Salad Dressing for 80¢ a bottle, bags of Inn Maid noodles, interior auto accessories such as clip-ons to hold tissue and sunglasses, plastic trash containers, car mats, even truck-bed mats for large and small trucks. Manager Gladys Bowman keeps stock rolling into this store, and on each visit you'll find new merchandise as well as the standbys you'll come to depend on.

Factory Direct
10737 Reading Rd. (Evendale)
733-0800

Fostoria Glass (the second oldest glass company in America next to Steuben) is also owned by the Lancaster Colony Corporation, and there is an outlet for these lead crystal and glass products in Monroe, Ohio. You'll see $10 crystal goblets in elegant patterns selling for $2 here, as well as more casual glassware. Expect to find wineglasses, carafes, bowls, sherbets, iced tea glasses in traditional patterns such as Jamestown and Whitehall, as well as contemporary designs. Both colored glass and clear are always available, and stock is made up of imperfect glassware plus discontinued patterns and colors.

Fostoria operates fifteen factory outlets in the United States, and they are always on major highway intersections so travelers have easy access to them. These stores draw customers from miles around.

Fostoria Glass Outlet
I-75 at Exit 29 (Monroe, OH)
1-539-9632

The China Closet sells sterling silver, silver plate, crystal, china, and kitchenware at discounts beginning at 20%, though some merchandise can be close to half of retail. All is first quality. Owner Bob Hertsenberg watches the newspapers for advertisements of department store sales and immediately drops his prices 10% below theirs. Then when the sale is over, he moves China Closet's prices back to their regular discount.

Brands always in stock are Reed & Barton, Wallace, and Gorham silver, Lenox, Wedgwood, and Limoges china, Colony, Durand, and Orrefors crystal. Cuisinarts, Copco enamel teapots, Krups coffee mills, Gerber steak knives—this store has variety. Bob will special order items at no extra cost, and bridal registry is available.

The China Closet International
3710 Paxton Rd. (Hyde Park)
731-7001

The China/Glass Outlet sells china, crystal, and stainless at about half of regular retail prices. Brands include Mikasa, Royal Doulton, Wedgwood, and many others. Burnes of Boston picture frames are available as well as nice acrylic pitchers, glasses, trays, and ice buckets. Stock changes often.

The China/Glass Outlet
11420 Montgomery Rd. (Harper's Crossing Center)
530-9700
1763 Monmouth St. (Newport Shopping Center)
581-9700

Pottery USA is a cavernous place offering all sorts of glasses—wine to brandy snifters, small table vases to huge red-clay pottery planters, shelves of candles, dried flowers, rolls of ribbon, wicker hampers and furniture, hurricane lamps, figurines, cookware, yarn—push a shopping cart around this supermarket of home accessories and I'll bet it will be overflowing by the time you get to the checkout counter. Great variety and prices here.

Pottery USA
Outlets, Ltd. (Kings Island)
398-3450

The Glass Barn is an old-time place where you can pick up all sorts of glasses, glass serving platters, souffle dishes, microwave casseroles—odds and ends and knickknacks that change constantly.

The Glass Barn
9216 Reading Rd. (Reading)
733-4121

36 Candle Tree manufactures novelty candles that are sold in retail stores—candles that look like a strawberry soda, a frosted cake, a white lacy wedding invitation, candles poured into a hollow log. Buy all these candle concoctions and many others at Candle Tree's factory, where you can also talk to staff about special orders.
Candle Tree
215 Dunn (Lockland)
761-5300

Specialty Cookware and Tableware

You want serious cookware—Calphalon or LeCreuset, maybe some beautiful copper casseroles. You're after best-quality cutlery, coffee makers, stockpots. You like to set a stunning table and that means Waterford crystal or maybe more casual Dansk. Your table setting vocabulary includes Haviland, Royal Copenhagen, Limoges—to name just a few. Or maybe you like Swedish-looking tableware with clean, sleek lines. Below is a list of stores where you can find all of these items. Each shop has its own distinctive collection.

The Culinary Emporium has great quality cookware and a food selection you'll find out more about in "Edibles," page 5.
The Culinary Emporium
Kenwood Towne Centre
793-2783
11439 Princeton Rd. (Tricentre)
772-1510

The 221 Store on the fourth floor of Contemporary Galleries carries designs with a Scandinavian flair.
221 Store
221 W. 4th St. (downtown)
621-3115

Closson's has top quality china, crystal, silver, stainless, best brands of cookware and accessories—a wide selection.
A.B. Closson Jr. Co.
401 Race St. (downtown)
762-5519
7866 Montgomery Rd. (Kenwood)
762-5545

Lazarus maintains a fine and fun selection of tableware, cookware, and gadgets. Check your phone directory for downtown and suburban mall addresses and specific department numbers.

Sterling Cut Glass stocks distinctive crystal—trays, barware, stemware, bowls, gift items. Much can be personalized.
Sterling Cut Glass
2107 Grandin Rd. (Hyde Park)
321-6151
1 W. 4th St. (downtown)
381-4646

Expect to find anything pewter including great dinner and salad plates at Pewter Place Engravery.
Pewter Place Engravery
Carew Tower, Suite 306 (downtown)
579-0736
Kenwood Towne Centre
891-0730

En Provence has lovely French country china—antique and contemporary—plus tablecloths, baskets, and other accessories.
En Provence
2722 Erie Ave. (Hyde Park Square)
871-9009

Cookworks carries a nice selection of cookware, gadgets, aprons.
Cookworks
435 Elm St. (Convention Place Mall)
721-2665

Giftique stocks unusual and beautiful china, silver, flatware, gift accessories.
Giftique
Kenwood Towne Centre
891-4100

You can pick up good-looking cooking-related gifts at The Panhandler.
The Panhandler
3446 Edwards Rd. (Hyde Park)
321-8062

M. Charles is a good place to find fine china, crystal, silver, gift accessories.
M. Charles
435 Elm St. (Convention Place Mall)
721-4666

Fine china, crystal, silver, gift accessories—Herschede's is a Cincinnati tradition for bridal registry. (See "Sparkle Plenty," page 154, for addresses and phone numbers.)

Newstedt-Loring Andrews is the place to find traditional, fine-quality tableware and gift accessories. (See "Sparkle Plenty," page 154, for addresses and phone numbers.)

For cookware, glassware, dishes, cannister sets, butcher blocks, picnicky kinds of things, kitchen accessories, try Cargo Express.
Cargo Express
Northgate Mall
741-8444
Eastgate Mall
753-6054
Florence Mall
371-3416

Any kind of cutting equipment—an especially wide selection of knives and scissors—can always be found at Hoffritz.
Hoffritz For Cutlery, Inc.
Carew Tower Arcade (downtown)
651-5865
Northgate Mall
385-5898

Pottery

If your choice in table settings runs to earthy, artist-made, hand-thrown pottery, visit Spring Street Pottery's showroom. Potters Allan Nairn, Michael Frasca, and Richard Aerni make large sculptural pieces you can view in public buildings all over town, but they always have smaller pieces such as platters, pitchers, teapots, mugs, vases, small and large planters at the showroom. Ask to be placed on Spring Street's mailing list. They have a once-a-year seconds sale usually in June or July at the pottery, and a Christmas sale at Memorial Hall on a Sunday a couple of weeks before the holidays.
Spring Street Pottery
1311 Spring St. (downtown)
381-1463

John Meinhart is the resident potter at Stoneware Alley, but the work of four or five other potters is sold here, too. Mugs, plates, bowls, cannister sets, colanders, animals—earthy to country looks are always on hand.
Stoneware Alley
4036 Hamilton Ave. (Northside)
681-5190

Bowls

Bob Fleming hand turns wooden bowls in small salad sizes, larger ones to hold fruit or greens, and makes complete salad sets. Bowls are walnut, cherry, maple, or butternut and each one is signed. Talk to Bob about special orders. He can make wooden dinner plates, dovetailed boxes, larger pieces of furniture such as tables, cabinets, reproduction antiques.
Fleming Woodworking
575-1715

Baskets

Longaberger maple-splint baskets have been made in Dresden, Ohio, since 1927. The fifth generation of this family business is seeing that today's quality is as high as it was at the company's inception. Longaberger baskets come in a multitude of sizes. Many are perfect as table centerpieces holding fruit or flowers, and there are market baskets, picnic baskets, gathering and laundry baskets, clothes hampers, cradles, so many more. All are artfully made, but also sturdy enough to withstand hard use.

Longaberger baskets are sold by company representatives who come to your home. They are not for sale in retail stores. Put together a group of people, and the representative brings basket samples, suggests how they can be used, takes catalogue orders, then delivers baskets six to eight weeks later. Longaberger basket presentations can be used as fund-raisers, too. Phone Madeline DeRose, the area representative, to arrange a presentation, and for more information.
Longaberger Baskets
891-7861

Greenery

Places to buy greenery and all the sundries that make them sprout more bountifully, experts to turn to for growing advice, plus yard accessories, all bloom in this chapter.

Don't know why your ferns are turning brown? Or why your grape ivy is looking peaked? Any question on horticulture or gardening can be answered with a phone call to the Civic Garden Center of Greater Cincinnati, a nonprofit volunteer organization dedicated to promoting interest and education in gardening and horticulture. Phone the center's hotline, 221-TREE, to ask what's wrong with your ailing plant. If staffers can't help you on the spot, they'll research your question and call you back. You can even make an appointment to have your plant examined at the center.

The center has a wonderful library—see "Libraries," page 126, for more information—plus programs that teach children how to grow and harvest their own food at garden plots scattered throughout the city. This is real hands-on experience. Volunteers and staff also advise neighborhood groups interested in forming community gardens.

You may visit the unique gardens on the center grounds, as well as its retrofit greenhouse, which shows how to use alternative energy to propagate plants. This place is truly a learning center for the hobbyist or the veteran gardener. Inquire about membership, which will keep you up to date on all lectures and workshops.
Civic Garden Center of Greater Cincinnati
2715 Reading Rd. (near downtown)
221-0981

The Hamilton County Co-op Extension Service is actually an extension of Ohio State University. It's an off-campus educational service equipped to answer any food and agricultural questions you may have. They know a lot about vegetable growing, spraying, flowers and lawns, pickling, canning, freezing, and storing perishables. For instance, if you want information on canning tomatoes, they'll send you pamphlets telling you exactly what to do. (Most brochures are free.) If the information you need isn't readily available to them, they'll go to the experts at Ohio State to get the answers. They'll

even answer urgent questions on the phone—say, if your freezer goes on the blink and you're frantic because everything is semi-squishy, they'll tell you exactly what needs to be cooked immediately, what can be refrozen, and what must be pitched.
Hamilton County Co-op Extension Service
11100 Winton Rd. (Greenhills)
825-6000

The Hamilton County Soil and Water Conservation District works hand in hand with the Co-op Extension Service. What information one doesn't have, the other does, so they refer to each other as a matter of course. But basically, county agents are equipped to help you with planting, mulching, gardening, soil erosion, ponds, or anything related to these subjects. They'll advise you on the phone, in person, or send you all the information you need. You can ask county agents why the maple trees in your yard are sickly, why your pond has become polluted; even soil testing can be arranged.

The district offers educational programs for grade school, high school, and college students, and conservationist speakers for groups and schools. Ask to be added to some of the district's mailing lists and you will be advised of when particular clinics are offered and when its annual sale of small trees will take place.
Hamilton County Soil and Water Conservation District
20 Endicott (Greenhills)
825-9765

Greenhouses

When the grass starts getting green, people begin to get plant fever. In spring, the garden stores and greenhouses are packed with people eager to spruce up their yards. Who has the pick of the crop? It's hard to say because there are so many places in Cincinnati where you can buy all sorts of good-looking plants. Nurseries, greenhouses, even neighborhood retail stores are flush with greenery. But there is a nucleus of old favorites among Cincinnati gardeners. Some operations have been in business for generations, lovingly nurturing seedlings into spectacular stock. Here are a handful of those most often mentioned by people with a green thumb. Call before you go to these places—some are open only during the prime planting season.

Delhi Flower and Garden Center
5222 Delhi Rd. (Delhi)
451-5222
135 Northland Blvd. (Tri-County)
771-7117

A.J. Rahn Greenhouses
4944 Gray Rd. (Winton Place)
541-0672

Nann's Florist and Greenhouses
7954 Cooper Rd. (Montgomery)
791-3811

Robert Funke Greenhouses
4798 Gray Rd. (Winton Place)
541-8170

Schumacher Greenhouses
4995 Winton Ridge (Winton Place)
541-8781

Bohrer Bros. Florist & Greenhouses
6183 Salem Rd. (Anderson Twp.)
231-7175

O'Rourke's Hardy Perennials
3436 Banning Rd. (Groesbeck)
923-3114

Durban's Greenhouses
533 McAlpin (Clifton)
861-7866

Bowen's Plant and Vegetable Farm
4162 Round Bottom Rd. (Newtown)
561-4047

The Old Green House
1415 Devil's Backbone Rd. (Mack)
941-0337

Benken Greenhouses
6000 Plainfield Rd. (Silverton)
891-1040

Mulch

Need mulch in quantity? Call Forrest Lytle and Sons, Inc., tree specialists, and have a truckload delivered. That's equivalent to approximately sixty of the three-cubic-foot bags, and the cost is much less when you buy it loose. If that amount is too staggering, you can still buy by the scoop—each is equal to eight three-cubic-foot bags. Or come to Lytle, fill whatever containers you wish, and take them home.

Lytle will also deliver a truckload of fresh, green wood chips, which are great for making pathways and dog runs but not good to use around bushes and trees. Phone for costs of all these gardening products, and check with other tree services and nurseries near you about buying from them by the truckload, too.
Forrest Lytle and Sons, Inc.
740 W. Galbraith Rd. (Finneytown)
521-1464

Organics

If you're strictly an organic gardener, head to Wooden Shoe Gardens to see their full line of organic fertilizers and gardening supplies, plus vegetable and herb starts. Owner David Rosenberg, who grows luscious greenhouse vegetables you can also buy at the gardens (see more about this in "Fresh Picked and Pick-Your-Own," on page 47), is an organic gardening expert. He'll do soil analysis and make recommendations for using natural products, he offers consulting services for your farm, lawn, or garden, and he's an interesting, caring person to talk to about growing anything without chemicals. Tucked into a hollow smack in the midst of the city, Wooden Shoe Gardens is a magical place to visit.
Wooden Shoe Gardens
5115 Wooden Shoe Ln. (Winton Place)
681-4574

Greenery

40 Flowers

Who are the best florists in the city? Who are the most creative, do the most spectacular parties and weddings, always work with customers to come up with ingenious ideas? I asked and asked. Here are some answers—those sworn by most often.

Dennis Buttelwerth Florists, Inc.
3438 Edwards Rd. (Hyde Park)
321-3611

Adrian's Flower Shop
Clifton & Ludlow (Clifton)
861-4232

Covent Garden Florist
2221 Beechmont Ave. (Mt. Washington)
232-4422

Louis the Florist
7416 Paddock Rd. (Carthage)
821-8530

Jones the Florist
1037 E. McMillan (East Walnut Hills)
961-6622

The Plant and Flower Market
9748 Montgomery Rd. (Montgomery)
793-3377

Del Apgar Florist
3275 Erie Ave. (Hyde Park)
321-2600

Cut-Rate Cut Flowers

Two cut-flower secrets for do-it-yourself arrangers.

Dennis Buttelwerth (see above) will give any customer a 40% discount on cut flowers from his cooler, as well as blooming plants in the store. All you have to do is pick them out, have them wrapped in clear cellophane, and take them home to arrange yourself.

Flowers, Flowers, Flowers, Unlimited is another place to gather armloads of beauties at lower than retail prices. Operated by Alan Lessure, son of Louis the Florist, this self-serve flower supermarket is packed with all sorts of varieties stored in refrigerated cases and stashed in huge pots all over the place. On a miserable winter day, I spotted daffodils, tulips, irises—welcome spring flowers in such dismal weather. This place does a land-office business—and should.
Flowers, Flowers, Flowers, Unlimited
Hyde Park Plaza
321-6116

Yard Art

If you want to give Mother Nature a helping hand, you will find a galaxy of yard art to plant on your lawn at Mi-San Pottery. Poodles, collies, burros pulling carts, families of deer, lions, frogs sitting on a bench holding fishing poles, metal windmills, globes on pedestals, any kind of fountain or bird bath you can think of is displayed in the front and side yards of this store. Truly you have to see the variety and quantity here to believe it.
Mi-San Pottery
8701 Cincinnati-Columbus Rd. (West Chester)
777-6545

Fountain Specialists are no slouch in the yard art department either. Want a small fountain or a Kings Island-size one? Check out this place. If you're interested in all sorts of statuary, flag poles, sundials, bird baths, fiberglass pools—anything you can or can't imagine in your yard, this place probably has it.
Fountain Specialists Co.
226 Main St. (Milford)
831-5717

Flower Foolers

You can't grow anything? Even fresh cut flowers don't make it in your house? The answer to your plight might be in a visit to the Posy Patch. This is a flower shop, but filled with a huge line of *silk* blossoms. More than 8,000 square feet contain 1,300 varieties that you can buy loose to arrange on your own or have designed for you. Prices range from a few dollars to a few hundred for the more exotic plants and posies. Caterers in search of table decorations shop here regularly.
Posy Patch
5819 Wooster Pk. (Fairfax)
561-9068

Herbs and Spices

As people have set aside their salt shakers in the quest for better health, they have turned to herbs and spices to make food more flavorful. That's why the sale of fresh herbs has sprouted, while growing your own in a patch outside or on the windowsill has become a passion. Even the use of non-culinary herbs—for bouquets, wreaths, and potpourri—has escalated. Here's where to find the pick of the crop. (Note: look for fresh herb plants in season, at many greenhouses throughout the city. See the preceding chapter, "Greenery," pages 38-40, for some prime locations.)

One of the best places to buy herb plants is at the once-a-year sale held on the first Saturday in May at the Civic Garden Center of Greater Cincinnati. (Look for more about the Garden Center in "Greenery," page 38.) Get there early because people from all over the city flock to this event—the entire driveway is covered with herb plants neatly arranged in alphabetical order. You can snap up hanging baskets of herbs and beginner herb kits containing a half dozen plants while how-to-grow demonstrations go on throughout the day.

In the fall, usually on the last Saturday in September or the first one in October, the Garden Center has an herb fair where you can stock up on dried herbs to take you through the winter. Besides the usual culinary ones, look for Chinese and Italian herb mixes and saltless salt which devotees swear by.

As the time for these events draws near, call the Garden Center to check specific dates and hours.

Civic Garden Center of Greater Cincinnati
2715 Reading Rd. (near downtown)
221-0981

Reminiscent Herb Farm has a field of herb plants grown without pesticides that you can buy fresh or dried. These include culinary herbs and everlasting flowers, as well as herbal teas and potpourris made on the premises. In season, you can purchase starter plants to grow yourself.

Classes in herb growing, and raised bed gardening, herbal crafts (such as wreath making and dried-flower arranging) are held here. Reminiscent Herb Farm is open year-round.

Reminiscent Herb Farm, Inc.
1344 Boone Aire Rd. (Florence)
525-8729

Shaker Herb Farm grows herbs—120 varieties—as well as scented geraniums and everlasting flowers. You can buy fresh herbs here only in the spring because drying is not done on the premises. But you can purchase all sorts of wonderful other dried herb products in their country gift shop whenever it is open.

Owner Bonnie Lindsay holds classes in dried-flower arranging and wreath making, as well as herb growing and herb drying. Bonnie also makes flower arrangements to order: everlasting flower wedding bouquets are her specialty. Using the language of flowers to make up these meaningful bouquets—like rosemary for remembrance and sage for wisdom—Bonnie says these have become a favorite with brides because they are lovely and fresh for the wedding, then dry beautifully and last for years.

Shaker Herb Farm is located in the former dwelling house of the Whitewater Shaker Settlement, founded in Harrison, Ohio, in 1832. The farm is open from May through December, and people are welcome to tour all of the historic premises (outside). To make sure you keep abreast of the many events that take place here, put your name on the Farm's mailing list when you visit, or give Bonnie a call.

Shaker Herb Farm
11813 Oxford Rd. (Harrison)
738-2939

Herbs and Spices

Pat Beckman, owner of the Wooden Onion, also lives in a historic house built in 1870 in Colerain Township. She generously opens both her herb gardens and house to garden clubs, and the visit includes a talk on growing herbs and making flower arrangements. Call to make reservations and to ask about the fee.

Pat also teaches beginning herb-growing classes in spring, dried wreath-making classes in August, and makes both fresh and dried Victorian-looking bridal bouquets that have become increasingly popular. Fresh herbs are for sale in late July and early August, but the rest of Pat's products (potpourris and dried arrangements) are available from August to Christmas. Phone for an appointment to visit.

Wooden Onion
385-9026

Debby Fogelman became so intrigued with her hobby of blending herbs and spices that it became a home-based business called Early American Scents. The bulk of her products are potpourris, which she says have such a wonderful aroma and long life because of the type and amounts of fixative she uses. She sells potpourri refresher as well.

Talk to Debby about some of the products she will whip up by special order only. These include bath salts, an after-sun moisturizer, massage oils, a splash-on insect repellent called Herbal Warmth that doubles as a muscle relaxer to quiet aches and pains when it is rubbed into the skin. Debby says she sells a lot of this 1800's formula she discovered in an herbal tome to outdoor sports enthusiasts. Phone her to place orders, which she will mail to you.

Early American Scents
232-7455

Murray Bros. has more than half a dozen old-time store locations (check the phone directory for the one nearest you), each packed with about 150 good-quality dried herbs and spices you can buy in bulk. The smallest quantity you can purchase is half an ounce and you'll be amazed at the difference in the price you pay when you carry home spices minus their fancy containers. Murray Bros. especially prides itself on its chili powder blend (it's as hot as a five-alarm fire), its pickling spices, vanilla extract, and sausage seasonings.

The Pasta Market (see "Edibles," page 5, for more on this store and the address) has a shelf of Dean and Deluca culinary herbs in nice round tins. Anyone who knows the wonders to be found in the Dean and Deluca food stores in New York will know that coming across these herbs in Cincinnati is a wonderful treat.

Mail-order herbs and herbal teas? The most wonderfully fresh, finest quality, are the lovingly grown hand packed ones you can buy in tins with authentic Shaker reproduction labels from the Shaker Community in Sabbathday Lake, Maine. They are still producing them as they always have for over a hundred years.

A sampling of the teas: camomile, catnip and clover, lemon verbena, and pennyroyal. The culinary herbs include basil, dill, oregano, and rosemary—just a few of the many they grow. These tins make glorious gifts for anyone—best of all for yourself. To obtain a free catalogue (which contains more Shaker products than just herbs) and to place orders, write to:

The United Society of Shakers
Herb Department
Sabbathday Lake
Poland Spring, ME 04274

Some of these same Shaker herbs and teas are available in one local store—The Shaker Seed Box Company (which you'll hear more about in "Museum Shops and Specialty Stores," page 96). Owner Steve Kistler had twenty-two varieties of herbs and thirty-five kinds of teas in stock when I last checked with him, plus Shaker vinegars and rosewater. Shakers use rosewater as a substitute for vanilla in some of their recipes. Worth a try! Or just splash it on your skin.

The Shaker Seed Box Company
6656 Chestnut St. (Mariemont)
271-7100

Bulk Buys

If you're taking part in a bake sale or revving up for holiday fruitcake making, you might need to buy herbs and spices in commercial quantities. Try finding them at the following places.

Squeri's Cash & Carry
49 Central Ave. (downtown)
579-0044

Makro
10765 Reading Rd. (Evendale)
554-3100

Cannery Row
416 Madison Ave. (Covington)
431-2687

Season and Spice mainly wholesales seasonings and spices to businesses and restaurants, but if you want to order in bulk—a pound is the minimum and that amount can be made up of a variety of spices—phone in your order and it will be delivered. If you want to stop in for a purchase, call ahead for an appointment because owners are mostly out making deliveries.

Season and Spice
9017 Reading Rd. (Reading)
563-7466

Fresh Picked and Pick-Your-Own

If your kids think apples grow in plastic bags at Kroger's or if you yearn for just-picked-that-day strawberries, it's time to get out of the supermarket and back to the farm to buy produce, maybe even harvest it yourself. There are many farms in the area that offer pick-your-own crops as well as markets on the premises where you can buy the day's bounty. However, if your back-to-the-land instincts are even more energetic than just picking stringbeans, there are cut-your-own-Christmas tree farms and nearby state and national forests where you can cut your own firewood. Roll up your sleeves and read on.

Kentucky Route 8 Farms

Head west on River Road, aim for the Anderson Ferry and drive aboard (one crosses the river every five or ten minutes), and you'll find yourself on Kentucky Route 8, which runs parallel to the river. Turn right and follow the road through Constance and then Stringtown (yes, Stringtown), and you'll find a bumper crop of vegetable stands owned by farmers who work the bottomland right on the river and produce some of the best-looking fruits and vegetables around. (Note: I've given you scenic directions. If you prefer the highway rather than the river route, what can I say?)

Not only can you buy from Route 8 vegetable stands, many of these farmers will let you pick your own fruits and vegetables depending on the size of their harvest and the time of year. Minimum amounts you can pick vary from farm to farm, and the lush season starts toward the end of June (though some stands open around mid May) and runs through fall. The general rule is that whenever vegetables start getting ripe, the stands are open—most seven days a week. Call first to check on open hours, to ask what fruits and vegetables are available, and if pick-your-own is possible.

The first stand you'll come to on Route 8 is Dolwick's, on the left. Vegetables include corn, tomatoes, kale, cabbage, zucchini, hot peppers, green peppers, and more. Sausage, bacon, and country hams are available in July. You can also pick your own beans at Dolwick's; the minimum is a bushel. Strawberries, too, but you must take six quarts. Other pick-your-own fruit is possible if there is some in the orchard.
Dolwick's
689-4465

McGlasson's is next on the right, and they have pick-your-own fall beans (these are terrific for canning), turnip and mustard greens, and tomatoes. A half bushel is the minimum.

The stand opens May 1 to sell bedding and vegetable plants, then cauliflower, tomatoes, apples, onions, cucumbers, and tiny new potatoes as the season progresses. In fall, the stand is flush with pumpkins, squash, apples, apple cider, and popcorn.
McGlasson's
689-5229

Next up is Parlor Grove, where you can pick your own tomatoes, apples, peaches, and green beans—half-bushel minimum. Vaughn Hempfling always has great-looking vegetables at his stand, along with honey, cider, Indian gourds, sorghum, and molasses in the fall.
Parlor Grove
689-4668

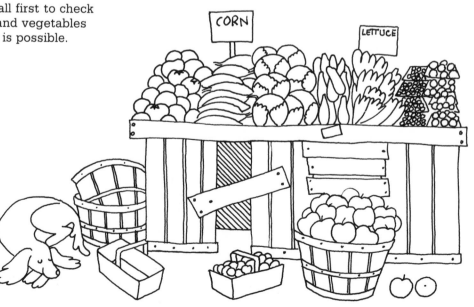

Valley Orchards, owned by Charles Hempfling (cousin of the Parlor Grove Hempflings), offers pick-your-own beans, peas, and tomatoes by the bushel or the half. There are pick-your-own apples and peaches when the weather is kind. The stand opens in April with asparagus, has bedding and hanging plants in May, then squash, cabbage, new potatoes, gorgeous gooseberries, red and black raspberries as the season heats up. Valley sells pumpkins in the fall or you can pick your own while you load up on cider, Indian corn, and popcorn at the market stand.

Valley Orchards
689-4992

Hartman's is way down at the end of the road, and offers pick-your-own tomatoes, potatoes, beans, Silver Queen corn, squash, cucumbers, onions, and pumpkins. There is always a full garden of vegetables, and you're allowed to pick any quantity you want. Market-stand crops are the same as the pick-your-own ones, and John Hartman cuts firewood when it starts to get cold. You're welcome to load up whatever you need. Just talk to him about the price.

Hartman's
586-8894

Other Farms and Orchards

Maplewood Orchard produces more than a dozen varieties of apples you can pick yourself with a picking pole they supply. A bushel is the minimum quantity. Vegetables such as sweet corn and green beans are sometimes offered on a pick-your-own basis, though you can always pick your own pumpkins in the fall. Picking time usually runs from the first weekend after Labor Day until the first week in November—weekends only, Friday noon until Sunday dark.

Maplewood's market is open seven days a week from early July until the end of December. It is always full of tasty cider, homemade apple butter and apple pies, peanut brittle, bags of ripe apples, huge and tiny pumpkins, squash, gourds, fresh vegetables, jams, and jellies.

Maplewood Orchard
3712 Stubbs Mill Rd. (Morrow, OH)
1-932-7981

At Reinking Orchards you can't pick your own, but you can buy their apple harvest and pumpkins as well as their homemade products: apple butter, cider, peanut butter, fudge, peanut brittle, and popcorn from July through March.

Reinking Orchards
Hwy. 48 (Aurora, IN)
812-926-2930

Rouster's Apple House grows forty different varieties of apples that are offered for sale in their market, which opens around July 4th and closes after Christmas. Besides crispy, top-quality apples, you can buy homemade apple cider, cider pops (like popsicles), jam, jelly, honey from local hives, apple butter and preserves made without sugar, plus three kinds of popcorn. There are five acres of berries you can pick yourself—blueberries, raspberries, and thornless blackberries. Call to be placed on Rouster's mailing list to find out what goodies will be available and their approximate picking times.

Rouster's Apple House
1980 State Rt. 131 (six miles east of Milford)
625-5504

At Twenty Mile Farm you can pick strawberries, a variety of beans—lima to green—broccoli, tomatoes, pumpkins, and other vegetables depending on which crops are most abundant. At their market, you can buy asparagus, Silver Queen corn, eggplant, zucchini, squash, popcorn, and other seasonal produce from mid-April until the end of October. Plans for the future include animals for children to pet—goats, rabbits, turkeys, and chickens.

Twenty Mile Farm
3394 W. U.S. 22-3 (Loveland)
683-7530

Fresh Picked and Pick-Your-Own

Minges Produce & Greenhouses is open year-round, though the pick-your-own season begins the end of May with strawberries, then continues with broccoli, cauliflower, peas, green and lima beans, tomatoes, green peppers, eggplant, and red raspberries. At the farm market you can buy all the pick-your-own crops, plus Silver Queen corn, watermelons, cantaloupes, jams, jellies, maple syrup, stone-ground flour, spices, Roseville old-fashioned-looking pottery—and more. In April, bedding and vegetable plants, shrubs, flower and vegetable seeds, mulch, and fertilizer are for sale.

Minges is always buzzing with activity. During the third weekend in October, which is when they hold their Pumpkin Festival, you can take a wagon ride to the pumpkin fields to pick your own. There is a petting zoo where kids can get close to deer, donkeys, goats, ducks, rabbits, and chickens. You can even grind peanuts to make your own peanut butter here.

Minges Produce & Greenhouses
10109 New Haven Rd. (Harrison, OH)
367-2035

The Ruoff Family Farm sells apples from their orchards plus plums, squash, potatoes, cucumbers, Silver Queen corn, beans, pumpkins, maple syrup, and honey at their farm market. In spring, you can visit the farm and see maple syrup-making demonstrations, cuddle up to pigs, sheep, goats, donkeys, chickens, ducks, and geese. You can take a two-hour tour of the farm (part of the tour includes a ride on a haywagon) if you call ahead for a reservation.

Ruoff Family Farm
9579 Brehm Rd. (Dry Ridge, OH)
385-7065

A & M Orchard has you-pick strawberries in June or you can buy them already in containers. Pick-your-own apples—Jonathan, Red Rome, Melrose, and Early Blaze—are ready by mid-September. You can buy pears, plums, prune plums, pumpkins, and Concord grapes, plus honey, jams and jellies, apple butter, popcorn, Indian corn, and squash at the farm market.

A & M Orchard
22141 State Rt. 251 (Midland, OH)
875-2500

Hidden Valley Fruit Farm has pick-your-own blackberries, raspberries, and strawberries early in the season, green beans, broccoli, sweet corn, squash, apples, pears, grapes, and pumpkins through the summer and fall.

Hidden Valley Fruit Farm
5474 N. State Rt. 48 (Lebanon, OH)
1-932-1869

Irons' Fruit Farm has pick-your-own strawberries, raspberries, blueberries, and cherries in June, then apples in the fall.

Irons' Fruit Farm
1640 Stubbs Mill Rd. (Lebanon, OH)
1-932-2853

Black Barn offers pick-your-own cabbage, cauliflower, broccoli, green beans, peas, lettuce, and strawberries in June, sweet corn in July and August.

Black Barn
1161 W. Ohio 63 (Lebanon, OH)
1-932-0433

Pick strawberries at Outaway Farm in June; cabbage, green beans, and corn in July.

Outaway Farm
2724 Case Rd. (New Richmond, OH)
734-2560

Pick strawberries at Pringle's Orchard in June, then apples, peaches, and pears through the rest of the summer and fall.

Pringle's Orchard
2697 Pringle Rd. (Goshen, OH)
625-1611

At Piney Wood Orchard you can pick apples, peaches, and pears from July through fall as well as grapes starting in early September.

Piney Wood Orchard
6701-A Woodvill Rd. (Morrow, OH)
899-3204

Bowen's Plant and Vegetable Farm has all sorts of plants for sale (see "Greenery," page 39) but features pick-your-own greens—turnip, mustard, spinach, kale, and collard—in the fall.

Bowen's Plant and Vegetable Farm
4162 Round Bottom Rd. (Newtown)
561-4047

Aichholz's Farm offers pick-your-own strawberries early in the season, then peas and beans later on. Their farm market is ripe with all sorts of good-looking vegetables such as corn, cucumbers, peppers, tomatoes, onions, cabbage—an abundant variety of produce—during the summer, then pumpkins, squash, and all shapes and sizes of gourds in the fall. Besides vegetables, the market has a deli, sells ice cream and other assorted food items. It has recently begun a catering service using its homegrown fruits and vegetables as part of the party fare such as a watermelon basket filled with fruits and vegetables. Pasta and artichoke salads, Chinese chicken wings, roast beef, and ham are popular, too.

Though the farm market closes around Christmas, the Flowers and Fine Gift Shop, in the rear of the farm market, is open year-round. In season, you can buy larkspur, dahlias, delphinium, and other fresh cut flowers, flower and herb plants, a good assortment of baskets, antique and contemporary silver and crystal, pottery, and other gift items.

Aichholz's Vegetable Farm
3950 Round Bottom Rd. (Newtown)
Farm Market: 561-2004
Flowers and Fine Gift Shop: 561-8919

Wooden Shoe Gardens has an organic fruit and vegetable farm market open year-round on Wednesday afternoons from 1 to 6. During the winter, produce is shipped in from all over the county by certified organic growers. But during Cincinnati's lush season, owner David Rosenberg offers his own primo varieties of lettuce to avid buyers (his specialty is limestone bibb), as well as produce from other local organic sources. Get there early because stock vanishes fast or order a week ahead and receive a 15% discount to boot. For large-quantity orders, you must give two weeks advance notice.

Wooden Shoe Gardens
5115 Wooden Shoe Ln. (Winton Place)
681-4574

The Farmer's Market, on the corner of Wilmer and Kellogg Avenues, near Lunken Airport, is where area farmers bring their produce to sell right from the back of their trucks. Look for them Monday through Friday during growing season, generally late in the day. This is a tradition that has been going on for years.

Farmer's Market
Wilmer & Kellogg Aves.

Other tailgate markets pop up all over town during the summer—it's hard to predict just where and when. Look for produce stands or trucks loaded with veggies in your neighborhood, or watch the newspapers for tailgate market announcements and schedules. In the past markets have been held at the parking lot of the Cincinnati Gardens in Swifton on Tuesdays and Saturdays; on Mondays at Nativity School, Woodford and Ridge in Pleasant Ridge, and St. Lawrence Church, 3680 Warsaw Ave., Price Hill; on Wednesdays in back of the Greenhills Shopping Center, 11000 Winton Rd., and United Methodist Church, Ebenezer and Bridgetown Rd. in Mack; on Thursdays at St. Therese Church, 2516 Alexandria Pike in Southgate, Kentucky, at Northminster Presbyterian Church, 703 Compton Rd., Finneytown, and the lot on the corner of Leggett and Medosh Ave. in Lincoln Heights. These are all likely places for markets to reappear.

Fresh Picked and Pick-Your-Own

48 Cut-Your-Own Christmas Trees

Here are a few of the Christmas tree farms in the area where you are welcome to cut your own. But be sure to watch the newspapers around Thanksgiving for announcements of more farms that may have mature enough fields of trees to be harvested.

Call Bezold Pines, which is a forty-five minute drive from downtown in California, Kentucky, to see if there is a good supply of trees and to ask directions. If the season has been dry, it's hard on the crop, but if Mother Nature has been benevolent, you can cut Scotch and white pine, starting three weeks before Christmas.
Bezold Pines
635-5283

Pine Achers, thirty-two miles from downtown, in Sherman, Kentucky, places ads in *The Cincinnati Enquirer* after Thanksgiving announcing their trees are ready. They grow Douglas fir, though other pines should be ready in a few years.
     The farm provides saws, helps people bale trees, and the owner says many families include a tailgate party in the tree-cutting occasion. Call for directions.
Pine Achers
606-428-1494

Stephenson Farm has thirty acres of trees—Scotch, white, and Austrian pine, Norway and white spruce. They furnish the saws, help in baling the tree and loading it into your car. Call for directions.
Stephenson Farm
5977 Oxford-Milford Rd. (Somerville, OH)
1-523-2275

Carl Halen's Christmas Tree Farm (about fifteen minutes from Northgate Mall) has mostly Scotch pines and Norway spruces. He prefers you bring your own saw, but will provide one if you need it, along with assistance if you're a novice cutter. Call for directions.
Carl Halen's Christmas Tree Farm
1321 Goos Rd. (Hamilton)
863-8982

Huber Orchard Winery has everything—you-pick vegetables, a huge farm market, cut-your-own Christmas trees, and a vineyard and winery. This place bustles most of the year. Strawberries, vegetables, apples, and pumpkins are available for picking. You can ride in a wagon out to the fields. Tour the winery to see wine being made—all the varieties from dry whites to sweet fruits are for sale by the bottle or the case. Special wine-tasting parties can be scheduled by reservation.
     Gift shops are full of country crafts—quilts and baskets to candles and soap. The farm market is filled with all varieties of fruits and vegetables, plus apple butter, jams, jelly, popcorn, candy, and pies. Then there's cheese, bread, and sausage—great wine-related edibles.
     Huber Orchard Winery is a distance from Cincinnati—it's twenty miles north of Louisville. Stop by if you're traveling near Louisville or head there for a special outing. Call or write for brochures, which will definitely whet your travel appetite.
Huber Orchard Winery and U-Pick Farm
Rt. 1, Box 202
Borden, IN 47106
812-923-9813 or 812-923-WINE

Harvest Your Own Firewood

If you would like some hearty exercise, an adventurous camping weekend, and free firewood for this winter, there are state and national forests within several hours' drive that will allow you to do your own harvesting. All forests have logging programs, and the firewood you will be allowed to cut is from the tops of trees loggers leave behind, fallen or dead trees, or those not suitable for commercial sawmills.

To harvest wood, you must obtain a permit from the forest rangers' office. These are open Monday through Friday, generally from 8 A.M. to 4:30 P.M., so if you can't cut wood during the week, you still have to get to the office before closing time on Friday, camp in the park overnight, and be up and ready for action on Saturday. (Some offices will send permits by mail, so phone.)

When you get the permit (some are free, others are not—call the ranger office for the current price), you will be informed of and given directions to the area of the forest where you may harvest wood. You can't just enter anywhere you please and start chopping. Also, you will be told the maximum amount you may gather per permit, which ranges from two to five ricks—that's a lot of wood!

Ranger offices may be some miles from the forest and the harvesting area may be twenty-five miles or more farther into the forest, so call ahead and ask about the roads. Some are rough skid trails that can only be traveled by four-wheel-drive vehicles, while other roads are easily traversed by regular pickup trucks or a family car pulling a rented trailer. Ask about campsites, too. Some are primitive, while others have all the amenities.

A last note of advice from the forest rangers: have good equipment. You'll need an ax and a chain saw with a spark arrester to prevent setting a fire. Rangers often make spot checks and will send you out of the forest if your chain saw could cause

danger. Also, come with a friend. If you are in a remote area and have an accident, you'll be able to get help.

Nearby forests include:

Hoosier National Forest, in Indiana, is about 65 miles west of Louisville. The ranger offices are at 15th and Washington Sts., Tell City, IN, about 50 miles southwest of Louisville (**812-547-7051**) and 608 W. Commerce, Brownstown, IN, about 60 miles southwest of Indianapolis (**812-358-2675**).

Wayne National Forest, in Ohio, has ranger offices at 4 Dalton Ave., Athens, OH, about 60 miles south of Columbus (**614-592-6644**) and Ironton, OH, 18 miles west of Huntington, WV (**614-532-3223**).

Daniel Boone National Forest, in Kentucky, approximately 20 miles southeast of Lexington has many ranger offices. One of the closest to Cincinnati is at 100 Vaught Rd., Winchester, KY, about 30 miles from the forest (**606-744-7676**).

Harrison Crawford State Forest, in Indiana, is 40 miles west of Louisville and the ranger office is 8 miles west of Corydon, IN, on State Rt. 462 (**812-738-8232**).

Clark State Forest, in Indiana, is about 20 miles north of Louisville and the ranger office is 2 miles north of Henryville, IN, off U.S. 31 (**812-294-4306**).

Handiest People in Town

Your new puppy has continental taste—she just chewed the toe off your best pair of Italian pumps. You came home from a party to find the pearl pin you were wearing (the one your grandmother gave you!) minus one of its pearls. Your three-year-old used your cherry dining table as a racetrack for his toy cars. Where do you go for help when these kinds of catastrophes strike? To some of the handiest people in Cincinnati. Craftspeople mentioned in this chapter can repair everything from antique silver to antiquated plumbing.

But my biggest nightmare in putting together a list of "the most wanted people in town" is that someone who has done an excellent job for me (and whose work other experts recommend) may have done a poor job for you—and that certainly can happen. What can I say? Nobody's perfect.

Furniture Restoration and Upholstery

Jim Henninger repairs and restores fine pieces of furniture of any period, can even duplicate a missing table leg so that it will match the other three down to the intricate carvings. A chair covered in four layers of paint is no challenge to Jim, who can restore inlaid pieces and upholster. He works for many antique dealers in the city and there's a waiting list for his services.
The Lost Art
6119 Madison Rd. (Madisonville)
272-1900

Bill Sears does great repair and refinishing of antiques and contemporary pieces. Just don't be in too much of a hurry for his services.
William A. Sears Finishing
8201 Camargo Rd. (Madeira)
271-0985

Wagner Restorations repairs and refinishes all types of furniture, even pianos. They will work on large pieces in your home that can't be removed (like cabinets), upholster furniture, refinish metal pieces such as copper and brass, will consult with you to design any kind of furniture you wish. Stop by the shop, which is in a big old church in the historic Seminary Square district in Covington.
Wagner Restorations, Inc.
Russell at 10th St. (Covington)
491-1292

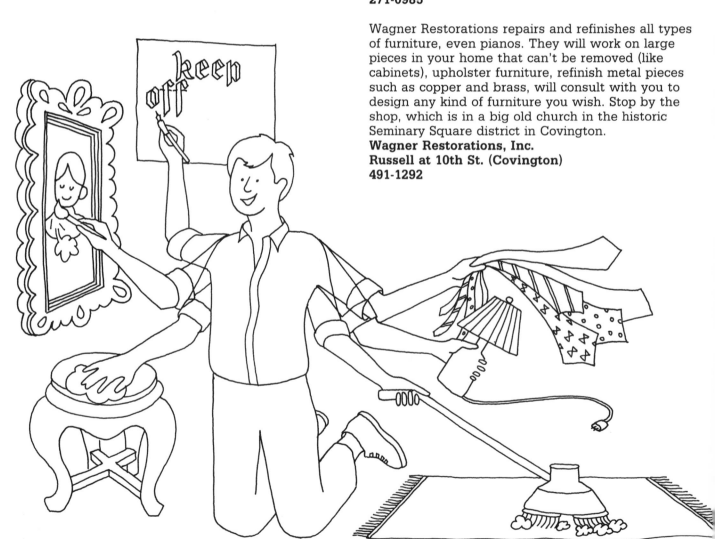

Walter Bednar apprenticed in Germany and can expertly repair furniture—contemporary or antique—as well as make most anything out of wood. He can do easy fixes like scratches, fabricate missing pieces, do delicate inlay work.
Mehrhoff Cabinet Shop
3501 Kleeman (Monfort Heights)
661-4592

Russ Bannister can upholster furniture in any material as well as refinish the wood. He put a new silk sling seat on a half-a-million-dollar bench Julius Caesar sat in. Think he can work on something of yours?
Acme Bannister Upholstery and Refinishing
6654 Montgomery Rd. (Kennedy Heights)
984-1960

Caning, Reed, and Rush Work
James Lewis reweaves furniture of rush, reed, willow, hickory, bark, rattan—almost any material that can be bent. Antique wicker is a specialty, though Jim also restores rattan frame furniture and recanes chair seats. He can work on museum-quality antiques to modern pieces.
James Lewis Reed Furniture Co.
3661 W. Galbraith Rd. (Groesbeck)
385-2589

Marci Clark repairs furniture made of natural materials such as cane and rush, can weave any seat pattern, and can fix anything made out of wicker. Marci breathes new life into broken baskets as well as furniture. She splices in new pieces, then uses herb or bark teas to give the patched areas an aged look. Call for an appointment.
Marci Clark
231-2836

Chair Taping
Steve Kistler of The Shaker Seed Box Company does chair taping in Shaker style. You can choose the seat pattern and the colors and be assured of authentic-looking results. (See "Museum Shops and Specialty Stores," page 96, for more about this store and the address.)

Piano Restoration and Tuning

The Player Piano Shop can completely restore any kind of piano: refinish the case, replate all the metal parts, restore the keyboard hammers. Even an old broken-down player piano can be put back into perfect working condition.
The Player Piano Shop
Showroom: 611 Main St. (downtown)
621-8153
Factory: 2029 Madison Rd. (O'Bryonville)
871-4626

People who own fine pianos depend on Ellen Sewell. She's a tuner/technician, which means she repairs and rebuilds. However, before she rebuilds, Ellen will tell you whether your piano is worth it. That's why people have Ellen look at a piano before they even consider buying it. She's a maestro.
Ellen Sewell
272-0693

Metal Replating and Repair
Cincinnati Plating Co. will repolish and repair silver, copper, brass, pewter, sterling, and chrome. This company will even tackle hard jobs like a spoon that has made a trip through a garbage disposal or a coffee pot minus a spout. New parts can be fabricated for existing pieces.
Cincinnati Plating & Repair Co.
13th & Broadway (downtown)
721-3446

The Tressel Co. is a firm Cincinnatians have trusted for years to polish and repair silver, pewter, brass, and copper.
Tressel Co.
811 Sycamore (downtown)
621-0905

Copper and brass only—St. Bernard Plating does wonders with these precious metals.
St. Bernard Plating
5560 Vine St. (St. Bernard)
242-4924

East Hills Plating and Repair cleans, replates, lacquers, and repairs silver, copper, and brass. They can also repair pewter, even refinish brass beds.
East Hills Plating & Repair Service
34 Washington Ave. (Bellevue)
431-7870

Handiest People in Town

Welding

John Feinauer can fabricate most anything from steel, from spiral staircases to window guards. He will make tedious repairs on antique wrought-iron many welders won't bother with.
John C. Feinauer Welding
4 W. 2nd St. (Newport)
291-3691

Tinsmith

Christopher Nordloh, under the company name of Lt. Moses Willard, makes reproductions of antique chandeliers and pierced-tin lighting fixtures that can be electrically wired or lighted with candles. All his work is strikingly authentic. Write for a catalogue of the complete line and enclose $4.50.
Lt. Moses Willard
1156 Hwy. 50
Milford, OH 45150
831-8956

Glass

Danny Howard can resilver antique mirrors as well as install new ones. He can cover an entire wall, if that's your pleasure. Custom-cut glass is his specialty, from creating new pieces such as pedestals to constructing an entire glass table. You can even bring Danny crystal goblets with chips and nicks to have them ground down and repolished.
Haglasco
211 York St. (Newport)
581-8810

If you want custom-made art glass—stained, leaded, or beveled panels for residences or commercial purposes depicting any theme you desire—the following two businesses can fill your needs. Architectural Art Glass Studio will also repair and restore antique art glass.

Kessler Studios
273 E. Broadway (Loveland)
683-7500

Architectural Art Glass Studio
6106½ Montgomery Rd. (Pleasant Ridge)
731-7336

Brush Restoration

You bought an antique comb, hairbrush, and hand mirror—a set that used to grace the top of dressing tables. You'd like to display them, only the bristles of the brush are decidedly tired. Cincinnati Brush Manufacturing Co. can remove the old bristles from the wood block inserted in the frame and replace them with nylon fibers in any gauge of stiffness you desire. They'll also replace bristles in antique fireplace brushes or worn-out contemporary brushes of any kind. They can fabricate a broom or brush for any job—just bring in an idea of what you want.
Cincinnati Brush Manufacturing Co.
2019 Central Ave. (downtown)
621-0370

Cincinnati Plating & Repair Co. (see their previous listing under "Metal Replating and Repair" in this chapter) can replace bristles in old brushes as well as replace combs and mirrors. They rejuvenate the whole set.

House Makeover

Say you want to put your home up for sale. Though it's in good condition, it just doesn't have enough charm to entice buyers. Call Anna Cassinelli of First Impressions. Merging her former profession as realtor and her talent as an interior designer, she knows exactly what a house needs to look good in

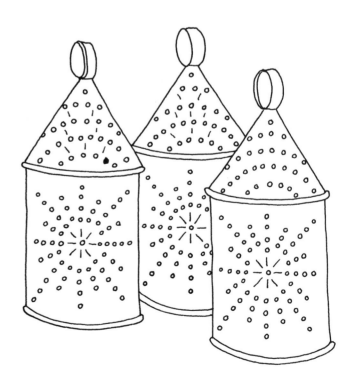

the marketplace. She comes to your home for an assessment, then transforms it with her own collection of objects. She hangs pictures, places knickknacks on tables, covers a table or two with tablecloths, drapes chairs with shawls or afghans. She'll spruce up a dull bathroom with mirrors, mats, and plants. Anna will even tell you what background music you should play when prospective buyers come to call. Clients I spoke to said Anna's fee was definitely worth it—they sold their homes on the first day they were shown.
First Impressions
751-3715

Building Restoration

Charles Dahlenburg is a building-restoration craftsman. He can restore exterior wood, plaster, repair doors, simulate old wood finishes, do carpentry, bring back antique mechanical systems to working condition. He can even repair antique plumbing by digging up vintage parts so that everything looks untouched. Charles trained at the National Trust for Historic Preservation in Tarrytown, New York, and has been rekindling Cincinnati buildings for fifteen years.
Charles Dahlenburg
491-6746

Art Restoration

Wiebold can conserve china, glass, metal, wood carvings, paintings—anything in the fine-art line except paper, textiles, and furniture. They routinely restore and repair museum-quality pieces and will do a fine job for you.
Wiebold Art Conservation Lab
413 Terrace Pl. (Terrace Park)
831-2541

Carolyn Von Stein is a fine-arts conservator who has worked on location to restore historic wall murals, and on everything else from paintings to wood carvings in her incredible studio overlooking the city. Her work is as impeccable as her taste.
Carolyn Von Stein
721-1033

Document and Book Restoration

See "Reading Matter," pages 120-124.

Doll Hospitals

See "Toys and Novelties," pages 98-102.

Mounting and Repairing Lamps

Virtually anything you bring to Palette Studios can be made into a lamp. Owner Paul Denight commonly wires antique pottery, glassware, and figurines. Those of rarity can be mounted without drilling so they do not lose their value. Palette repairs lamps, recovers shades, and custom makes shades out of any material as long as it is pliable. This includes suede, chintz, even wallpaper.
Palette Studios
2501 Woodburn Ave. (Walnut Hills)
961-1316

Walls

Marbling, faux treatments, stenciling, glazing, air brushing, sponging, ragging—Gary Lord can do any sort of hand-painted wall finish and restore old ones. Show him a page from a magazine and he can reproduce it in your home, even faux marble painted floors and contemporary floor designs such as triangles and squares.
Wall Options By Gary Lord
542-5069

Eileen Kleinman can stencil Victorian or Colonial designs on your walls, a Noah's Ark wall graphic in a nursery, even a Rousseau-like scene. She can do floor stencils, too. Call her with ideas. She'll come up with the drawing, then do the painting.
Up Against the Wall
984-1951

Handiest People in Town

54

Hardwood Floors

For laying beautiful hardwood floors, staining, sealing, refinishing, cleaning, and waxing, call these two fine companies many builders and homeowners depend on.

McSwain Hardwood
554-0270

Bluford Jackson & Son
831-6231

Carpet and Upholstery Cleaners

Gfroerer cleans wall-to-wall carpeting and area rugs, as well as any kind of antique or rare floor covering such as Orientals, Aubussons, classic American woven rugs with care and understanding of their value. They repair, refit, refringe—do all sorts of maintenance as well. Upholstery is treated with the same fine respect.
The Gfroerer Co., Inc.
241-4209

Security/Amirkhanian has an outstanding reputation for carpet and upholstery cleaning services.
Security/Amirkhanian
242-1431 (Cincinnati)
727-6000 (Erlanger)

Fiber Seal

Fiber Seal is recommended by many interior designers to protect fine upholstery, carpets, fabric wall coverings, and drapes. Their spray treatment forms a protective sealant on fabrics that prevents smudges and spills from becoming permanent stains.
Fiber Seal of Cincinnati
321-8887

Dry Cleaners

Everyone has his own dry cleaning horror story. There isn't one company I could get people to agree is best. Still, Batsakes emerged as the blue-ribbon favorite—for cleaning hats and clothes. Expensive knits come back the same size from Batsakes and knit tops are kindly folded over hangers, not jammed on them like shirts so the shoulders are out of shape. The runner-up choice was Widmer's—and they pick up and deliver, which is a decided asset. Both do laundry and alterations.

J&G Batsakes Dry Cleaners
605 Walnut St. (downtown)
721-4030

Widmer's Dry Cleaners
2016 Madison Rd. (O'Bryonville)
321-5100

Reweaving

Rips, tears, burns, and worn spots on fabrics? You need someone to assess the damage, tell you whether the garment is worthy of the cost, and whether the finished work will really disguise the injury or look sadly patched. You can depend on these three reweavers.

A-1 Miracle Weavers
18 E. 4th St., 2nd floor (downtown)
381-3753

Wizard Weavers
2701 Observatory (Hyde Park)
871-5750

Banasch's
108 E. 7th St. (downtown)
721-5210

Down Comforter and Pillow Repair

See "Bedding," pages 32-33.

Antique Clothing Restoration

Both Mary Fisher and Jennifer Gleason (they are friends, but they work on their own) do impeccable antique wedding-gown restoration. They can remake a family heirloom to fit a contemporary-size woman: rejuvenate, repair or restyle any delicate vintage garment—old white cottons to '20s beaded evening gowns. You'll find out more about these two talented women in "Wearables," page 20.

Mary Fisher
491-6746

Jennifer Gleason
431-1974

Ties Narrowed

Wide ties stuck in the back of your closet can be narrowed to any width you specify so you can add them to this year's wardrobe. Sound appealing? Call these two specialists. (Although this service is performed at A-One's main location, you can drop ties off at any of their branches.)

A-One Cleaners
731-7950

Widmer's Dry Cleaners
321-5100

Monograms

If you'd like something monogrammed—from guest towels to the lining of your coat—in a variety of attractive letter styles, try these two stores.

Monograms Plus, Inc.
Valley Center (Roselawn)
761-7587

Koch Sporting Goods
131 W. 4th St. (downtown)
621-2352

Shoe and Leather Repair

Kathman's can repair, dye, clean, weatherize, and restyle shoes. This even means intricate jobs such as rounding off pointed toes or making round ones pointy. Bernie Kathman and his son Buck can bring most any shoe back for a second walk around the block (even ones used by dogs as teething rings) and will honestly tell you if a shoe isn't worth fixing. Alterations on leather goods such as purse straps and belts are made here, suede garments are cleaned, orthopedic shoe prescriptions are filled.
Kathman Goodyear Shoe Repair
108 W. 6th St. (downtown)
621-7541

Brems Shoe Co. is one of the few remaining places in town where you can order custom-made shoes of the finest available leather. Not stylish shoes, though. I'm talking about the lace-up or sensible strap kind—standard models. Orthopedic shoes can be made to order (tiny to a size 17) and no prescription is too hard to fill. All repairs can be speedily handled.
Jacob D. Brems Shoe Co.
923 Vine St. (downtown)
721-3914

Though any Marmer store can fill shoe prescriptions, the one in Western Hills Plaza has a Prescription Footwear Clinic where shoes to fit people with specific problems such as arthritis, diabetes, any foot trauma are kept in stock to be adapted to the customer's problem. Molds of feet can be cast here for custom shoes as well.
Marmer's
Western Hills Plaza
661-4507

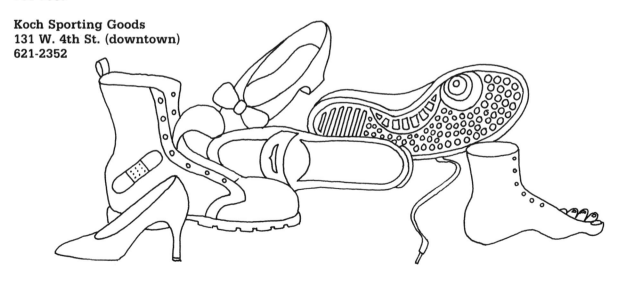

Handiest People in Town

Jewelry Repair

Frank Jones, owner of S&L Jewelry Co. (see "Sparkle Plenty," page 154, for complete information), can fix any piece of jewelry worth repairing, from replacing lost stones to rejoining a broken gold chain. He will candidly tell you whether the piece you bring in can justify the work and the cost—which is one of the reasons Frank is so popular. He can create an earring to match one you've lost, restyle old jewelry, even make new baubles from old gold jewelry by melting down the original.

S&L Jewelry Co.
37 W. 7th St., 4th fl. (downtown)
241-7359

Calligraphy

If you want a document or award handwritten in perfect script, call on a calligrapher of the caliber of Roman Wilshanetsky. He's a member of the Society of Scribes and Illuminators and hand letters children's books, charters, diplomas, declarations, and awards. Roman does not do mass-production work such as invitations or placecards but will refer you to people who do.

Roman Wilshanetsky
Home: 941-2943
Office: 471-2364

Bernie Berg will address invitations, hand letter seating charts, place cards—whatever you desire—in beautiful script. Talk to him about your special order.

Calligraphy by Bernie Berg
351-1234

Party Planners (more about them in "Home Entertainment," page 85, and "Party Paper and Office Supplies," page 91) can arrange calligraphers to do any sort of party writing. They can even find people to address your Christmas cards—just drop off your list and your cards and they'll take care of the rest.

Party Planners
793-3388

Signs

Need a sign for your booth at the craft fair, or for some other special occasion? Bring Pat Watson your idea or logo and he'll paint any sign on cloth, vinyl, paper, posterboard, or wood at a reasonable price.

Pat Watson
205 E. 8th St. (downtown)
241-1350

Vacuum-Sweeper Repair

Yes, there really is a person who will pick up your ailing vacuum sweeper, fix it, then deliver it the next day. His name is Howard Lucas, and he performs these mercy missions all over the city. He encourages regular service calls so that he can keep your sweeper in good running order rather than have you call him after it's given out. But no matter what the problem, Howard repairs all makes and models.

Howard Lucas
825-4473

Lawn-Mower Repair

Drop off your lawnmower at Swallen's Lawn Mower Repair Shop in the fall and they'll clean it, sharpen the blades, change the oil, put in new plugs, check the air cleaner, and store it until spring for $24.95. If the mower needs more work, they'll charge more, of course. Pickup and delivery are possible, too, but they will also cost you extra.

Swallen's Lawn Mower Repair Shop
4861 Spring Grove Ave. (Winton Place)
681-5079

Come Clean

Tell me the person who would rather scrub the kitchen floor than go for a walk in the woods. But jobs like that need to get done somehow, sometime. So, whether you're after someone to help you clean, products to make unpleasant jobs you have to do yourself easier, or soaps to make bath soaks silkier after you get the chores done—read on.

Get Organized

Your closets are a jumble. You vow you'll organize this mess one day—when you have time. But that day never seems to dawn. You just keep rooting through the chaos in your cupboards, swearing good intentions that never come to pass. Wouldn't it be wonderful if you could wave a magic wand and have everything put right for you? You can.

Call Debbie Hettesheimer, one of the most organized people I've ever met. Known as a "design organizer" for homes and offices, Debbie assesses your storage problems, makes drawings showing how to store materials more efficiently, then does it all for you.

Debbie came to my rescue bringing two assistants. In a day and a half, they untangled my hangers and substituted no-snarl ones that could be hung in layers. She destroyed my "towering inferno" of sweaters and set up a honeycomb system of rows of tubes, then rolled each sweater inside a tube, non-wrinkled and in plain view. She hung my belts on racks, color-coded my blouses and skirts (light to dark, summer to winter), separated my mixed-up sweatsuits into a ready-to-exercise system. She went through hall closets, mating mittens, scarves, overcoats—nothing escaped her whirlwind path. The only thing I had to do was get out of Debbie's way and learn how to fold things her way. She created space where I thought there was none and discovered clothes I hadn't seen in years in the backs of closets.

Debbie has all the supplies to create her system, which you buy along with her design services. Ask for an estimate.
The Debbinaire Way
771-4520

Edward Ruben calls himself a closetologist—he's a closet doctor who makes the best house calls in town. Edward organizes laundry rooms, attics, garages, outside storage areas, clothes closets. He's a remodeler who has a mill shop to create good-looking wood systems that can be color-coordinated with any room in your home.

Call him for a free consultation. After that, he will draw a plan for you. Edward doesn't roll sweaters like Debbie Hettesheimer; he creates bins. Should your existing closet rods need to be removed, he will replaster and paint so everything looks as good as new, even better, with his handiwork in place. He can also build outside storage areas hidden within tables, planters, even a fence, to stash the garden hose and all the tools that are spilling out of your garage.
Closets and More
984-MORE

Come Clean

The California Closet Company will send a designer to your home to measure your closets, take clothes counts, and then come up with a design for an organized system using their products. Or you can do the homework yourself and bring measurements to the store, which will net you a 25% savings. (Pantries, laundry rooms, and hall closets can be organized by designers, too.) If you're a do-it-yourselfer, California Closet Company has all sorts of closet-organizing accessories in the showroom ready for you to take home and install. All products are wood; there are three grades to choose from.
California Closet Company
I-275 & Mosteller Rd. (Sharonville)
772-0300

Cleaning Services

The popularity of cleaning services has skyrocketed as dual-career couples with little spare time need help to keep their homes livable. There are many fine companies that fill this need in Cincinnati, but recommending any of them is a chancy business. A service one person raves about may do a terrible job in another person's opinion. What *clean* means to people can't be found in a dictionary. So, hesitatingly and with trepidation, I offer the following three services—just to help you out in a pinch. They have been wholeheartedly recommended by people I trust.

My Maid, Inc. performs mostly residential general housecleaning services, though they will also do laundry and ironing, wash windows on the inside, even perform "relocation services," which means cleaning an empty house from top to bottom. Cleaning crews bring their own equipment, supply their own waxes and polishes, and can often do a job with just twenty-four hours notice. They work primarily east of I-75.
My Maid, Inc.
232-8731

Brenda T. Grier, owner of Bucketts, Mopps and Raggs Housecleaning Service, is a cheery, accommodating woman who will come to your home, assess your needs, tell you how long it will take to do the job, give you a price, and send a crew to do the work in speedy time. Brenda services the entire city, doing residential cleaning jobs, even washing dishes and doing laundry, but no ironing or windows. One person, whose home Brenda's crew cleaned before he moved into it, swears by her service. Clients arrange key drop-offs with her or simply give her a key, so Brenda's crews can set things right while they're at the office.
Bucketts, Mopps and Raggs Housecleaning Service
751-8473

Merry Maids is a franchise operation, one of 325 businesses in forty states now being called the "McDonald's" of the cleaning industry. Their two-person teams attack your messy house. One does the "wet work," the other the "dry work." They start at the top of each room and work down, vacuuming and dusting all the little places most people often miss. Their system is scientific and thorough. Owners Rich and Bobbi Levin will come to your home to give you an estimate. The price includes bringing all their own equipment and cleaning products. However, they will use yours if you prefer.
Merry Maids
821-9595

Industrial Cleaning Supplies

You doing the cleaning? Then do it faster, using potent industrial cleaning compounds. A person working in a commercial kitchen doesn't have time to scrub grease off stove parts, not to mention that awful glob of stuff hanging from the exhaust fan. He has a solution he can drop the dirty part into, pull it out, and it's clean.

Well, where do you get these products? From industrial suppliers who will sell to retail customers. Such things as laundry detergents, upholstery shampoo, dishwashing compounds, scrub soap for cement floors, furniture polish, heavy-duty garbage

cans, buckets, mops, every kind of broom and brush imaginable, and zillions of other things. You'll find brands you recognize from the grocery shelves and other names you won't, though they may be made by the same companies but for commercial use.

Here's a good starting list of places to investigate.

Phillips Supply Co.
1 Crosley Field Ln. (Queensgate)
579-1762

Saalfeld Paper Co.
2701 Spring Grove Ave. (Camp Washington)
542-7100

Hillside Maintenance Supply Co.
2331 Gilbert Ave. (East Walnut Hills)
751-4100

Herz-Weil
7623 Production Dr. (Roselawn)
821-3200

At J&S there is a huge supply of cleaning aids in their cash-and-carry store, or phone for a catalogue and ask for delivery, which comes in handy when you're buying a hundred-pound box of detergent and have no one to help you carry it inside your home. Small-order delivery can be arranged as well. Staff will advise you on which products to buy and will help arrange group purchases so customers can buy in quantity to qualify for bigger discounts.
J&S Soap and Supply
2043 Harrison Ave. (Fairmount)
661-5087

Cincinnati Brush Manufacturing Co. is filled with every kind of brush imaginable—upholstery, car wash, blacktop, paint brushes. There are brooms galore and even lambs' wool dusters with five-foot-long handles to reach spiderwebs on the ceiling. If you can't find the brush you need, this company will make it for you! All sorts of cleaning compounds, work gloves, garbage cans are also sold here.
Cincinnati Brush Manufacturing Co.
2019 Central Ave. (downtown)
621-0370

Big Jobs

Do you and your neighbors want to tackle cleaning up all the debris that's collected on your street? For a job that energetic, call Clean Cincinnati for assistance. You can have a Supercan delivered to your street and load it with old boards, car mufflers

abandoned next to the curb, washers, water heaters—whatever you've been wanting to get rid of for ages. After the one to three days you've reserved the Supercan for, the truck that delivered it comes and hauls it away.

Note that Supercans are dinosaur-size and look like a gondola coal car. Needless to say, your street must be wide enough to accommodate its girth and length. And the Supercan is not allowed to obstruct fire hydrants or street signs or be a traffic hazard.

How do you get such a wonder? Phone Clean Cincinnati and ask the staff to send you a form (which a representative of your community council must sign). Then mail it back at least three or four weeks prior to your proposed clean-up date. These huge containers are in heavy demand from the beginning of April until the beginning of October. No wonder—this service is free.
Clean Cincinnati
352-4910

Go Soak

You're exhausted from all this heavy-duty cleaning. Well, even thinking about it makes you want to soak in a hot tub. Check out the following two stores for all the soaps, lotions, and oils you'll need to treat yourself right.

Crabtree and Evelyn has soaps in every shape imaginable, made from all sorts of natural ingredients: guest bathroom soaps, animal-shaped soaps for children, oils, lotions, bath accessories, including a friendly yellow rubber duck you might like to take a soak with.
Crabtree and Evelyn
Westin Hotel (downtown)
421-6273

Caswell-Massey, one of the oldest chemists and perfumers in America, is flush with flower-scented soaps, those made of oatmeal, glycerine, buttermilk, tomato, tangerine, even blocks of Castile soap you can slice pieces from and use just as your grandparents did. There are dozens of skin care products, beautiful brushes, combs, even shaving brushes and mugs, straight razors and strops, which are all hard to come by. Phone for a catalogue so you can see their whole wondrous collection.
Caswell-Massey
Carew Tower Arcade (downtown)
421-6200

Cars

60 If the interior of your car looks like a combat zone, there are professional auto reconditioners who can perform rejuvenating wonders. They can even bring the exterior up to snuff with the interior if you ask for a total job.

Many of these car wizards perform less drastic clean-up services, too. You can make arrangements to have them pick up your car while you are at work, hand wash (even wax) it, clean the interior, and then have it delivered to you before the end of the day. Ask about arranging this on a weekly basis if you really want to keep your car spiffy. (Note: my experience with pickup and delivery services is that they can be spotty. Many companies say they will do this—and do. Others will—until they become too busy to keep it up. Dependability can change quickly.) Also, you *can* drop your car off yourself at any of these places.

An intensive interior-reconditioning job generally means nothing inside the car is left untouched. They vacuum and shampoo the carpet and upholstery and remove all stains, redress leather seats, scrub the car ceiling, and put windows, knobs, seat belts, mirrors, the trunk in like-new shape. Exterior work includes hand washing; removing tar, oxidation, stains, old wax; cleaning vinyl, rubber, plastic, and chrome; hand waxing and buffing the body. You can also ask them to redress the tires and clean and repaint the engine. Prices will depend on the amount of work you want done, who's doing it, and the condition of your car. But if you definitely want more maintenance than a drive-through car wash can provide, here are some places that perform meticulous auto-care services.

Asco Reconditioning's pickup and delivery services are available on the east side of town—mainly Anderson Township, downtown, Hyde Park, Montgomery, and Kenwood.
Asco Reconditioning
165 E. Main St. (Batavia)
732-9211

Phone for an appointment with Autoworld owners Fred and Judy Tiemeyer, who do impeccable, personal work. They will even restore classic cars and make house calls for vintage autos exceeding $100,000 in value.
Autoworld (West Chester area)
777-2973

Owner John McGrath of Finishing Touch will pick up and deliver in Montgomery, Blue Ash, Madeira, Indian Hill, Kenwood, Sharonville, Tri-County, Mason, West Chester. This place does fine, dependable work and regularly cleans up Jags, Mercedes-Benzes, BMWs—you know. You can bring your RV, truck, or van here, too.
Finishing Touch
8647 U.S. Rt. 42 (West Chester)
779-2120

If you drop your car off at Butler's, you can arrange to be taken to work and picked up later in the day in a Cadillac limousine. They will also pick up and deliver your car for you, and they do A-1 service.
Butler's Auto Cleaning Specialists
8181 Camargo Rd. (Madeira)
271-1000

Quality Car Cleaning picks up and delivers in a three-mile radius of Blue Ash, Montgomery, and Deer Park.
Quality Car Cleaning
4452 Sycamore Rd. (Rossmoyne)
984-8323

Professional Auto Care will pick up and deliver in Blue Ash only.
Professional Auto Care
5011 Cooper Rd. (Blue Ash)
891-0957

Calvin Cross picks up and delivers free in the downtown area; ask him about the charge for service if you're further away. Calvin's been doing cars for fifteen years, has owned this business for two, and promises a detailed, top-quality job.
Calvin's Auto Laundry
425 E. Court St. (downtown)
241-WASH

Other Restorative Services

Someone dropped a cigarette on your back seat and burned a terrible hole in your upholstery. Or maybe a person with a sick sense of humor slashed your convertible top. Or your garage was flooded in a rainstorm and so was your car. Who can repair the results of these disasters? Try Jim Hayden. This large operation also installs sunroofs and custom vinyl car roofs, replaces upholstery, makes seat covers—it can do all sorts of auto reconditioning.

Jim Hayden's Auto Top
3154 Exon Ave. (Evendale)
563-8828

Max Interior Design can do any kind of interior car restoration—these folks are so adept at it that they have brought a 1950 Mercury and a 1949 Buick back to life, even a 1927 Rolls-Royce. They can customize a car interior—like building a bar in the back seat—as well as installing sunroofs, doing van conversions. Talk to them about what you need.

Also talk to the owner about a man named Jim Farr a.k.a. Dauber, who works out of this shop as well as others in town. Dauber is an artist among car buffs and is known as the best striper in Cincinnati. No vinyl stick-on stripes for him. He paints them on, and he paints them on some of the best cars in town. Dauber also paints stripes on racing cars, and can paint any design on any car you want.

Max Interior Design
1565 Harrison Ave. (Fairmount)
661-7433

Bill Roell can paint your entire car, or paint pin stripes, racing stripes, flames shooting down the sides, but no murals. He can do a classic paint job on a BMW or transform a Corvette by painting it pearlized gold. Talk to him about any custom job you can dream up.

Bill Roell Paint Shop
17 W. 18th St. (Covington)
291-7596

The Larry B. Daniels Co. is recommended by most of the expensive foreign-car dealers when people ask who does the best paint job in town. Daniels guarantees the car will look just like it did when it came off the showroom floor when he's finished with it, and to back up that promise, he completely disassembles the car to paint it. Don't expect work to be done in a few weeks and do expect to pay top dollar for a job of this caliber. Craftsmen here take time with cars in the Porsche and Ferrari class. Mercedes-Benzes and BMWs are routine in this place, but Daniels will also work on domestic cars.

The Larry B. Daniels Co.
4003 Plainville Rd. (Madison Place)
271-1746

Larry Kramer can build a car (like a hot rod) from scratch or redesign any car. He can lower the roof, extend the fenders, change the wheel base, fit a newer, bigger motor, and install air conditioning in a vintage car. Larry likes nostalgia cars best—'50s cars are the most popular right now, with 1950 Mercurys leading the pack. You can't be in a hurry for Larry's services. He's booked for a year in advance.

Larry Kramer Custom Cars
2437 Beekman St. (Fairmount)
921-0306

Need hubcaps? You can find just about any kind for any model car dating as far back as the 1940s at Red-Fox Dealer Supply, otherwise known as "The Hub Cap Daddy." These hubcaps are the originals, not replicas, which makes this store a real treasure trove. And what's not in the store may be out in the garage, so keep looking.

Red-Fox Car Dealer Supply
7450 Vine St. (Carthage)
948-8083

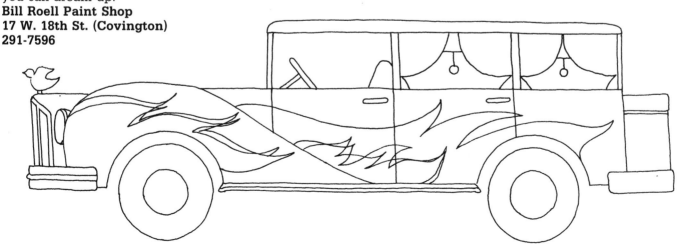

Cars

62 You can find wheel-cover look-alikes at A-One Dealer Supply. Insignias on these are similar to the original hubcaps, but definitely not the same, which might make purists shudder. But if you've lost a few hubcaps in street craters during a bad winter, you may be happy to save some money buying replicas.

Bring the wheel covers you have left so you can match them as closely as possible by looking through A-One's catalogue. Staff will fetch your choice from the warehouse to see how it looks with what you've got. If it doesn't work too well, they'll keep bringing others until you find a style that fits.

A-One Dealer Supply
5517 Fair Ln. (Fairfax)
272-1595

Spradlin Imported Auto Parts has every kind of accessory and cleaning supply imaginable for foreign cars, including waxes fit for a Rolls-Royce. You can buy orthopedic car seats here—just the right prescription for people with back problems. Made to replace the original car seat, they provide lumbar support, can be electrically heated and adjusted, and for their roughly $3,000 price, they do all sorts of other wonderful tricks.

Spradlin Imported Auto Parts
2021 E. Kemper Rd. (Sharonville)
771-7777
3972 Edwards Rd. (Hyde Park)
731-5900
8090 Beechmont Ave. (Anderson Twp.)
474-5810

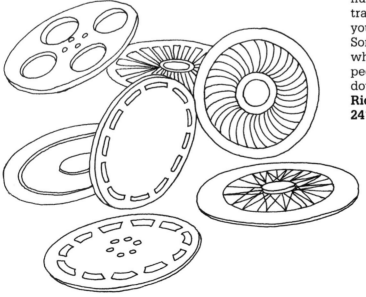

Get A Hearse

You want a car more unusual than anyone else's and you don't mind being a bit macabre? Go see Carl Woerner, who sells vintage hearses and ambulances—lots of Cadillac models—because he says they're not only beautifully and expensively made vehicles—but they sure get you noticed when you drive up in one. Ask him about the time he took a carload of people to the drive-in in an ambulance or the time he picked up a date in a hearse.

Who are Carl's serious customers? People who use hearses and ambulances like trucks for moving and hauling, rock groups who lug around equipment, college students. These cars have low mileage and a good price—though some eat gas like nothing else you've ever driven. I love talking to Carl about these cars—his enthusiasm is contagious. But I did not like it when my son caught the fever and we almost wound up with a black hearse a block long parked in our driveway.

C-W Coach Sales
7444 Vine St. (Carthage)
821-6200

Share the Ride

Do your car a real favor and use it less. Call Rideshare, an information center on pooled rides that has a computer matching system to get people who live and work in the same area to travel to work together. They also offer "park and ride" information on where you can park your car free all day and then take public transportation. They can provide you with van pool information on getting downtown from outlying areas.

Rideshare's objective is to decrease the number of people who drive alone to lower the traffic volume, which will lead to cleaner air. And your pocketbook will benefit, as well as your body. Some insurance companies give discounts to people who car pool. And any car carrying three or more people can park free at Riverfront Stadium Lot #3 downtown. Call for additional information.

Rideshare
241-RIDE

Who'll Watch the Kids?

Whether you need an occasional babysitter or full-time help, you want someone responsible to watch your children. Who can you turn to? The agencies mentioned in this chapter—with a mild disclaimer. A service that provides excellent child-care professionals for one person may disappoint another. Like cleaning services, opinions are extremely subjective. Though the agencies mentioned in this chapter have been highly recommended by people who have used them, be sure to carefully interview anyone you are thinking of hiring to make sure they meet your special requirements.

Comprehensive Community Child Care (4 C's) is the most important source of child-care information in Cincinnati. This agency helps parents evaluate child care and puts parents in touch with child-care providers. Staff can send you free brochures telling you what to look for in a day-care center and how to interview people who will take care of your children, even send you a list of babysitting services. If you are interested in a day-care center for your child, 4 C's will refer you to one in your area and tell you what services it offers. If you only need after-school child care, 4 C's can direct you. They can assist you with infant care—in your own home, someone else's, or tell you which day-care centers are licensed to take care of babies.

4 C's only refers to licensed facilities that meet their standards—and they are very particular. Call 4 C's if you need information or assistance with any aspect of caring for children.
Comprehensive Community Child Care
621-8585

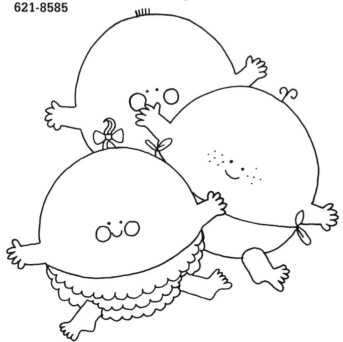

If you've missed work in the past to care for a sick child, you'll be happy to know about Kid Kare. It's professional supervision for children six weeks to fifteen years of age by licensed pediatric nurses at St. Luke Hospital. From 6 A.M. to 6:30 P.M., sick children are cared for, given meals, and entertained for $16 per ten-hour day. Care for less than eight hours is $2 per hour.

Whether your child has something contagious or just a stomach ache, St. Luke's program is a lifesaver if you need to be at work and your child needs supervision. Just phone two hours before you intend to drop off your child, and fill out pre-admission forms when you arrive. Consider doing the paperwork in advance so that everything will be in place when an emergency strikes. Note that daily admission depends on space availability, but right now St. Luke has sixteen beds—enough to meet current demand. Phone St. Luke for more information and ask that a Kid Kare brochure be sent to you.
Kid Kare
St. Luke Hospital
85 N. Grand Ave. (Ft. Thomas)
To obtain information:
572-3277
To reserve Kid Kare:
572-3610

Domestic Connection maintains a drop-in center for children from eighteen months to twelve years of age. For a yearly family registration fee, members can bring children to this clean, cheerful place filled with up-to-date play equipment for however many hours they need children supervised—for a day or just while they run errands. Domestic Connection provides all sorts of in-home domestic assistance, too. Phone to see if your child-care needs can be met by their personnel.
Domestic Connection
3318 Erie Ave. (Hyde Park)
871-MOMS

Rock-A-Bye is one of the oldest sitter registry services in the city. Grown children who were cared for by Rock-A-Bye babysitters are now calling the service for their children. That's solid reference. Rock-A-Bye provides babysitters for the evening, for an entire weekend, live-ins for parents on vacation, or to watch children at home while Mom is in the hospital having another. Maternity nurses can also be provided.
Rock-A-Bye and Family Care
721-7440

Who'll Watch the Kids?

64

Jack and Jill Babysitting Service has been in business twenty-six years providing reputable, dependable sitters to Cincinnati families. They will book occasional evenings, overnights, sitters to stay with children while parents vacation, and maternity nurses.

Jack and Jill Babysitting Service
731-5261

Apple of Your Eye can help you find full-time or part-time help or someone for continuous care, which is babysitting the same days or hours each week. They can also provide sitters for occasional evenings, overnights, and vacations, plus maternity nurses. Call and leave a message on the answering machine. You will be contacted within a couple of hours.

Apple of Your Eye Referral Service
530-0999

Friends of the Family is a referral service providing a full range of personalized home and family care services. This company interviews potential workers to fill your needs, then sends them to you so that you can interview them yourself. For housecleaning aid, for someone to do shopping and errands, child care, babysitting, pet sitting—give them a call to see if they can come up with someone to help.

Friends of the Family
489-1688

Home Management Services acts on behalf of parents to locate child-care and domestic help by placing advertisements, then interviewing and screening applicants. Parents are responsible for the final hiring decision.

Home Management Services
232-4711

Child Care Professionals, Inc. worked with the College of Mt. St. Joseph to set up a child-care curriculum in 1986. The college coursework in subjects such as infant and child development, home management, family communication, nutrition, and others is directed by the Education Department and certifies students to take care of children. Graduates who are referred to as nannies, masters, and governesses are then placed in private homes by Child Care Professionals, Inc. The agency staff matches family needs with the skills of these professional care givers by making in-home family visits.

For quality help of this kind, expect to pay a salary in the range of $150 to $350 a week, though $200 is an average starting wage. And remember nannies care for children, cook for them, provide transportation to school and appointments, travel with the family while caring for the child. They do not do domestic chores.

Child Care Professionals, Inc.
561-4810

North American Nannies Institute is a nanny school and employment agency for its graduates, who are placed all over the country. There is a waiting list for these talented students, and no wonder. They are trained in child development theory, guidance, discipline, infant care, cooking, creative art and movement by Dr. Judy Bunge, a Ph.D. in Child Development and Director of the Institute.

Families are screened so that nannies can be found to match their particular needs. Starting salaries are generally $200 per week.

North American Nannies Institute
61 Jefferson Ave.
Columbus, OH 43215
614-228-6264

The Au Pair in America program can give American families child-care help while young British and English-speaking Europeans between the ages of eighteen and twenty-five have a place to live for a year that gives them an inside view of American family life. The host family provides the au pair with a private room, full board, at least $100 a week, and inclusion in family outings, some social events, and vacations. The au pair helps look after children, helps bathe and feed them, can be asked to watch them when parents are not at home, should assist with light housework and other pre-arranged duties. Everyone benefits.

Au Pair in America
100 Greenwich Ave.
Greenwich, CT 06830
800-243-4567

Senior Services

There are many agencies that provide crucial services for older adults such as delivering prepared meals, operating adult day-care centers, providing home health aides. How do you find these kinds of help without making a morning's worth of phone calls? Try these pivotal sources.

The Council on Aging of the Cincinnati Area actually develops many programs for seniors or contracts them out. That's why phoning for information here generally yields answers right away. Staff will point you to activities at a nearby senior center, can explain what adult day-care centers actually provide and give you names to contact, can tell you about educational opportunities and how to apply for financial assistance, arrange home-delivered meals, do employment placement, counsel on housing opportunities—these are just a sampling. Whether you need advice on how to pick a nursing home for your parents or want to arrange for someone to drive them to the supermarket once a week, this is a good place to get the information.

Council on Aging of the Cincinnati Area
721-1025

United Home Care helps older adults remain as independent as possible at home. An intake person gathers information on what the senior needs, does an in-home assessment, then comes up with suggestions to fill those needs, plus the names of people who can actually do the jobs, whether it's physical therapy, light housekeeping and meal preparation, telephone reassurance, total care, or a combination of many services. United Home Care has fingers into all the home-care agencies in the city—they pull the care package together saving you endless hours and frustration.

United Home Care
621-8989

United Way Information and Referral has every helpful agency in the area on its computer so phone callers are immediately directed to specific people who can deliver the services they need. (See "Help: Get It—Give It," page 161, for complete information.)

United Way Information and Referral
721-7900

Senior Services caseworkers go into the home to investigate seniors' problems, then solve them. One of the agency's primary responsibilities is to monitor senior protective services, to supervise homebound, older individuals so they are not financially or physically taken advantage of. This agency is equipped to be the representative payee for Social Security payments should a senior not be able to take care of his finances, even assume powers of attorney.

Call Senior Services if your parent needs a gerontological assessment. This is crucial if your parent needs help and you don't know exactly what kind or how to arrange it. Social workers do a complete workup, calling in other professionals, then they hold a family conference presenting community resources that can fill in the gaps. After a care structure has been set up, staff will monitor these services to make sure the quality of care remains high. This is an extremely valuable service, especially if the parent who needs care is in a different city than his children.

Senior Services can provide diverse assistance, so whether you need home-delivered meals, or you want to know about shared housing units in the city, this supportive and protective agency is a good one to turn to.

Senior Services
721-4330

Pro Seniors is a law project for the elderly whose primary job is to provide free legal assistance to people over sixty years old. Whether you need help in drawing up a will, want to know your rights as a nursing-home resident, need to find out about Medicare eligibility, this agency provides concrete assistance.

Pro Seniors, Inc.
621-8721

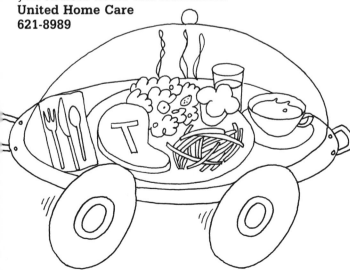

Body and Soul

Feeling fit and looking it, too—that's the credo of the '80s. So to help you stay in perfect shape, you're about to be introduced to people who can advise you how to eat right, tell you how to shed stress, beautify your body, even put you in touch with heavenly bodies by contacting the spirit world.

You Are What You Eat

Never mind the latest food gurus, fad diet books, megavitamin regimens—you want the real story on what food you should be eating. Phone the Greater Cincinnati Nutrition Council hotline at 721-7900. Dieticians can tell you the nutritional value and calorie content of any food product, advise you whether a particular food is right for your special diet (high-cholesterol, salt-free), evaluate diet books, tell you about food additives and artificial sweeteners, send out brochures providing much specialized diet and food information. The Nutrition Council will also recommend nutritionists who are in private practice, should you want a personal consultation. Ask about the agency's speakers bureau, about membership, which entitles you to their newsletter, *Food for Thought*, about whatever special services they may presently be offering.
Greater Cincinnati Nutrition Council
621-3262

Never before have so many people sought the help of nutritionists. But doesn't it make sense? If you're a marathon runner, a food expert can tell you exactly how to fuel your body with the energy it needs. If you must eliminate, say, sugar from your diet, you can speak to someone who can work out a menu that is adaptable to your life-style and palate. All of the registered dieticians in private practice who I mention below do not pass out magic diets. They do share valuable food information so you can eat more intelligently on your own. A few will even accompany clients to the supermarket to show them how to put better food alternatives in their shopping carts, will teach them how to crack the code on labels so they will know how to make all the right choices. These nutritionists are adaptable—they'll work with you to satisfy your particular health needs.

Diann R. Rivkin, R.D
871-7828 (Hyde Park)

Susan G. Riches, R.D.
441-3330 (Ft. Thomas)

Ruth Edwards, R.D.
574-9932 (Western Hills)

Jeanne Houston
671-1011 (Fairfield—Tri-County)

Anda Lou Gouge
525-6382 (Florence)

Joan Stoffregen
231-1144 (Anderson Twp.)

Anne Marie Erb
232-6173 (Anderson Twp.)

Expand Your Horizons

You want to find someone who gives great massages, does acupuncture, can help you manage stress. You want to know about retreat centers in the area, health food restaurants, upcoming body/mind workshops. There are two quarterly newspapers in Cincinnati that deliver this very information.

New Lifestyles explores all aspects of personal growth and alternative living in Greater Cincinnati. Editor and publisher Suzanne Collins has even put together a *Healing Arts Directory* that lists every kind of practitioner: massage therapists, holistic physicians and therapists, hypnotists, rebirthers, tarot readers, many others. Suzanne knows these people and is familiar with their skills, so her newspaper and her directory are extremely helpful. *New Lifestyles* is available free at assorted health food stores and bookstores throughout the city. Or you can buy a subscription for $7.50 per year. The *Healing Arts Directory* is $2.50 plus 50¢ postage.

New Lifestyles
5397 Country Lane
Milford, OH 45150
831-7377

The Greater Cincinnati Resource Directory is distributed free at about 150 locations in Cincinnati: health food stores, bookstores—look for it. It contains all the information you need to find psychics to rolfers, natural childbirth to martial arts classes. It is a fine source of regularly updated information. A subscription costs $7.50 per year.

Greater Cincinnati Resource Directory
3514 Burch Ave.
Cincinnati, OH 45208
871-4950 or 244-9066

Body Work

Some people like a gentle massage; others want a deep tissue treatment. Some prefer the Oriental approach, which means the massage therapist works mainly on pressure points, or a Swedish massage so that the therapist smooths out muscles with the palms of his hands. How can you find a massage therapist just right for you? Look in the two publications I just mentioned. Phone some of the therapists who seem like likely candidates and ask about their techniques. You may have to try out several to find the person who best suits you. Also, ask your friends who they go to for massage. Sometimes that's the easiest and best way. However, to help along your search, here are a few people and places I've heard good things about and/or I've tried myself.

Body Comfort Therapeutic Massage
321-6362

Jeanne Miller
321-6411

Karen Rommé
542-0259

Kate Walker
221-6245

Gary Matthews
1-444-2834
Answering service:
244-3114

John Degg
581-6932

The following places offer massage, but also facials, face and/or body waxing, makeovers, manicures, pedicures, a full line of hair services. You can choose any or several of the services or sign up for all of them—some offer a day's worth of treatment for a special price. Bliss! (Note that Slend-O-Form serves women only, offering facials, massage, controlled ring rollers; Mitchell's does everything but massage.)

Patricia Stewart
8 Fountain Square (downtown)
721-1557

Phyllis at the Madison
2324 Madison Rd. (Hyde Park)
321-1300

Body and Soul

Joi Skin and Hair Center
2128 Madison Rd. (O'Bryonville)
321-4681

Dazzles
3074 Madison Rd. (Oakley)
321-5777

Slend-O-Form Studio
18 E. 4th St., 11th fl. (downtown)
621-3878

Mitchell's
9823 Montgomery Rd. (Montgomery)
793-0900

Let's Make Up

You want a professional to advise you about
makeup so you can learn to accentuate your best
features. Call About Face. Owner Eileen Shapiro
listens to what your preferences are, helps you use
makeup to match your life-style. She uses fine-
quality cosmetics, many of which are recommended
by dermatologists, that do not irritate your skin. She
can make you sparkle for a special occasion, often
does entire wedding parties.

    Eileen also works with people who have had
facial surgery. She can handily disguise scars,
camouflage birthmarks and teach clients how to do
it, too.
About Face
7979 Reading Rd. (Roselawn)
761-9700

Ellen Levin is a makeup artist who works with
dermatologists and plastic surgeons. She is an
expert at disguising eyelifts, facelifts, bruises,
birthmarks, pigmentation problems, scars due to
shingles and acne. She regularly works with
serious burn cases, has even recreated a mouth
with makeup. Ellen sees patients in doctors' offices
right after surgery, or in her studio. She does
glamour makeup, too, which Ellen says adds zip to
the serious side of her business.
Ellen Levin
9404 Main St. (Montgomery)
984-0960

You don't need a professional to make you up. You
can do just fine on your own, but you'd like to use
cosmetics that have not been tested on laboratory
animals. Where do you find cruelty-free products in
Cincinnati? Contact Jayn Meinhardt. She is a
representative for the Paul Penders skin care line:
cleansers, eye cream, hand creams, skin-care
products, bath products, deodorants, hair-care
products, a variety of makeup. Phone or write her
for catalogues, price lists, to place orders, to find
out what local retail stores carry some of these
products. Jayn sells them at her home from 2:00 to
4:00 on Sunday afternoons.
Jayn Meinhardt
1501 E. McMillan (E. Walnut Hills)
Cincinnati, OH 45206
961-5555

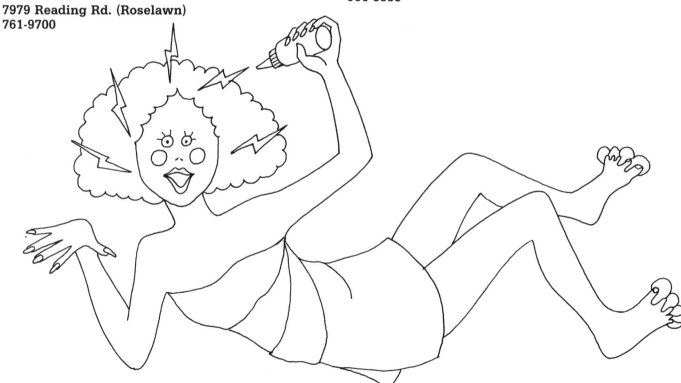

Health Resorts

Sans Souci, housed in a spacious colonial home on a grand eighty-acre estate, is in Bellbrook, Ohio, near Dayton. This health resort, owned and operated by Susanne Kircher, offers residential, weekend, or day-long programs specializing in weight control and general health. The agenda includes exercise, walks, aqua dynamics, dance classes, slimnastics, yoga, cooking classes, meditation walks, stress management, smoking-cessation classes, makeup, pedicures, manicures, massage. Open from May through October, Sans Souci has had national recognition for its excellence.

Sans Souci
3745 W. Franklin Rd.
Bellbrook, OH 45305
1-848-4851 or 1-435-9778

Kerr House, twenty minutes south of the Toledo Airport, is an oasis of Victorian charm. If you are looking for pampering, make reservations here. Your body and spirit will be rejuvenated after a week-long stay because your daily regimen begins with breakfast in bed, is followed by massage, facials, a variety of exercise sessions, sauna treatments, and ends with a healthy gourmet dinner served by candlelight. How nice.

Kerr House
Grand Rapids, OH 43522
419-832-1733

Oh, My Aching Back

All you need is something to relieve your aching back. Try The Back Care Shop. It stocks twenty different types of back support cushions, cervical pillows, braces, chairs, tools such as rakes and shovels designed for people with back problems, all sorts of sleeping aids.

The Back Care Shop
7390 Hosbrook Rd. (Kenwood)
793-7335
765-G Eastgate South Dr. (Mt. Carmel)
752-5200

Star Trek

You want to connect with the spirit world. You're not a skeptic; you believe in psychics. Well, there are many people in the area who say they have such extrasensory powers. Some of them advertise in the quarterly publications I mentioned previously in this chapter. Here are four you may want to consider.

Margeurite Bolden is an ordained minister and a psychic spiritual counselor. By entering into meditation, she blends with the higher aspects of a person's nature and becomes clairvoyant. Then she shares her insights by acting as a conduit between the person she is counseling and the person's spirit guides.

Margeurite Bolden
351-4953

Carmen Cohen lives north of Hamilton and has quite a following among Cincinnatians. She gives clients a twenty-minute reading, then they may ask questions.

Carmen Cohen
868-1939

Esther Shelton says her God-given spiritual gift came to her four years ago and is growing stronger all the time. She shares her insight with people who come to her with questions about their inner selves and personal problems. Esther says, "God gives the answers. I tell the person what feedback I receive."

Esther Shelton
356-1368

Linda Hauser can touch someone's hand or sit next to a person and symbols flash through her mind. When she relates these symbols to whoever she is with, they have special meaning for that person. Linda is also a medium, an ESP advisor, and she gives readings to those who are open to this spirit-inspired information.

Linda Hauser
351-2514

Body and Soul

Edward Kluska, owner of the New World Bookshop, became fascinated with the potential of astrology in the early '70s. Since then, this M.A. in psychology has taught many astrology classes and offers a complete consultation service. Says Ed, "Astrology is a sophisticated tool which can help us discover our deepest needs, motivations, and dimensions. I aspire to help people gain greater self-understanding, develop their potential, make wiser decisions." Phone New World for information on Ed's many astrological services.
New World Bookshop
336 Ludlow Ave. (Clifton)
861-6100

Cool It

If you'd like to settle a conflict amicably, whether it's a property dispute with a neighbor or an even hotter topic—your divorce—you might want to give mediation a try. It's a more pleasant alternative to "My lawyer will be in touch with yours." The Cincinnati Mediation Center works with clients who have difficulties to find common overlapping interests, then helps them negotiate with each other. Even high-conflict problems—custody, alimony, family disputes—can be solved with mediation if disagreeing parties work at it. Phone the Cincinnati Mediation Center for more information on this empowering process.
Cincinnati Mediation Center
221-8744

Like Mother, Like Daughter

Deborah Smith-Blackmer and her mother, Miriam Smith, are clinical social workers in separate private practices. By examining the crucial issues that have allowed them to forge a flexible, sympathetic, loving relationship, they have developed a workshop that makes women in the group aware of how they were mothered and what kind of mothers they have become because of it.

During these workshops, Deborah and Miriam do dramatic readings from literature to illustrate their points. For instance, the poignant passage from *Uncle Tom's Cabin* when the mother and daughter talk to each other on the night before they are to be separated allows workshop participants to talk about their own experiences of painful separation from their children. Women relate to the universal mother-daughter problems presented through literature that makes them feel open enough to talk about them to each other. These workshops are powerful because Miriam and

Deborah are skilled, sensitive group facilitators. Optimum group size is twenty-five to thirty women, but Miriam and Deborah have done presentations for as many as 300. Phone well in advance to schedule sessions. These are busy women.
Deborah Smith-Blackmer
Miriam Smith
281-4033

Growth Oasis

The spirit at Grailville Conference Center, situated on 360 rolling acres of Loveland farmland, comes from the Grail, the movement that operates the facility. It is dedicated to justice, peace, liberating ways to live, human development and creativity, spiritual search, social responsibility and international awareness. That's quite a lot, but it accounts for the peaceful feeling of Grailville, which is why businesses, social service and religious organizations, all sorts of groups book the conference grounds for all-day meetings, overnight programs, week-long retreats. It's a perfect place to be introspective, get energy from within, become better charged when you leave.
Grailville Conference Center
932 O'Bannonville Rd. (Loveland)
683-2340

The Joy Outdoor Education Center is a year-round conference/retreat center situated on 315 rolling forested acres in Warren County. Lee Snooks, the director, will work with companies and organizations—adults to teenagers—to tailor group sessions that build confidence, teamwork, leadership, and group communications. Learning to walk—as a group—a rope course that gets progressively more difficult certainly is a good example of how these qualities are fostered. Learning how to get everyone in your group over a fourteen-foot wall is another way.

This place is becoming increasingly popular with businesses who realize executives need a chance to get out of their everyday environment to understand how to deal with it better. They come away from Joy with increased personal confidence, better group-communications skills, are more poised under pressure, and are better decision makers.
Joy Outdoor Education Center
Box 157
Clarksville, OH 45113
381-8689

Pet Projects

Duplexes for dogs? A four-poster for Rover's afternoon snooze? A psychologist to soothe your tabby's trauma? Acupuncture for animals? You bet. From canine beauty salons to gourmet pet treats—all of these secrets will now be unleashed.

Veterinary Specialists

Sure you take your pet to a fine veterinarian. But did you know there are specialists in town who have been board-certified in their fields, having completed years of training *after* they graduated from veterinary school? Your vet may refer you to one of these specialists should your pet have a disturbing problem, but for your own information, here's who to call.

Dr. Patrick Breen, dermatologist, specializes in skin diseases of mainly dogs, cats, and horses. Many are due to allergies that manifest themselves in animals as skin problems. He also commonly treats infections and hormonal skin complications.
Dr. Patrick Breen
4725 Cornell Rd. (Blue Ash)
489-4644

Dr. Kerry Ketring, an ophthalmologist, treats dogs and cats as well as rabbits, snakes, birds of prey, and all exotic animals. Dr. Ketring performs cataract surgery, treats glaucoma, removes foreign objects from eyes. Many breeds have inherited eye diseases, so he checks out breeding stock as well as puppies.
Dr. Kerry Ketring
All Animal Eye Clinic
1174 W. Kemper Rd. (Forest Park)
825-0805

Dr. Bruce Butler, a surgical specialist, performs all types of surgery, but is especially trained in sensitive procedures such as spinal and chest operations as well as total hip replacements. He commonly treats arthritis and hip problems. He can mend nasty fractures with a bone-plating technique, which involves inserting bone plates and screws.
Dr. Bruce Butler
Tennessee Avenue Animal Hospital
1381 Tennessee Ave. (Bond Hill)
242-2141

Dr. William Rogers, internist, is a sophisticated diagnostician in areas such as the heart, abdomen, pancreas, liver, and kidney. He is able to come up with answers through extensive tests for pets with difficult-to-diagnose problems.
Dr. William A. Rogers
931 State Rt. 28 (Milford)
831-7400

Besides maintaining an extensive animal practice, Dr. Marvin Cain is also a board-certified acupuncturist. Owners swear by the success of his techniques.
Dr. Marvin Cain
Mt. Healthy Animal Hospital
9199 Pippin Rd. (Mt. Healthy)
931-9127

The Spay Neuter Clinic, badly needed in the pet world, came into existence several years ago. This clinic performs spaying and neutering only—no other surgical techniques—at reduced fees to encourage control of the pet population. Animals must be at least six months old to qualify for the operation.
Spay Neuter Clinic
1712 Blue Rock (Northside)
541-4510

Pet Projects

Mind Your Manners

Dr. Robert Andrysco is an animal behavior specialist, having received a Ph.D. in the combined studies of psychology, psychiatry, and veterinary medicine. Common canine problems Dr. Andrysco deals with are trouble with housebreaking, destructive chewing, excessive barking, digging up the yard, aggressive behavior. He also deals with cats who urinate and defecate anywhere but the litter box, destroy personal property, are aggressive. Dr. Andrysco feels much of this behavior is normal animal activity—it just doesn't fit into our human environment. By advising owners on how to modify their behavior as well as their living quarters, pets will straighten out.

Dr. Andrysco is based in Columbus, but books appointments in Cincinnati several times a month through Dr. Kerry Ketring's office. After he consults in person with patients, he continues treatment via phone consultations. Often, he can prescribe the entire treatment by phone. Dr. Andrysco also offers individual dog-obedience classes in Columbus—seven one-hour sessions for any dog older than eight weeks. "Why wait until your dog is six months old to get rid of puppy traits like chewing up your couch?" says Dr. Andrysco. Makes sense to me.

Dr. Robert Andrysco
Columbus:
614-486-9861
Cincinnati:
825-0805

Bob Diehl and Peggy Turvey are owners of the Cincinnati Dog Training School, and each has specialized dog training expertise. Bob specializes in training hunting dogs, even works with terriers for gaming trials. Peggy teaches obedience classes at the Shadybrook Armory on Tuesday nights, as well as puppy kindergarten for as young as eight-week-old pups. Says Peggy, "I work on housebreaking, teach them to come when they're called, heel on a leash." Peggy also teaches search and rescue tracking, which means dogs learn to follow a person's trail and pick up articles he has dropped along the way. She teaches sporting dogs to do field work—private classes only. Peggy actually goes out in the field with clients.

Both Peggy and Bob work with animal behavioral problems. They will come to your home together if you have a large animal that is especially aggressive, or they will come alone depending on whether the animal responds to a male or a female handler. They observe your pet's behavior and see how he interacts with you so they can tell you why he is doing, well, what he is doing. For instance, does your dog rush past you to get through an open door first? That shows who is number one in your house—your dog is dominating you. Peggy or Bob will explain how to tone down this aggressive trait. They commonly deal with dogs who are jealous of new babies, hate your kitten, tear up furniture, chase cars, soil rugs.

Cincinnati Dog Training School
941-1536

If you have show business aspirations for your pet, look up Joy Ryan at her shop, Dolled Up Doggies. She's trained dogs for three productions of *Annie*, for *The Wiz*, to host a trivia talk show on television, for numerous television commercials. Joy must see if your dog has the temperament to be a star before she will work with him, and he must have above-average intelligence. But she also teaches house manners, which are invaluable to any dog owner, such as training a dog not to jump on guests when

they arrive and not to climb in their laps at dinner. She can train dogs to fetch the morning newspaper, to ring a bell instead of scratching the door to let you know they want to go in or out, even to answer the phone by picking up the receiver when it rings, laying it on a table, and then barking into the mouthpiece. Do they take messages? She hasn't gotten that far yet. She'll also come to your home to work with canine behavioral problems: aggression, housebreaking, digging up the yard, destroying the furniture.

Joy teaches basic obedience classes as well—group or private lessons. She will train dogs to be street smart, teaching your pet to heel next to your baby's stroller instead of dragging you and your child down the road, to be calm if you walk him on thoroughfares with a lot of traffic. Joy holds puppy classes, too, even gives individual lessons by training through play. In her spare time, Joy grooms all breeds of dogs and cats, even bunnies.

Dolled Up Doggies
3859 North Bend Rd. (Cheviot)
662-7309

To teach your dog to show off, who do you turn to? Laura Kling trains dogs for the show ring— confirmation training is what it's called. Laura teaches dog owners to present their dogs at shows or shows dogs for their owners. She is a professional handler—all breeds. Laura owns a world-famous Golden Retriever who has collected many prizes. She says, "I give classes at the Shadybrook Armory in Hartwell on Tuesday nights, but sometimes I will have a dog come and live with me for a while so he will learn to sparkle in the ring. One dog I worked with couldn't walk in a straight line before I took him in, but now he's doing fine. I build their confidence through love, but I also let them know who is boss."

Laura Kling
574-8479

Head Trip

Beatrice Lydecker is an Oregon-based animal psychic. She has ESP with animals. By tuning into the animal's wavelength, she finds out what is bothering him and then tells his owner. Beatrice says she can tell you why your dog is not happy, not eating, is excessively barking, chewing furniture, acting openly aggressive, seems emotionally off balance. She says vets call her for a second opinion when they can't find anything physically wrong with a pet. These animals may tell Beatrice they don't like their new home, their owner's new husband, or being left alone so often. Beatrice even works with racehorse owners whose animals aren't performing. "Sometimes they aren't happy with their stalls," she says.

Beatrice talks to dogs, cats, horses, and birds, gives seminars all over the country to show owners how to tune into their animals' feelings just as she does. Beatrice is phoned by people all over the country for consultations. These cost $20 for fifteen minutes, $30 for half an hour, $45 for an hour. To make an appointment for a phone consultation, call 503-297-2746 or 503-738-8480. If you can't reach her at those numbers (she travels constantly), leave messages for her at 503-232-5710, and she'll phone you.

Beatrice also has 15,000 people on the mailing list for her newsletter. To get on her mailing list, write to:

Beatrice Lydecker
Nutrition Now, Inc.
3363 S.E. 20th St.
Portland, OR 97202

Pet Projects

Oh, My Aching Back

Many people have believed in the health benefits of massage for years. However, the trend has recently mushroomed as converts to active sports have realized how much massage soothes aches and pains besides increasing their overall sense of well-being. Massage for animals was sure to follow. And it has, because it relieves the pain of arthritis, helps big dogs with hurtful hip problems, aids animals in regaining their mobility after surgery, stimulates poor circulation.

Talk to Gary Matthews about massage for your aching animal. Although he's a licensed massage therapist for humans (more about him in "Body and Soul," page 67), Gary has a special feel for all creatures. They respond to his open and accepting nature as well as his touch, which is gentle but firm. Gary says he has worked on dogs, cats, goats, even turkeys and chickens. If you need further references, talk to my German Shepherd.

Gary Matthews
1-444-2834
Answering service:
244-3114

Gourmet Treats

Munchies for dogs? The ultimate canine treat is Oz Farm Natural Country Dog Biscuits. Gary Matthews and his wife, Ginger, are the baking duo, and they supply discriminating stores all over the city with their delicacies. Or you can phone Oz Farm for special orders. These biscuits contain no preservatives or bone meal. They are made with vegetable shortening, whole wheat flour, honey, and wheat germ. They smell terrific and though I haven't noshed on them yet, people who have say they are tasty spread with peanut butter. Oh yes, dogs like them, too.

The biscuits come in two sizes, and are specially decorated for all the holidays (hearts at Valentine's Day, green and red at Christmas). Ginger and Gary have even made up biscuits decorated with the Star of David for Passover, but will be happy to make these treats year-round for owners of canine princes and princesses. They'll personalize biscuits with your dog's name, bake giant biscuits for any occasion—talk to Ginger and Gary about individual orders.

Oz Farm Natural Country Dog Biscuits
1-444-2834

Just Another Pretty Face

The ultimate place to take any dog to get groomed and beautified is the Bow Wow Boutique. Owner Karla Addington is a certified master groomer who can take care of all 127 breeds. In fact, Karla won first place in the Creative Competition in the 1987

International Competition in New York, where she beat out representatives from eleven other countries, so you can be assured that when your dog leaves Bow Wow he will look appropriate for his particular breed. Getting a terrier cut when you're a pedigreed poodle is downright embarrassing.

Bow Wow Boutique is also an information center for dog owners. Karla will talk to prospective buyers about what different breeds require, which dogs best suit their lifestyles, discuss training and behavioral problems. All of this information is free since Karla feels strongly about being a pet-owner counselor; pet owners have tremendous confidence in this generous woman.

Bow Wow Boutique also stocks any kind of equipment or apparel dog owners could fancy. These items include beds, from a brass four-poster to all sorts of nifty pillows, pet car seats, life jackets for doggie swimmers, heavy-duty nylon pet carriers you can sling over your shoulder. There are no ordinary dog biscuits here. Dog treats include croissants, bagels, pizza slices, or the whole pizza. Clothes for the well-dressed dog run the gamut from a rack of T-shirts with clever logos to sweaters—argyle, Shetland, you name it. Formal dogs can snap up a tuxedo and top hat or a fake-fur jacket, while those favoring a casual look can choose a camouflage number or a plaid jacket with a tam to match. Rhinestone cowdogs can browse through a case packed with jeweled collars.

Karla's business, as well as her fame, has spread. In addition to her hub Pleasant Ridge location, she has recently opened two new Bow Wow Boutiques.

Bow Wow Boutique
6201 Montgomery Rd. (Pleasant Ridge)
631-3939
405 Scott St. (Covington)
491-3939
Town & Country Kennel & Cattery
1051 Meredith (Mt. Healthy)
522-BEST

Ritzy Digs

If your dog's living quarters need rehabbing, David Breiner can fix them up in style. The yard of his shop is packed with about 150 ready-to-go dog and cat houses in all sizes, shapes, and colors. Dave makes all of them from two-inch-thick Styrofoam sheets sandwiched between electroplated steel for insulation. He cuts all door openings toward the corner of the house so there is a good, warm, sheltered area where your dog or cat can curl up. All houses have wall-to-wall shag carpeting and are priced according to size. Windows, automatic watering trays, heat tapes installed in the floor, as well as anything else you may want included, definitely cost more than standard models. But Dave takes custom orders in stride. He has built raccoon houses, rabbit hutches, and duplexes complete with picture windows for two St. Bernards.

David Breiner Wood Shop
5370 Rt. 4 (Fairfield)
829-7782

The Pets-N-Such departments at the half dozen Van Leunen's stores in Greater Cincinnati, as well as the Pets & Supplies departments at Swallen's stores, are brimming with pet houses, beds, loungers, all sorts of supplies. I spotted fluorescent rocks to spruce up your fish tank, mirrors and swings to entertain your pet parakeet, extravagant cat scratching-post tunnels, doggie perfume, a wide assortment of collars and leashes. For pet staples and for fun stuff, check out these stores. Also check out their locations and phone numbers in your phone directory.

Pet Projects

Home Away From Home

You hate leaving your pet at a kennel while you are on vacation. Town & Country Kennels, new on the Cincinnati scene, can ease your separation pangs. Owner Barbara Schwartz, who has raised dogs for more than thirty years and has done obedience and confirmation training, consulted with veterinarians all over the country, as well as the Humane Society, before she built this state-of-the-art facility.

For instance, Barbara thoughtfully put her twenty-six cat units away from the dog runs so felines are not intimidated. She had special air units installed in the cat area because cats are so susceptible to upper respiratory ailments. Dogs will be walked however many times a day you wish (extra charge for this), be allowed to run in a fenced-in area, will be fed what you specify—even delicacies. If your dog seems homesick, Barbara will spend time with him, cook him some special tidbits, maybe take him into the kitchen with her for a while to get him to start eating. There are isolation areas so, should an animal become ill, it will not infect the others. There is also an attendant on duty twenty-four hours a day at Town & Country so the dog's last "out" is at 11 P.M., first "out" is at 6 A.M. This is definitely kind to animals' innards; many kennels are not as accommodating.

Barbara will offer animal photography services, arrange for animal portraits, sell stained-glass panels with animal motifs, or have one custom made at your request. Dog grooming is available through the Bow Wow Boutique located on the premises.

Town & Country Kennel & Cattery
1051 Meredith Dr. (Mt. Healthy)
522-BEST

Have a Heart

When you bring an Easter bunny home, it's cute—for a while . . . until the kiddies get tired of fondling it. Too often, it's soon banished to a pen out back where it's uncared for and forgotten. Sad. Next Easter, why not do something happier for everyone? Take in a homeless dog or cat from the Society for the Prevention of Cruelty to Animals (SPCA). These animals are just waiting to be adopted—any time of year. Also note, the SPCA has good educational programs open to the public. Staff will even come to schools and talk to groups, bringing live animals and slides. The SPCA investigates charges of cruelty, rescues trapped, abandoned, or marooned animals, answers all sorts of animal-related questions on the phone.

Society for the Prevention of Cruelty to Animals
3949 Colerain Ave. (Northside)
541-6100

If you spot an orphaned baby wild animal or bird, of course you want to help. But even though your intentions are good, your interference can permanently separate it from its parents. So before you rush out to administer aid, watch from a distance for a while to see if the parents return. Also note that injured wild animals can be dangerous, so call the following experts for directions in handling them. Remember it is against the law to make pets of many species of wild birds and animals. Though you probably won't get into trouble by helping out orphans for a while, it is illegal to keep them permanently. And while raising wild animals, you imprint them with human qualities, making them unfit to survive in their natural environment when you release them. Again, phone these experts for explicit directions so this does not happen.

One source of aid is the Raise and Release Program of the Cincinnati Zoo. By phoning this volunteer organization made up of people equipped to care for all sorts of animals such as snakes, bats, birds of prey, mammals, bees, and hornets—really anything that walks, crawls, or flies—you will be put in touch with just the right care giver. You can also phone the Hamilton County Park District. Staff will give you good advice or point you to experts who can take care of that specific animal.

Raise and Release Program
281-3700

Hamilton County Park District
825-0615

For The Birds

For any kind of wild bird related items—a large variety of seed mixes, bird baths, feeders, binoculars, bird-theme sweatshirts and mugs, video cassettes to help you identify birds, books—go to Wild Birds Unlimited. Owner Todd Graham is knowledgeable about birds and will recommend the proper seeds to attract a colorful variety to your feeders.

Wild Birds Unlimited
7688 Camargo Rd. (Madeira)
271-1887

Feed mills also stock bird seed in bulk so that you can keep your yard chirping all year round. Whether you want a few pounds or hundreds, you can get good variety and great prices. Feed mills also stock chow for a large number of animals, rabbit pellets to livestock feed. Dog food and cat food can be bought in large bags. So can kitty litter. Many stock other animal sundries as well: leashes, water bowls, all sorts of treats. You can even find large bags of charcoal, grass and vegetable seeds, fertilizer, bales of straw. Investigate these places.

Reading Feed Mill
9359 Reading Rd. (Reading)
733-5520

Ben Riesenberg Sons, Inc.
200 Smalley Rd. (Lockland)
554-1630

Leisgang Country & Garden Store
4423 Bridgetown Rd. (Bridgetown)
574-4423

Final Resting Place

When a loved pet dies it is traumatic. Many owners find some solace in laying to rest their beloved animal friends in a lovely place. Such a place is The Pine's Pet Cemetery. Operated by Jean and Tom Lawton, an extremely caring couple, the grounds are exquisitely maintained. All sorts of exotic animals are buried here, as well as dogs and cats. Even six humans are buried next to their pets as per their requests. There is a chapel on the grounds family members can use at their discretion, and Jean says, "Many children have their first brush with death when they lose a pet. Parents can make this experience less jolting when they show children how to say good-bye with love and dignity."

The Pine's provides cremation services as well as burial, will pick up deceased pets at home or at a veterinarian's office. The Lawtons frankly and openly discuss prices and all arrangements. They will be happy to mail brochures.

The Pine's Pet Cemetery, Inc.
764 Riley Wills Rd. (Lebanon, OH)
579-8250

Arrive In Style

You want to make a splashy entrance for a special occasion. You're thinking of pulling up in a chauffeur-driven Rolls-Royce, maybe swooping down on someone's front lawn in a hot-air balloon, or hiring a jet for the grandest of getaways. Here's how to make all your high-flying arrangements.

Limos

There are lots of limousine companies in Cincinnati. I've tried to single out some who have traffic-stopping vehicles, some with sedate stretch Caddys for more formal occasions, some with handy vans, some who offer special services—like city tours. Whoever you deal with, ask about minimum hours of rental and the cost. Also be sure what uniform the driver will be wearing. One friend who hired a limo had a bad experience. The Cadillac was fine, but the driver showed up in jeans and a baseball cap. State what you expect—up front.

Sandra Q. Woosley, of Ride the Great White, drives an awesome ultrastretch all-white 1959 restored Cadillac that is twenty-eight feet long. The tail fins alone look like they could reach from Fountain Square to Riverfront Stadium. This car stops people in their tracks when Sandra pulls up in it. Needless to say, that's just the effect her passengers want. Sandra does weddings and anniversaries in this baby she has fondly dubbed "The Great White," also romantic lunches—she picks up a couple at work, arranges for lunch to be served in the car, drives around downtown for an hour. Talk to her about a nighttime version of this midday rendezvous, complete with champagne and hors d'oeuvres. Sandra will work with people to make all sorts of motorized parties possible. She also does mundane things like airport pickups.
Ride the Great White
244-2600

Call Classic Carriage Limousine if you want to hire a 1958 Rolls-Royce or a 1932 Duesenberg Phaeton (valued at $800,000 since only thirty-four were ever made). These cars can be rented for any occasion—specialties are weddings (a red carpet is even rolled out of the car), bringing mother and baby home from the hospital. King of the Queen City Tour is one and a half hours around the city with lunch served on a silver tray, wine sipped out of a silver wine goblet—service to match the vehicle.

This company has access to other vintage cars in the event you have big plans for a deluxe occasion. But they do routine around-town pickups and deliveries as well.
Classic Carriage Limousine
637-1919

Just in case your travel needs include a computer, a wet bar, a TV, and a cellular phone, call Progressive Limo. The car that is outfitted with all this equipment is a 1986 white stretch Lincoln Town Car that has had six feet added to it, making it a seventy-two-inch rolling office. Progressive has other Caddys and Lincolns in its fleet, too, and does proms, weddings, and many corporate runs.
Progressive Limousine
681-LIMO

"The Starship Enterprise" is a six-door black stretch Cadillac that has a mirrored divider between the driver and the passenger compartment. "Why did you have a mirror installed?" I asked the owner. "So you can see yourself riding inside such a gorgeous limousine," he answered. I should have known.

Butler's Limousine Service has other limos besides this extra-glitzy one, all of which are silver and have been equipped with stereos, color TVs, bars, and phones. Chauffeurs wear uniforms, even a tuxedo if you wish. Ask about weddings and other special-occasion packages.
Butler's Limousine Service
271-1000

River City Limousine provides luxury cars—stretch Lincolns and Cadillacs—and uniformed drivers who will drive you to any appointment around town, even out of town. Talk to the company about a trip to Churchill Downs, Chicago, or New York. City tour packages are available as well as rentals for any special occasion.
River City Limousine
481-2800

Carey/Barr Limousine Service does corporate accounts, proms, and weddings in its formal stretch cars and has just added a white stretch Lincoln Town Car with all the fixings to its impressive fleet.
Carey/Barr Limousine Service
531-7321

Washington Limousine, Inc. has been in business for years. They have standard limousines, stretches, coach buses, even twenty-six vans. They'll take anyone anywhere with a couple of hours notice. A driver picked up my family and me at the airport one Labor Day along with our dog, three cats, and a summer's worth of luggage. He solemnly loaded all of us into the van we had requested, drove us smoothly home, and never batted an eye at his strange entourage.
Washington Limousine, Inc.
221-0074

Door to Door Transportation Services, Inc. has regularly scheduled van trips from Cincinnati to a number of cities in the area—Louisville, Indianapolis, Detroit, Cleveland, more. Prices are reasonable and it sure beats making a tiring, one-day round trip on your own. You can also charter these comfortable, nicely kept vans for in-town or out-of-town use. I hired this company to ferry thirty out-of-town guests staying at a downtown hotel to my home for dinner and then back to the hotel again. They were easy to work with, prompt, and reasonable. Call for details on their many services.
Door To Door Transportation Services, Inc.
641-0088

Get a Bus

When you want to take a crowd to Keeneland for a day at the races, why not charter a bus? Need to get a wedding party from the church to the reception? Have a luxury bus waiting and start the party on board—with champagne and all the trimmings. One bus company owner told me a bride chartered a bus to drive her from home to the church so she could stand up and not wrinkle her dress. Now that's style! Whatever occasion you need mega-person transportation for, and whether the trip is local or cross-country, talk to the following companies to arrange luxury travel.

Croswell Bus Line, Inc.
724-2206

Charter Bus Service
251-7900

Royal Travel
721-6614

Traveline Charter Service
829-8290

Horse-Drawn Carriages

You're old-fashioned, sentimental. Could a horse-drawn carriage suit your mood? If so, these two companies are highly recommended.

Royal Carriage Company provides elegant antique-reproduction carriages driven by formally attired professionals in 1880s garb for wedding parties, downtown tours, all sorts of special events—talk to them about your plans.
Royal Carriage Co.
721-0001

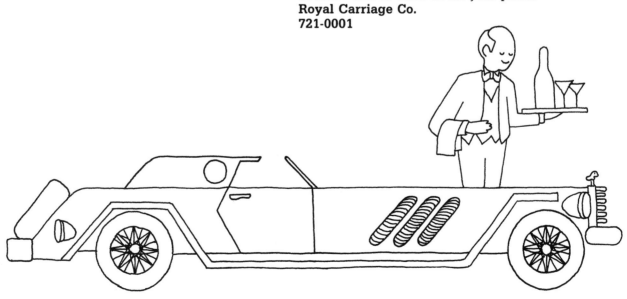

Arrive in Style

Norman Flagge, owner and driver of A. Horse & Carriage, wears a frock coat and breeches when he drives his original 1880 Rockaway carriage. His personalized service is available for unique occasions as well as city tours. Right now, he can be reached through Royal Carriage.
A. Horse & Carriage
721-0001 or 535-0160

Riverboats

You want to charter a paddle wheeler—traveling via the Ohio River is your grand plan. Phone BB Riverboats and inquire whether the *Mark Twain,* which can accommodate sixty people, is available for you and your crowd. BB Riverboats has all sorts of boats for charter, and you'll learn more details in "Stopoffs." But if you want to set your own course, have any kind of meal—casual to elegant—served aboard, book entertainers to amuse you and your guests while you're afloat, give them a call.
BB Riverboats
261-8500

Planes

You're a high flyer. You want to rent a jet and you'd also like it stocked with snacks, some beverages, a fruit or veggie tray, please. It's possible. Just phone these four air transporters and ask what planes in their fleet match your fancy and your pocketbook.

Jet Air, Inc.
871-8878

Schmidt Aviation
984-5880

American Air Services
871-2004

Cardinal Air Training
321-5822

Balloons

You think drifting through the clouds in a hot-air balloon looks romantic. Well, you can arrange a champagne flight in one, a sunrise or sunset sendoff, even a private party (some accommodate a group of people). Talk to these two companies about any heavenly plans.

Balloons Unlimited
581-6966

Aerosport Hot Air Balloons
871-4564

Great Places to Have a Party

If you're fed up with the same kinds of parties given at the same old places, these suggestions just might spark your social life.

Museum and Historic-Home Galas

If you want to host an event that is truly memorable, consider having a party at a historic mansion or museum. See if you can rent any of the unique places mentioned in "Queen City's Crown Jewels," pages 128 to 130. Some museums are available for business, social, or philanthropic groups only. Some are happily open to private parties. Most have strict rules about the use of their valuable premises: number of people, smoking, food, and alcohol—inquire about all of them. But to give you a glimpse of how special your party can be, here's what some of these museums offer.

Historic Southwest Ohio has jurisdiction over two locations: the Hauck House on Dayton Street, downtown, and Sharon Woods Village. The Hauck House and the Hayner House in Sharon Woods Village are both rentable for special occasions.

It doesn't take much to make a party elegant at the Hauck House because it is so spectacular. There are parquet floors, terrazzo halls, marble mantels, and painted ceilings. What a setting for a chamber music recital and then a gorgeous sit-down dinner, a small wedding—whatever you can dream up. There's even a glorious harp in residence and a jewel of a garden you can use when weather permits. The number of guests must be limited to forty-nine, one of three caterers approved by the association must be selected to provide party fare, and galas must be scheduled when the Hauck House is closed to the public. Inquire about other strict usage regulations designed to protect the house's priceless appointments.

The Hayner House, a fourteen-room Greek Revival structure in Sharon Woods Village, would be fine for an old-fashioned country party. From November through April when the village is closed to the public, you can use three adjoining rooms in the house, which are not furnished then. This place is just right for a midwinter bash.
Historic Southwest Ohio
563-9484

Could anything be more impressive than having the entire Cincinnati Art Museum as the backdrop for your next party? Social and philanthropic groups and business organizations that have $25,000 to spend can rent the museum facilities. Just think of dancing in the musical-instrument gallery, having dinner in the Near and Far Eastern wing. Three hundred people can be accommodated for a sit-down dinner, 500 for a reception. You can rent portions of the museum, too. For instance, $5,000 will get you a single gallery for an evening—ask about which ones could be made available.

According to Gretchen Mehring, coordinator of public services at the museum, "Companies that rent the museum facilities do so because they want to support it. The museum allows them to use its facilities as a way of saying 'thank you.' However, if private individuals want to be generous, we'd be inclined to talk to them as well. But definitely, no weddings." Phone Gretchen for more information.
Cincinnati Art Museum
721-5204

The Taft Museum makes its premises available to museum-affiliated organizations, nonpartisan, nonpolitical adult community groups whose programs and/or purposes are related to the arts. No private personal parties are permitted. Still, if you qualify to rent the Taft, you can use the exquisite garden for daytime events, high teas, cocktail parties, or dinners. Indoor galleries may be rented as well, but requests may be denied if the event conflicts with exhibition schedules.
The Taft Museum
241-0343

Great Places to
Have a Party

Hillforest, an Italian Renaissance villa built in Aurora, Indiana, by distiller and brewer Thomas Gaff in 1852, has a breathtaking view of the Ohio River. The interior is a five-star Hollywood movie set for a wedding, not only because of the exquisite formal parlors, but especially because of the grand staircase the bride can descend. However, the house may be rented for a variety of occasions as long as none of them includes serving alcohol, though wine may be offered on the porches. Food is fine anywhere.

Guests are also welcome to tour the thirteen rooms of the mansion on their own or arrange to be guided through it. Do note that because the house is situated on a steep hill, you may want to think twice about scheduling functions in snowy months. Getting to the summit can be treacherous, which is why the house is closed from December 23 to May 1. However, Hillforest is only a forty-minute drive from downtown Cincinnati.
Hillforest
812-926-0087

Peterloon, the Georgian mansion built by John and Irene Emery in 1928 to 1930, has a style that makes you feel you are visiting a home in seventeenth-century Europe. Though it has magnificent grounds and formal paneled rooms filled with important art objects, the estate has a comfortable, warm feeling, showing it was where a large family grew up. Charitable, nonprofit groups and businesses may rent Peterloon's facilities for workshops, luncheons, and dinners—discuss all the particulars with the staff.
Peterloon
791-7600

The Toedtman School of Music is housed in the former summer residence of John Hauck, built in 1904. This mansion, situated on grounds hosting formal gardens and complete with leaded-glass doors and a porch that wraps around the entire front of the house, is available for parties. Because the staircase is so dramatic, the house—like Hillforest—is also commonly rented for weddings. But any kind of party can be accommodated—summer ones on the porch and spilling out on the grounds are pretty special. Talk to Melissa Toedtman about a party including a musical recital. Since the house is a music school, she can arrange piano concerts, chamber music—all sorts of melodic entertainment for guests. Then you can serve food as simpatico as the music.
Toedtman School of Music
12171 Mosteller Rd. (Sharonville)
772-7900

Adventurous Affairs

What could be more fun than having a child's birthday party at the Cincinnati Zoo? Kids tour the Children's Zoo, have hamburgers or hot dogs, cake and ice cream, even receive party favors. Parties (generally tailored to four- to eight-year-olds) can be booked from April to September.

Adult parties at the zoo can be as imaginative as you are. In warm months, zoo staff will erect tents that can hold up to 600 people on Peacock Pavilion. Dinner, dancing, any theme party complete with decorations can be accommodated. Hosts can even arrange to have animal houses kept open in the early evening so their guests can tour the grounds. Other outdoor functions can be held in one of the zoo shelters; indoor events for up to seventy people can be booked in the boardroom. Call the zoo for additional information.
The Cincinnati Zoo
Group sales:
281-4701

If you really want to spice up your business or social functions, phone the Natural History Museum. They'll custom tailor a party to suit your fancy, but consider their suggested activities: a barefoot tour of the cave, edible insects and other "natural" foods, an update on little-known prehistoric wonders you certainly didn't learn about as a kid. The museum also offers a two-hour riverboat cruise down the Ohio while you absorb all the facts about how it contributed to the development of the Ohio Valley. Musical entertainment offsets the heavy subject matter on how massive glaciers rearranged Cincinnati's landscape. You can even book an all-night cruise. The adventure begins at the museum so you can learn about all the creatures that fly, crawl, slither, and hoot in the night. Then at 1:00 A.M. buses take your group to a riverboat for a real live look at the night. Breakfast is served at 5:00 A.M., after which your party is bused back to the museum.

Kids can have exciting parties, too—three themes. Choose the Sunshine Birthday and partygoers will do everything under the sun; the Astronaut Birthday features a trip to the Planetarium to view the night sky as it looked on the day the birthday boy or girl was born; at the Dinosaur Birthday, the birthday child adopts his or her own dinosaur. All parties include a staff member to provide games, prizes, ice cream and cake, soft drinks, balloons.

Cincinnati Museum of Natural History
621-3889

Do something really dramatic. Buy out the house for a performance at the Playhouse in the Park. Have dinner catered before the show or enjoy a picnic outside with the city skyline as your backdrop. This party would be memorable. Talk to the person in charge of group sales to work out all the arrangements.

Cincinnati Playhouse in the Park
421-5440

Any group or company can rent the College Football Hall of Fame for meetings, dinners, or functions of any kind. It's also available for private parties, meetings, fashion shows, wedding receptions—even proms have been held here. A nice feature is that guests have the run of the place while parties or meetings are being held. Four different films as diverse as Fred Flintstone explaining the game of football and the greatest football bloopers are shown continuously. There are computer quizzes, a game that either boos or cheers according to how skillful you are at kicking field goals, and a walk-through time tunnel that depicts the history of football.

Minimum number of people should be twenty, maximum is 450. For hour-long meetings up to those that last a week, arrangements can be made by calling the group sales manager. Cost depends on the group size and the length of the function.

College Football Hall of Fame
Group Sales Manager:
241-5410

Casual Fun

Rent the Stone Valley Dance Barn for private parties—it can hold up to 150 people. Owner Tom Stone will call your square dance and provide the music. Ask him about the clog dance group that will perform at your party. Tom may also be agreeable to calling dances at functions you give in places other than his dance barn. Talk to him about it.

Stone Valley Dance Barn
Rt. 3, Box 1 (West Harrison, IN)
637-5183

For blue-jeans blasts—try a hayride. Handle Bar Ranch has been hosting picnics and hayrides for years. The facilities include a ball field, spots to sit around a campfire—that is, after you've exhausted yourself from an old-fashioned square dance. Handle Bar staff are accommodating. They'll help you make arrangements that will please your particular group.

Handle Bar Ranch
825-9222

Great Places to Have a Party

Sunrock Farm in Wilder, Kentucky, specializes in hayrides. Owners Frank Traina and Debbie Pendock will even customize routes. Choose one that winds along the river valley with great city views or take an urban ride around downtown Cincinnati. In winter everyone snuggles under blankets and pretends the hayride is a "sleigh ride." When you return to Sunrock after the ride, torches light the driveway. You can sing around the campfire, have a square dance or party in the paneled shelter, take a (daytime) tour of the farm, which has been set up as an environmental education center. Frank and Debbie raise geese, wandering peacocks, and other assorted farm animals. So, whether you go to Sunrock to learn about the natural environment or just to have fun, the place is always full of surprises.
Sunrock Farm
781-5502

Parties in the city parks are popular because there are so many beautiful lodges and picnic areas you can rent. But weddings in the parks are popular, too. Favorite spots with brides and grooms include the gardens around the arboretum in Mt. Airy Forest, the Temple of Love Gazebo in Mt. Storm Park, and the bandstand in Burnet Woods. A beautiful view of the Little Miami Valley can be seen from the pavilion in Alms Park, where early-morning rising-sun ceremonies would be spectacular. In Eden Park, the Murray Seasongood Pavilion is available as is the quaint little gazebo near Mirror Lake, plus the one near Krohn Conservatory right on the corner of Martin Drive. Call the park board officials in charge of booking weddings and other parties to find out about permits, charges, and what dates are available.
Cincinnati Park Board
352-4080

Energetic Amusements

For a party that's really out of this world, have one on the planet Photon, which is located in Springdale. Become part of this humanoid video game by suiting up in a stereophonic helmet, a chest pod, a battery-pack belt and arming yourself with a laser pistol. All the equipment you're wearing tracks and relays other players' moves, tells you if you've been hit while you crawl through tunnels, bunkers, a maze, wind your way through fog on the trail of other players. This live video-game palace can be rented for private parties before or after it's open to the general public. Call to find out about group rates and the cost of having food catered.
Photon
310 W. Crescentville Rd. (Springdale)
671-1612

Think your lively group would like to roller-skate, play miniature golf, bat some baseballs in an indoor batting cage? Call the Fun Factory to book a party—for adults or children. Birthday parties for children four to thirteen years old are popular here!
Fun Factory
1631 Sherman Ave. (Norwood)
631-1311

Gymnastics parties for children are favored by many mothers. The idea is to get the wiggling, squiggling kids out of the house and directed by a professional. Everybody has a great time!

Queen City Gymnastics hosts parties for three- to six-year-olds that include active participation in a gymnastics class by all the wee guests. Queen City even supplies invitations, gives the birthday child a T-shirt, serves juice, but the hosts are responsible for other refreshments.

At the Hyde Park Gymnastics Center, staff members supervise a gymnastics party session for eight to ten children. Have your refreshments at home first or bring them to the gym—your choice.

Queen City Gymnastics Center, Inc.
11658 Deerfield Rd. (Blue Ash)
489-7575

Hyde Park Gymnastics Center
3130 Wasson Rd. (Hyde Park)
321-1003

Moveable Feasts

Check out the limo services mentioned in "Arrive in Style." Many offer city tours with champagne and gourmet meals during the drive. Buses, hot-air balloons, airplanes, and riverboats can also be your party setting. Phone the services mentioned in that chapter to see what you can set up.

Home Entertainment

You like to entertain at home, whether you have a few people over for a casual dinner or invite a large crowd for a more formal occasion. The only problem is that these days you don't have the time for preparation. Well, instead of forgoing something that gives you pleasure, hire stand-ins to give you a hand. In this chapter, I've served up party planners, caterers, places you can pick up ready-to-serve food, entertainers—the works. So phone your friends, then the people mentioned on the following pages, sit back, and relax.

Party Planners and Caterers

Rochford Kennedy and Co., Ltd. is a special-events management firm that can plan and execute every detail of any kind of special event, huge or tiny. From big bashes such as staging the Mason Dixon Steeplechase to weddings or intimate dinners, Mary Margaret Rochford, former public relations and fashion director of Saks Fifth Avenue, has a knack for planning and coordinating with flair. Any theme, any cuisine—you can give her the specific plan or tell her to come up with all the ideas and just walk away knowing your party will be done with cachet.
Rochford Kennedy and Co., Ltd.
579-0202

Party Planners is a special-events coordinating agency. Owners Judy Petricoff and Ronnie Shore can handle every detail of any party, no matter how large or small. In fact, they do major events for many corporations. From invitations and tablecloths to flowers, balloons, ice sculptures—everything—they can produce the entire package or any part of it you desire.
Party Planners
793-3388

Robert A. Dressler can come up with gorgeous food for parties—any size, any theme, even follow recipes you specify. He brings impeccably polite, well-dressed help who will set your table and set up the bar. When your guests leave, Bob will leave your kitchen in such good shape you won't know anyone has been around. Bob has his own supply of silver and serving pieces, a variety of fine-looking dishes, and glasses. He can take care of rentals—from tables and chairs to tents and limousines—even arrange for flowers and other decorations. Truly, if you want to be a guest at your own party—for six or 600—phone Bob. He'll also prepare dinners you can serve yourself or any single course such as desserts or hors d'oeuvres.
Robert A. Dressler Catering
271-9000

Catherine Headley does beautiful parties. Her buffet tables can be spectacular, whether it's a summer picnicky-type spread or for a more elegant occasion. And her food is just as good as it looks. She's flexible enough to tailor any party to your specific needs, can supply help, arrange for rentals, take care of every detail. Catherine will also prepare food for you to serve on your own, if you phone her in advance.
Catherine Headley Catering
631-8839

Michele's Catered Cuisine is relatively new on the scene, but Michele Groene and her partners, Ricklie Vordenberg and Suzanne Baird, produce food that is fresh and imaginative looking, creatively garnished, and fine tasting. They will cater big parties, bring help, and arrange rentals or prepare food you can serve yourself. They'll even deliver it. They work extremely hard to please clients.
Michele's Catered Cuisine
793-FOOD

Elegant Fare can custom cater anything from a box-lunch picnic to a white-glove reception. Staff can accommodate ten people or hundreds. As an example of their ingenuity, for one customer who didn't want to use flowers as a centerpiece, Elegant Fare staff created a bird of paradise out of a pineapple, cascades of fruit clusters for every table. For a Victorian wedding, they researched food popular during that era and prepared a beautiful authentic spread.

The chef, who formerly was with the Delta Queen and Grossinger's, a famous resort in the Catskills, can cook all sorts of ethnic dishes—ask.

Home Entertainment

Elegant Fare also tries to accommodate occasions that demand strictly kosher cuisine and will prepare food at a certified kosher kitchen to meet dietary requirements. They'll deliver any kind of food you specify if you want to serve it yourself.

Elegant Fare
489-4035

The Chafer is getting a ground swell of word-of-mouth acclaim these days. Their food is versatile, tasty, and nicely served. One well-traveled food maven requested Mexican specialties for her dinner party and raved about the dishes that were created for the occasion. The Chafer can handle large or small crowds, can bring all the equipment and serving personnel you require.

The Chafer
271-2500

You can pick up carry-out gourmet food at Heart Bakers—nice-looking chicken and pasta salads, homemade bread and soups (ask for thick potato leek), imaginative desserts such as a heart-shaped linzer torte. Basically, Robert McGrane of Heart Bakers can come up with any food you want, will deliver it, can even accommodate in-home parties—buffets to sit-down dinners. His is an inventive approach.

Heart Bakers
36 W. 5th St. (downtown)
651-4278

Epicuriosity, the gourmet-to-go shop in O'Bryonville, is a great place to stock up on frozen entrees, hors d'oeuvres, and soups that are kept in the store's freezer. For yourself, or for company, they certainly come in handy. You may special order take-home food and Epicuriosity staff will cater parties. Dishes like pasta primavera, eggplant parmesan, salmon and pasta in dill cream sauce are popular in summer; desserts like white chocolate mousse with raspberry sauce and their apple pie that customers swear is the best in the free world are building Epicuriosity an enviable reputation.

Epicuriosity
1983 Madison Rd. (O'Bryonville)
871-3037

For an outdoor barbecue your guests will never forget, phone Jerry Hart or Bill Thomas. These two chefs bring whole pigs, lambs, steamship rounds of beef on a twenty-foot boat trailer, then roast the animal on a spit over an open fire (oak or hickory charcoal) in your backyard. These animals take up to eight hours to cook, and the caterers supervise the barbecue and the carving. The rest of the meal is up to you. And note these beasts can feed from seventy-five to 500 people. Also be careful about inviting vegetarians to this kind of feast—it can offend sensitivities. Carnivores love it.

Jerry Hart
271-5253
Bill Thomas
561-4960

On the other end of the food spectrum is Whole Foods Cuisine. Partners Gale Howe and Valaree Hemighaus will prepare food you can pick up and take home or cater an event for you. No animal or dairy products are used, so you can expect imaginative dishes such as leek kasha pie with baked red beans and sauteed carrot tops, barley lentil salad with corn and grated carrots, millet and butternut squash with an assortment of marinated vegetables. If good health and good food is the combination you're looking for, call Whole Foods Cuisine.

Whole Foods Cuisine
Valaree Hemighaus
681-9272
Gale Howe
861-4440

Inventive and artistic are the two words to describe Christos & Drivakis's natural foods fare. This restaurant has developed an avid and loyal following. If you'd like to serve the food you love to eat in the restaurant to guests in your own home, phone Valerie Stroud, one of the owners. You can choose dishes on the menu or Valerie can create whatever you like. But the standard Christos dishes are pretty special: Baingan Chatni, an Indian curried stew of chunky eggplant, potatoes, broccoli, and peas, covered with saffron rice or couscous; Lumache Gesualdo, giant shell noodles filled with spinach, Italian seitan sausage, and a ricotta-style tofu cheese covered with tomato sauce. Got the picture? Christos desserts are as fine as the entrees.

Valerie told me one busy customer orders a month's worth of dishes, asks her to have them individually wrapped so he can stock his freezer. This way he always has a great-tasting meal to come home to. That's treating yourself right.

Christos & Drivakis
701 E. Epworth (Winton Place)
541-8333

The Pasta Market will cater cocktail parties, office luncheons, buffets, provide food for all occasions—you pick it up or they'll deliver. The menu includes their own freshly made pasta and sauces, homemade salads and soups—turn to ''Edibles'' (page 5) for all the great-tasting details. But phone owner Steve Shifman to discuss catering possibilities.

The Pasta Market
8110 Montgomery Rd. (Kenwood)
745-9022

Hickory Jim's makes great authentic Southern barbeque, cole slaw, Brunswick stew, ribs, smoked chicken, a host of Southern-style country desserts like banana cream pie, peanut butter pie, chocolate angel food cake, and rice pudding. Pastry chef Richard Prince bakes three or four special desserts daily. Inquire about seasonal specialties such as pumpkin or sweet potato pie for the holidays. Phone this take-out restaurant to order large amounts of their zingy homemade food if you're in the mood for down-home country cooking, and ask about their catering services. Owner Jim Edgy will work with you to create all sorts of menus, will supply just hors d'oeuvres if you wish, can even do wedding and birthday cakes.

Hickory Jim's Southern Bar-B-Q
4785 Red Bank Rd. (Madisonville)
561-9966

Jeff Thomas and Tim Mendenhall, co-owners of Annie's Pub and Restaurant, have a world of food and catering experience. Tim was formerly chef at The Elms and Jeff was general manager of Rusconi's and R.S.V.P. restaurants. They joined forces in their catering firm aptly called Partners in Cuisine, which drew many loyal customers, but gave up that business for their recent restaurant venture, Annie's Pub. If you like country cuisine, Tim and Jeff will accommodate carry-out orders. Just pick what's on the menu. You'll find dishes like country paté meatloaf, salmon cakes, egg pasta tossed with asparagus, cream, snails, bleu cheese, and parmesan. Tim's spoonbread is outstanding. So are his desserts. Apple pie, hot vanilla doughnuts smothered in bittersweet chocolate brandy sauce, strawberry shortcake. It's hard to choose. Phone Jeff or Tim for to-go food details, and about their sending a server to assist you and your guests.

Annie's Pub and Restaurant
9700 Constitution Dr. (Williamsburg in Hartwell)
761-8483

You'd love to serve good Indian food at home. Then order ahead at the tiny restaurant/food store called India Quality Foods. The restaurant may be small, but the food speaks mightily for their expertise. Your guests will be delighted.

India Quality Foods
268 Ludlow (Clifton)
961-4184

Antipastos, pasta primavera, Italian cheese trays, any Italian specialty from Barresi's restaurant or next-door deli can be cooked up for the crew you want to entertain.

Barresi's Italian American Restaurant
4111 Webster Ave. (Deer Park)
793-2540

China Gourmet is in a class by itself in the Chinese food category. Owner Bing Moy avoids tired Oriental dishes and continues to produce authentic, original dishes that have built him a fine reputation. Phone China Gourmet about cooking for at-home parties.

China Gourmet
3340 Erie Ave. (Hyde Park)
871-6612

Many restaurants will provide food for your parties. Phone your favorite ones and see what you can stir up.

Scenery and Props

Your party theme is Arabian Nights, so you need some fiberglass camels as decorations, maybe even some horses. Or you're thinking of an Oriental bash, or a circus theme, or you'd like chandeliers, waterfalls, and fountains. Call Decorative Rentals for any kind of scenery. They can do an entire set or supply you with a single prop like a ten-foot-high Eiffel Tower, life-size columns, huts, bridges, spaceships, enough greenery to turn your garage into a park.

Decorative Rentals
2720 W. McMicken Ave. (University Heights)
559-1425

Entertainment

If you're looking for talent to liven up your next party, think about tapping the expertise of all those energetic students at the School for Creative and Performing Arts. There is a theater company capable of producing a complete variety show as well as a symphony orchestra. Also available are

Home Entertainment

choirs, chamber music ensembles, dancers who perform ballet, modern, or folk pieces, mime groups. Be sure to ask about the SCPA Christmas carolers, who will come to your party dressed as Oliver Twist urchins during the holidays. All of these kids are special. I've never seen an audience that wasn't completely enraptured by any performance. Phone the school's booking office for additional details and rate schedules.

School for Creative and Performing Arts
421-2680

Talented College Conservatory of Music students register with the school's Concert Bureau to gain performing experience and to meet their education expenses. Classical, rock, jazz—you can book any kind of musician for recitals, dances, or weddings. Groups perform Broadway show tunes. There are barbershop quartets. Vocalists will sing wedding solos. You name it—these students can do it. Just phone the Concert Bureau with your request and staff will give you the names of able students. Then it's up to you to make the arrangements with the student. Also the bureau does not set prices. Fees are based on the mutual agreement of the employer and the artist.

College Conservatory of Music Concert Bureau
475-4551

Showstopper's Talent Agency represents a kaleidoscope of performers: bands that play jazz, Dixieland, bluegrass, and soft rock, comedians, dancers, magicians, mimes, musical-theater groups, palm readers, psychics, puppet shows. I've just reeled off a few of the performers this agency books. Owners Mary-Bob Rubenstein and Carolee Schwartz have so many contacts they are able to come up with unique, quality entertainers to fit any party theme. For instance, Showstopper's can put together a mime workshop for a children's birthday party. The mime applies makeup on the children, then includes them in the act. A ballet dancer can teach a dance class; a robot will play Simon Says. Actors can mingle with adult guests and do a pickpocket routine. A woman dressed as a bag lady rummages through guests' plates, turns to a surprised gentleman and says, "Look what's happened to my life since you dumped me." Tell Carolee or Mary-Bob what act you want; they'll create it. From cabaret shows to a full-scale musical production with words and music written just for you, Showstopper's is singularly creative. They have a long list of satisfied corporate clients as well as private-party repeat customers.

Showstopper's Talent Agency, Inc.
631-7469

Someone gets murdered during a party at your house. Well, that's one way to liven up the evening. Call Madcap Productions; they'll supply the actors who will pretend to be participants in this drama. They'll argue, then someone will keel over at the table—he's been poisoned. Or a body will be found in the bathroom by a guest. (Make sure the person who discovers the "corpse" has a strong heart!) An actor then says, "I'm the inspector. Don't anyone move." And the guests surely don't. Then everyone is questioned. Clues are leaked. These parties are intriguing and very popular.

Jerry Handorf and Beth Kuttelman of Madcap also produce gangster parties, Romeo and Juliet comedy productions, life-size puppet shows. They involve the audience in most of their productions, even costume people and bring them on stage. Madcap is the resident company at the Children's Zoo in the summer, performs at many schools and for many corporations.

Madcap Productions
921-5965

The Wayne Martin Puppets perform at schools, for civic organizations, in the city parks, on television, in the movies, with the Cincinnati Symphony Orchestra, at your home if you wish to book them. Wayne Martin produces shows for children and adults, uses hand puppets, rod puppets, life-size puppets, marionettes. There are seasonal productions, some that incorporate show tunes or classical music.

Wayne Martin Puppets
481-7666 or 922-5155

You're not apt to forget Colonel Charlie Riley if you've ever seen him perform. This Colonel Sanders look-alike puts a huge top hat over his entire head, paints a face on his chest (his breasts are eyes, his belly button is the mouth) and, by flexing his stomach muscles to make them look like moving lips, pantomimes playing "Sweet Georgia Brown" and other songs with a saxophone and trumpet he puts in his navel. You have to see this act to believe it. Colonel Riley brings his own stage, lights, and music. He has been performing these numbers for thirty years. Phone him. He'll send you photos if you ask.

Colonel Charlie Riley
342-7898

You'll find out all about dance lessons at The Flying Cloud Academy of Vintage Dance in "Learn Your Lesson," page 144, so for now, let's zero in on how you can have a vintage ball with the Flying Cloud Troupe as entertainment. But first, what are vintage dances? They're the ones your grandparents enjoyed: schottisches, mazurkas, quadrilles, galops, polkas, waltzes, so many more.

Richard Powers, director of The Flying Cloud Academy, revived these dances, teaches them to many enthusiastic Cincinnatians, holds historic balls. The Flying Cloud Troupe, which consists of twenty-five people, can stage a performance at a costume ball you might like to give. The troupe will perform one out of every three dances and call the rest of them so your guests can follow. Everyone has a wonderful time. (This troupe is famous! They did the dancing in the Warner Bros. movie *North and South*.)

The Flying Cloud Academy of Vintage Dance
321-4878

Check "Extras from Sports and the Performing Arts," pages 131 to 133, for more entertainment possibilities. You may be able to book all sorts of professional ensembles such as groups from the Opera, Playhouse in the Park—check them out.

Kidstuff

At an art birthday party, children provide their own entertainment with supervision by Patty Grant of Creative Crafts. She or one of her assistants runs the entire two-hour birthday party for four- to twelve-year-olds from beginning to end. And they bring all the supplies except the birthday cake, asking the mother or father to supply an undecorated one.

During the first hour, children sit at a table and decorate a plain paper tablecloth and plates with nontoxic markers. The birthday child decorates his cake while the guests garnish frosted cookies. After they all sing "Happy Birthday," craft creation begins. Each child makes four projects in four different mediums. These are the favors he will take home. Patty matches projects to age groups, so designs range from painting rocks and making dolls

from clothespins to turning tennis balls into puppets and gluing together rocket ships. There are weaving and building projects as well. Patty, who is just finishing a master's degree in art therapy, has examples for children to follow, but encourages them to be freewheeling and not make replicas. She wants to build self-esteem. The charge is $4.50 per child and there must be a minimum of ten children; maximum is thirty.

Creative Crafts
662-3892

Former teachers Pat Shryock and Joyce Kormos are now known on the children's party circuit as Polka and Dots. When they retired to rear their own small children, they created clown characters to delight little ones at birthday parties on a part-time basis. They have been so successful they are decidedly full-time these days. Drawing from their teaching experience with squirmy kids, they have put together entertainment that keeps four- and five-year-olds involved and interested. They do a puppet show, magic tricks, can play the harmonica and accordion, even pass out rhythm instruments to their audience. Everyone plays and sings. They juggle, paint children's faces, make balloon animals—parties can be tailored to any specifications.

Polka and Dots the Clowns
Joyce Kormos
683-1900
Pat Shryock
891-6667

Party Paper and Office Supplies

Pretty paper and party accessories plus all the office materials you need to make big-time business deals—here are some first-rate suppliers.

First off, some of the most innovative notecards, from nature scenes to art cards, can be gathered from gift shops nestled in museums, the downtown public library, the zoo—places like that. Unique specialty stores such as The Magic World of Serendipity, Fancy This, Inc., The Shaker Seed Box Company, always have handsome gift enclosures, notecards, and stationery, too. Be sure to keep all of these places in mind when you go shopping—you'll learn specifically where they are and what they offer in the "Museum Shops and Specialty Stores" chapter.

Cards and Accessories

There are some outstanding all-occasion party-paper stores in town. These carry an array of invitations and stationery from fine companies like Crane and Pineider to those that have all kinds of sayings already printed on them. You can match paper plates, napkins, matchbooks, cups to many of the invitations, and quite a few can be personalized. Paper supplies with holiday themes sweep through these stores with the seasons, and most carry colorful wrapping paper and ribbons. Some stock wedding accessories like bridal books, wedding registers, quill pens, and garters. So the next time you have a celebration of any kind, here's where to pick up the non-edible fixings.

Mary Hopple has outstanding taste—from stunning embossed cards made of handmade paper to clever invitations, this store is beautifully packed with party and stationery products.
M. Hopple & Co.
21 E. 5th St. (Skywalk)
579-9458
7565 Kenwood Rd. (Kenwood)
791-6426

Besides all sorts of party supplies and invitations, Parchment & Presents stocks some unusual gift items—such as crystal picture frames and kaleidoscopes containing semiprecious stones.
Parchment & Presents
Kenwood Mall
891-1777

In addition to paper, On Occasions, Inc. sometimes has boxes of Krön chocolates in stock—look for them especially around Valentine's Day.
On Occasions, Inc.
3416 Edwards Rd. (Hyde Park)
321-7898
280 E. Sharon Rd. (Glendale)
772-7898

This small shop is an outlet for Contempo paper products.
The Paper Warehouse
2430 E. Kemper Rd. (Shapely Outlet Center)
771-BAGS

Party Palais offers discounts of 20% on wedding invitations, but better yet, this store is organized so that every kind of paper product related to a particular party theme is arranged together on shelves. You don't have to have an imagination if you shop here—the store has everything laid out for you.
Party Palais
7750 Beechmont (Anderson Twp.)
232-0031

Balloons to table covers that look like cloth, wedding accessories to party favors for kids and adults. All-occasion greeting cards and invitations—Celebration is a complete party store.
Celebration
234 E. 6th St. (downtown)
421-1233

Party Planners has handmade paper, fine paper, and fun paper, plus all sorts of invitations and party accessories. (See more about the company's complete party service in "Home Entertainment," page 85.)

Party Planners
4337 Creek Rd. (Blue Ash)
793-3388

Identification Specialists gives a 20% discount on wedding invitations and accessories such as matches, napkins, wedding party gifts.

Identification Specialists
2957 Montana Ave. (Westwood)
662-1720

Party Supplies has plastic cutlery in about fifteen colors, twenty colors of plates, napkins, and tablecloths, decorations, helium balloons at good prices.

Party Supplies
8314 Plainfield Rd. (Deer Park)
891-4245

Cappel's has party supplies all right—silk flowers, aisle runners, streamers, and bells, to name a few reception decorations, walls of ribbon and bows, rolls of wrapping paper, tablecloths, napkins, plastic glasses. In-the-know party givers and handicrafters have always found Cappel's to be one of the most fertile sources of supplies.

Cappel Display Co.
920 Elm St. (downtown)
621-0952

Wholesale and Off-Price Paper and Party Supplies

Buehler Paper's Cash & Carry stores have plastic and paper plates, cups, coffee stirrers, cocktail straws, doilies, placemats, wedding aisle runners—the Blue Ash warehouse is packed with tons of party as well as hospital supplies, such as bed pads and adult diapers. This large paper distributor sells products in large quantities so you can get a price break. Or if you're overwhelmed by having to buy 25,000 cocktail straws even if they are priced at $27.30 or a roll of 4,000 carnival tickets for $4.30, you can buy in smaller numbers.

Buehler Paper's Cash & Carry
4699 Malsbary (Blue Ash)
891-9065
2nd & Court St. (Covington)
581-5070
2206 Beechmont Ave. (Anderson Twp.)
231-4273

Saalfeld Paper Co., another wholesale paper distributor, is agreeable to selling to retail customers. Again, their variety of paper products is as endless as their warehouse, so anything you even think you might need is probably here (along with cleaning compounds, cases of glassware, a room entirely filled with baskets—the kind florists and fruit stores use). Check out this place carefully.

Saalfeld Paper Co.
2701 Spring Grove Ave. (Camp Washington)
542-7100

Premiere has picnic supplies, decorations, twenty-five colors of plastic cutlery as well as plates, napkins, and cups to match. Look for plastic table covers in a variety of hues, aluminum baking pans, bathroom tissue, giftwrap by the foot or the jumbo roll.

Premiere Party and Paper Supplies
8784 Colerain Ave. (Groesbeck)
385-4060

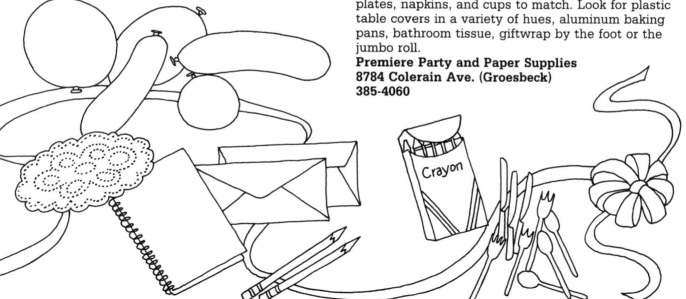

Party Paper and Office Supplies

92 The Paper Factory is one of the busiest stores at Outlets, Ltd. and it should be. It carries dozens of rolls of wrapping paper, ribbons, bows, stacks of business envelopes, packs of legal pads, typing paper, all sorts of stationery, spiral notebooks, coloring books, napkins, plates. That's just a few of the products always on hand at definitely friendly prices. Be prepared to buy more than you thought you would (everyone leaves carrying big bags) and spend less than you figured.
The Paper Factory
Outlets, Ltd. (Kings Island)
398-2777

The Francoise Greeting Card Co. wholesales novelties and greeting cards to clubs, church and school groups, which resell them as money-raising projects. But walk-in customers can qualify for Francoise's wholesale prices, too, which are about 35% less than list prices. Many manufacturers' lines of cards are in stock here—from inspirational notes and special-occasion greetings to those with blank interiors so you can jot down whatever you wish. Decorated recipe cards, postcards, even novelty stationery items can be found here. There are shelves full of gift items at Francoise—everything from keychains and photo frames to oven mitts and stick-on-telephone pens. This is a good place to look for little fun giveaways.
Francoise Greeting Card Co.
631 Main St. (downtown)
241-8281

Keep Makro and Squeri's Cash & Carry in mind if you need paper products in bulk—cases of bathroom and facial tissue, stacks of cups and plates, all sorts of aluminum baking pans. Makro has aisles of office supplies, too. Look for complete information about Makro in "Off-Price" (page 103), and see "Edibles" (page 9) for more about Squeri's.

Office Supplies
Calendars (desk and wall), appointment books, fountain pens, flo pens, typing paper, legal pads, paper clips, file boxes—any item you'd need to run an office can be purchased from stores selling office supplies. Many of these stores are located quite near the courthouse, downtown, so legal eagles hurrying by can pick up provisions. Look for school supplies at office outfitters, too. These places have always smelled like September to me.

Spitzfaden
629 Main St. (downtown)
721-1885

Gibson and Perin
121 W. 4th St. (downtown)
621-2592
138 E. 6th St. (downtown)
241-0495

Elgin Office Equipment Co.
810 Main St. (downtown)
621-1616

John R. Green Co.
411 W. 6th St. (Covington)
431-5568

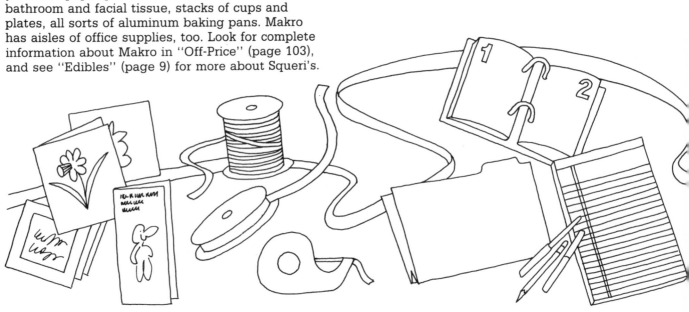

Museum Shops and Specialty Stores

You want to pick up a gift that's unique—it doesn't have to be expensive, just thoughtful. Something the person will truly appreciate and use—not stick in a drawer out of sight. Find these hard-to-find presents in museum gift shops, where the money you spend will also support worthy causes. This chapter includes other notable shops as well.

Museum Shops

The Cincinnati Art Museum Gift Shop has fine museum-reproduction jewelry, art books, coloring books, superb posters, slides from the permanent collection. There is a caseful of "little items" perfect for kids to buy their parents and a superb collection of notecards and postcards. If you're always on the lookout for creative small presents, buy some arty postcards and tie the packet with a ribbon. Friends can use them as invitations, gift enclosures, thank you notes, or slip them into a bag when traveling.
Cincinnati Art Museum Gift Shop
Eden Park
721-5204

The Cincinnati Fire Museum Gift Shop sells fire-fighting related items. There are small wooden fire trucks and other toys and models, T-shirts with the museum's logo, plastic fire hats that have "chief" printed on them, coloring books, placemats, and prints of antique fire-fighting apparatus.
Cincinnati Fire Museum Gift Shop
315 W. Court St. (downtown)
621-5553

The Cincinnati Historical Society Gift Shop has mainly books, prints, and photographs dealing with Cincinnati history. When the society makes the move to Union Terminal (more about that in "The Queen City's Crown Jewels," page 128), look for an expanded shop.
Cincinnati Historical Society Gift Shop
Eden Park
241-4622

Cincinnati Museum of Natural History Collectors' Shop has a great collection of archaeology, geology, astronomy, and other nature books. Gift items include rocks and minerals, rock-collecting equipment, Indian and Eskimo artifacts, and jewelry made with minerals and semiprecious stones. There are always wonderful novelty items here, many of which are dinosaur-related.
Cincinnati Museum of Natural History
Collectors' Shop
1720 Gilbert Ave. (near downtown)
621-3889

The Cincinnati Nature Center Gift Shop has a terrific variety of bird feeders (some of which can even defy squirrels), John Ruthven and Charles Harper art posters, notepaper and postcards, dried wreaths, stuffed animals and puppets, a solid collection of nature books, especially those dealing with animal and bird identification.
Cincinnati Nature Center Gift Shop
4949 Tealtown Rd. (Milford)
831-1711

The Cincinnati Zoo Shop has every animal-related gift you can imagine: cards, stuffed animals, books, T-shirts, jewelry, educational toys and puppets. This place provides a wildlife shopping experience.
The Cincinnati Zoo Shop
3400 Vine St. (Avondale)
281-4701

Museum Shops and Specialty Stores

The Contemporary Arts Center Bookstore is one of my favorite places for notepaper and postcards, and I always delight in their supply of arty-looking pencils and ballpoint pens to use as stocking stuffers. Look for a new-fashioned singing teakettle designed by Michael Graves, outdoor bells designed by Paolo Soleri, aprons decorated with Picasso prints, and a poster collection that college kids love for their dorm rooms.
The Contemporary Arts Center Bookstore
115 E. 5th St. (downtown)
241-4428

Nature's Niche Gift & Book Shop is the gift and bookstore for the Hamilton County Parks, and it always has a fine variety of well-designed bird feeders, bird seed blended specially for the shop to attract diverse flocks, nature books, and gift items made of natural materials.
Nature's Niche Gift & Book Shop
Farbach-Werner Nature Preserve
3455 Poole Rd. (Groesbeck)
923-3665

The College Store of the Hebrew Union College—Jewish Institute of Religion has unique handcrafted Judaica including menorahs, mezuzahs, kiddush cups, and seder plates as well as cookbooks, art books, books related to Jewish studies.
The College Store
Hebrew Union College—
Jewish Institute of Religion
3101 Clifton Ave. (Clifton)
221-1875

Krohn Conservatory Gift Shop has lush houseplants from the everyday to the exotic (like gorgeous orchids and unusual ferns) at reasonable prices. There are plant-growing accessories, sundials, bulbs, plant kits, and books.
Krohn Conservatory Gift Shop
Eden Park
352-4091

The Music Hall Centennial Shop benefits the Cincinnati Ballet, Opera Guild, and Symphony Orchestra. That's why you'll find all sorts of music-related items here like Nutcracker dolls, novelty music boxes, cassettes, T-shirts that have such things printed on them as "Fa-la-la-la-la," notecards resembling piano keyboards. The shop is open one hour before performances at Music Hall and at intermission.
Music Hall Centennial Shop
1241 Elm St. (downtown)
621-1919

Friends Shop of the Public Library of Cincinnati and Hamilton County has one of the best selections of notecards in town (Ansel Adams to Shakespeare) plus great-looking totes and book bags. Look for bookends—petrified wood ones from Arizona, animal carvings from Africa, brass bookends made in Philadelphia, bookmarks, book covers, educational toys, activity books, terrific posters— really any book-related gift item. This shop is extremely popular and stocks items people always come back for.
Friends Shop
Public Library of Cincinnati and Hamilton County
800 Vine St. (downtown)
369-6920

Sharon Woods Village Shop, located in the John B. Hayner House in the historic village, sells antiques, antique reproductions, ornaments, dolls, miniatures, wreaths, a fine selection of books on antiques and history-related subjects—everything that fits the mood and period of the village.
Sharon Woods Village Shop
Sharon Woods Park (Sharonville)
Hwy. 42
563-2503

The Taft Museum Shop has lovely jewelry, porcelain, enameled and cloisonné vases and bowls, Chinese decorative pieces, books, and notecards.
The Taft Museum Shop
316 Pike St. (downtown)
241-0343

The Playhouse in the Park's gift kiosk is located in the theater lobby and is open before and after performances and during intermission. Want a *Little Shop of Horrors* people-eating plant bank, or a T-shirt that says "Come Playhouse With Me"? Buy them here.
Cincinnati Playhouse in the Park Gift Kiosk
Eden Park
421-5440

Clovernook Home and School for the Blind has a gift shop filled with lovely handwoven articles made in the school's weaving shop. Reversible cotton rugs with multicolored warp come in a variety of sizes and besides being good-looking, they're perfect water- and dirt-absorbers and wash beautifully. They're durable, too. Placemats are made in white and other colors; some sets have napkins to match. There are also tablecloths and baby blankets.
Clovernook Home and School for the Blind Gift Shop
7000 Hamilton Ave. (North College Hill)
522-3860

Everything in the Carnegie Arts Center Gift Shop is made by Greater Cincinnati artisans and artists: jewelry, pottery, handwoven scarves and shawls, clothes made of antique fabrics, baskets, ceramics, and quilts.
Carnegie Arts Center Gift Shop
Robbins & Scott Sts. (Covington)
491-2030

The Warren County Historical Society's Gift Shop has an outstanding collection of Shaker replicas— pegs, boxes, and baskets, as well as other antique reproductions such as pottery, pewter pieces, and candlesticks. Many local artists supply this shop with their crafts, which makes it well worth the drive to Lebanon.
Warren County Historical Society Gift Shop
105 S. Broadway (Lebanon, OH)
1-932-1817

Other Specialty Shops

Bonnie Wittenbaum, the owner of the Magic World of Serendipity, jam-packs her shop with good-looking and whimsical merchandise without ever crossing the line to cutesy. She has a good eye. She also has more Bybee pottery than anyone else in the city, as well as Bennington pottery and Louisville stoneware. Other American handcrafts include leaded-glass sun catchers, art glass objects, wine goblets with pewter stems, many baskets, handwoven throw rugs, and an outstanding collection of notecards, gift enclosures, postcards, and wrapping paper. Cotton ribbon can be purchased by the bolt or the yard. Bonnie will make up gift baskets containing any assortment of items you find in the store and always has good suggestions for hard-to-buy-for people.
Magic World of Serendipity
6902 Murray Ave. (Mariemont)
271-1400

If you are interested in Shaker furnishings and accessories, you can find fine reproductions at The Shaker Seed Box Company. Look for all sorts of small boxes, seed boxes, peg rails, clocks, chairs, rockers, tables, case pieces with drawers. Proprietor Steve Kistler, who is a Shaker expert, can have furniture made by special order and can have chairs retaped in Shaker style in quite a large variety of colors. Small items such as notecards, placemats, herbs and spices, Shaker-style gardener's smocks are also abundant here.

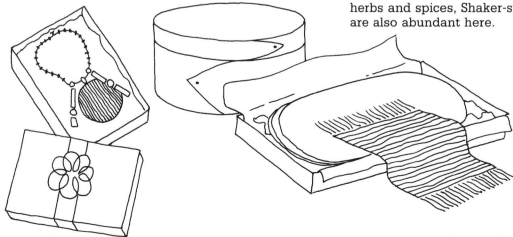

Museum Shops and Specialty Stores

Steve's tasteful shop has now expanded into an art gallery where Shaker art labels, spirit drawings, counted cross-stitch pieces (a popular one is "Hands to Work, Hearts to God"), and posters are displayed. Shows change every two months.

The Shaker Seed Box Company
6656 Chestnut St. (Mariemont)
271-7100

The Grailville Art and Book Shop is more than a reliable source for meaningful books on women's issues, religious search, spirituality, and social concerns: it is an interesting place to find one-of-a-kind art objects. Many are taken on consignment from artists sympathetic to Grailville's goals. There are also handcrafts from Third World countries and a good selection of inspirational and non-religious cards and posters. Try to combine a trip to the store with a walk around the serene grounds.

The Grailville Art Book Shop
932 O'Bannonville Rd. (Loveland)
683-0202

Fancy This, Inc. is filled with so many assorted items: cookware, placemats, baskets, mugs, nicely decorated plastic barware, doormats (plain or personalized), picture frames, a good collection of notecards, and all sorts of wrapping supplies such as paper, colorful bags, tissue, gift enclosures.

Owners Ann Pease and Pam Salatich are helpful in suggesting items to make up custom gift baskets, and talk to either of them about having a wooden model of your house or someone else's done by a local artist. Just submit photos of the house from all angles, and the artist will produce a hand-cut, hand-painted miniature.

Fancy This also has a computer poet in residence. Feed it the name of the person you want to send a greeting to, along with a few of his traits and the special occasion you have in mind, and the computer comes up with two limericks—fun and sentimental. After you choose one, the greeting will be printed on any blank card you select. Welcome to the future!

Fancy This, Inc.
8416 Vine St. (Hartwell)
821-0844

Linden Noll is virtually wall-to-wall, floor-to-ceiling European gifts and collectibles. A sampling: folklore-theme table linens; antique-look jewelry from Sweden, Germany, and Holland; imported dolls; traditional folk costumes for children and adults—flowered dresses and aprons to Lederhosen, shirts, and vests. There are Christmas ornaments year-round (including hand-blown glass ones), hand-painted Easter eggs from Hungary and Germany, old-fashioned Valentines and other special-occasion cards. There is much emphasis on holiday gifts. Take time to browse through Linden Noll. There is much to see in every nook and cranny.

Linden Noll Gift Haus
514 W. 6th St. (Covington)
581-7633

Country House has American country reproductions from handwoven throw rugs to all sorts of baskets. Many small gift items are always in stock, but custom orders of quilts, furniture, lamp shades—almost any item in the store—can be accommodated.
Country House
7801 Laurel Ave. (Madeira)
271-1074

The Green Apple has cut-crystal pieces—vases, bowls, salad bowls, trays, and tureens—as well as a wide selection of picture frames, which are always thoughtful presents. Some in stock are made of terra cotta, Lucite, metals—contemporary to Art Deco styles. Children's clothes, stuffed animals, cookware, handmade silver Israeli jewelry—this shop always has a fine supply of gifts.
The Green Apple
6200 Montgomery Rd. (Pleasant Ridge)
531-0622

Margaritaville stocks everything Mexican: all sorts of pots and vases, sets of stoneware dishes and bowls, glassware, handwoven wool throw rugs and wall hangings, cotton dresses and shirts, silver jewelry from the silversmiths in Taxco.
Margaritaville
2034 Madison Rd. (O'Bryonville)
321-9779

Gloria Nadel sells a variety of gift items, a large part of which are made of Lucite, by appointment only. Picture frames, desk plates, clipboards, museum cases for collectibles, table pedestals are in stock, or you can have them custom made. Talk to Gloria about bathroom accessories, even lamps and tea carts. All of these items are sold at a discount.
Gloria Nadel Designs
351-2530

Looking for a Cincy souvenir? Try the Cincy Shop. Ballet, zoo, opera, city-skyline posters are always present. So are Reds and Bengals souvenirs and dozens of T-shirts and sweatshirts bearing local sayings.
Cincy Shop
26 Fountain Square Plaza (downtown)
579-1435
Swifton Commons Mall (Roselawn)
731-7227
Tri-County Mall
671-1271

The College Football Hall of Fame Gift Shop is where to shop for football fans. Pennants, mugs, coffee cups, wristbands, headbands, trash cans, sweatshirts represent almost every college.
College Football Hall of Fame
5440 Kings Island Dr. (adjacent to Kings Island)
241-5410

If you've been to a dozen places and you still can't find what you need, try Pier I Imports. Mugs, mats, wicker furniture, vases, boxes, soap, candles, cookware—anything for the house can be found in Pier I stores. They're great places to buy furniture at modest prices and all sorts of small presents for any occasion. Gypsy clothes—colorful cotton separates—are now part of their everyday stock. Check the phone directory for the store nearest you.

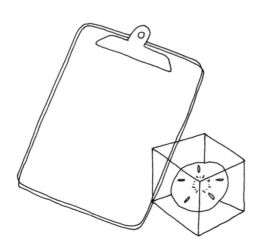

Toys and Novelties

You can buy toys most anyplace in town—in supermarket-type toy stores that carry every brand you see on television, department stores, discount stores, and variety stores. But in this chapter, I've rounded up some of the special shops in the city—those that carry squeezable, unmotorized dolls and stuffed animals, places to buy teaching toys, fun stores packed with magic tricks and novelties.

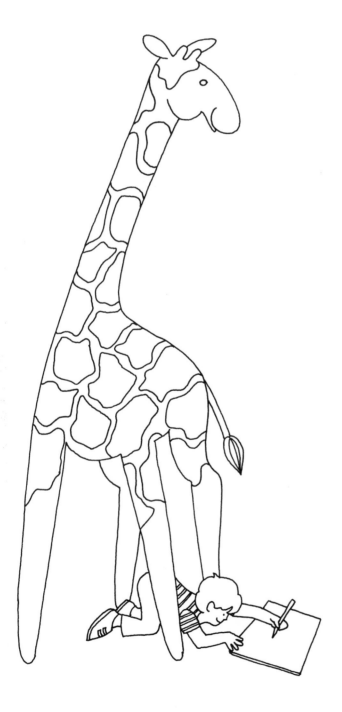

Toys

If you're looking for Steiff stuffed animals; Madame Alexander, Corolle, Götz (the best European and American dolls); Brio and Lego trains, toys, and building systems; sturdy, educational blocks, puzzles, and games from preschool to adult; you-build-it models; science experiments—in short, as close to F.A.O. Schwarz stock as you can find in Cincinnati—check out these blue-ribbon toy stores.

Larson's Toys & Games
33 W. 5th St. (downtown)
241-3455

The Toy Shop
Westin Hotel (downtown)
721-TOYS

Main St. Children & Adult Toy Store
9416 Main St. (Montgomery)
891-1050

King Arthur's Court
Hyde Park Plaza
871-6031
7840 Cooper Rd. (Montgomery)
Check Directory Assistance for this new listing.

Dolls and Stuffed Animals

Blooming Dolls and Things carries antique and modern classics, American dolls such as Madame Alexander, European ones such as Lenci and Kathy Kruse. You'll find wooden Pinocchios from Italy that have two adjustable nose sizes, Nutcracker dolls, nests of dolls from Russia—large and tiny sets. This store also carries doll-related items such as cradles and clothes, and its restoration and repair services even include stitching up a new wardrobe. Expect to spend $1 to $5,000 when you go shopping here.
Blooming Dolls and Things
8376 Vine St. (Hartwell)
761-7997

All My Children Doll Shop has many plush animals including Steiff, and all sorts of dolls made in America including porcelain ones, even a doll resembling Joan Crawford. European brands include Zaps, Lissi, Götz, and Helmut Engel. You'll find doll clothes, cradles, even real children-sized furniture such as upholstered wing chairs, a harvest table with ladderback chairs, sturdy work tables.
All My Children Doll Shop
2732 Erie Ave. (Hyde Park Square)
871-8442

Offerings at the Doll Gallery range from classic Raggedy Anns priced at $29.95 to incredible collectibles that must be handled with care because they cost $15,000. There are hand-painted wax-over-porcelain dolls, bisque dolls, some made by international artists. Notice the $4,000 Italian doll with long auburn hair who looks like Hamlet's Ophelia in her long, flowing dress; owner Phyllis Sanders describes her and the other dolls in this category as contemporary art. Most items in the store are collectibles rather than dolls you'd actually play with, but you can find teddy bears and baby dolls a small child would love among the museum-quality stock.

Doll Gallery
9514 Kenwood Rd. (Montgomery)
791-6606

Animal Haus Ltd. is a teddy bear supermarket. The store carries twenty-seven top brands from all over the world. There are country bears, campers, schoolgirls, and grandpas. There are also many classic teddies as well as a good number dressed in period clothes. What a collection!

Animal Haus Ltd.
7784 Montgomery Rd. (Kenwood)
984-9955

Walk into the Doll Clinic and you walk back in time. The cases out front are filled with dolls from the 1890s to the present time. They have sweet faces, beautiful clothes—you'll recognize all the old friends you played with as a child.

The back of the store is closed off by a door marked "Surgery." All repair is performed here—operations such as patching heads, rerooting hair, replacing eyes and teeth, fingers and toes. When I was there, a teddy bear that had been loved into a pancake was being restuffed. There are racks of clothes and drawers full of doll parts. Clothes can also be made to order.

Owner Betty Bryant buys as well as sells vintage dolls and stuffed animals. And believe me, before you discard the old dolls that need to be cleaned out of your closets, have them appraised here. Seeing price tags on dolls like ones I had given away made me a true believer in their incredible value.

Doll Clinic
528 Main St. (Covington)
291-1174

Dollhouses and Miniatures

If you're in the market for a dollhouse—from a Swiss chalet to a Victorian mansion, even a tiny house that's a replica of your own—plus furniture to fill every room, try the following stores.

Unicorn Miniatures
1028 Delta (Mt. Lookout)
871-2823

Treasures Forever
3540 Blue Rock Rd. (White Oak)
385-9145

The Sow's Ear
11182 Reading Rd. (Sharonville)
563-5577

Treasure House Gallery
1518 Dixie Hwy. (Park Hills, KY)
291-3412

Trains

You love trains. Then visit The Crossing some Saturday—that's the only day of the week the shop is open. The Crossing buys, sells, and repairs vintage Lionel, American Flyer, and other brands of trains that have become valuable collectibles.

Seems that the "golden age" of Lionel trains began after World War II and continued until the '60s when extensive use of plastic began. Then interest in new trains slipped while interest in older models raged. People from all over the Tri-State who know the value of classic trains make tracks to The Crossing. Now that you know about it, you can climb aboard.

The Crossing
2435 W. McMicken Ave. (Clifton)
651-2424

The Garden Railway Co. is a train gallery, *not* a hobby store—for they specialize in handmade trains from the Orient and Europe. Besides representing products for some of the most famous international train makers, Garden Railway can construct a railway in your backyard that is a moving sculpture. Built to your design, it will be complete with bonsai trees, rocks, ponds, and railroad ties to create natural scenery. The trains that will run on these are made specifically for outdoor use. Garden Railway is an incredibly special place. You have to visit the store to see for yourself.

The Garden Railway Co.
2009 Madison Rd. (O'Bryonville)
321-9949

Toys and Novelties

100   Teaching Toys

The John R. Green Co. sells such marvelous school supplies that any parent could entertain a child for a year just picking through the store's shelves. There are hundreds of painless skill-teaching games, about every school subject and for all age levels, such as Alpha Mat (a language arts floor game), Vowel Bingo, Syllable Safari. There are puzzles, clocks to teach telling time, terrific wall hangings about subjects as far-ranging as dinosaurs and the solar system. Look for all sorts of craft supplies to make clothespin and pipecleaner people, and art supplies including brushes, paints, and paper for novices and serious artists.
John R. Green Co.
411 W. 6th St. (Covington)
431-5568

You can buy Discovery Toys in your own home (they are not sold in retail stores) if you put a group of people together. Then, for hosting the event, you get 10% of the evening's sale in either money or toys.

    Company representatives talk to the group you've assembled about the appropriateness of toys for children of a particular age and demonstrate how parents should work with their children and the toys for maximum pleasure and minimum frustration. And note that each Discovery toy is nontoxic, made to span at least one year of a child's growth and development, and covers at least two educational concepts. From newborn toys that teach sensory and motor skills to adult games of strategy and planning, these toys are excellent. Call Judy Davis, the area manager, for information on contacting one of the more than seventy-five representatives in these parts and setting up a party.
Discovery Toys
351-1031

The Learning Tree is operated by Carol Cimini and Kim Stahl, who are interested in getting people to know more about educational toys they feel children would love to play with—outside of school. Call them about home parties for eight to thirty people for which hosts get up to 35% of the proceeds. There are more than 300 items to choose from, including activity books, records and tapes, learning games, and toys that cover everything from language arts to science.
The Learning Tree
829-8900

The Blue Marble is a bookstore devoted to children. It sells cloth books for babies, nursery rhymes, fairy tales, books for beginning readers, literature, fiction, information, reference, foreign language books, books for parents who want to read up on the special problems of children, books for teachers.

    If that isn't enough, The Blue Marble also carries educational and musical toys, European toys such as those made by Ambi, Kiddicraft, and Brio, wooden games and soft toys made by Students Craft Industry of Berea College, records and tapes. This lovely Ft. Thomas store is adjacent to several others that sell crafts. You may want to explore all of them when you visit.
The Blue Marble
118 N. Ft. Thomas Ave. (Ft. Thomas)
781-0602

The Schoolbell, a fairly new children's bookstore, has a modest supply of children's books that the owner says is growing. There are books for infants to fourteen-year-olds, fiction and nonfiction, learning books for children, and how-to-parent books for adults. In addition, The Schoolbell carries European wooden toys, puzzles, games, and stuffed animals.
The Schoolbell Books & Gifts
9466 Montgomery Rd. (Montgomery)
891-4994

Magic

You're a trickster. Plastic ice cubes with flies inside, glasses that dribble, snapping gum—you love the stuff. Or maybe you're a serious magician. You're after wands, capes, scarves, big stage illusions. Here are three places to find them, all of which have magicians in residence to help you make just the right selections.

Playing cards are a specialty at Haines House of Cards, but they carry a complete selection of magical apparatus.
Haines House of Cards
2514 Leslie Ave. (Norwood)
531-6548

Wm. H. Brewe Magic offers small pocket tricks to large stage illusions as well as custom building for magicians.
Wm. H. Brewe Magic
1685 Harrison Ave. (Fairmount)
251-4218

At Venture III you can find small tricks and stage magic—from caring people who take time to explain them patiently. The store was packed with kids the Saturday I stopped in.
Venture III
6016 Montgomery Rd. (Pleasant Ridge)
531-2100

Novelties

Companies that supply prizes and games to school carnivals are flush with items you can use as birthday-party favors for small children, or for Halloween giveaways instead of candy, or for fun on any occasion. What kinds of things can you find? Plastic spider rings, rubber snakes, crickets, flying propellers, tiny dolls, false teeth and moustaches, little purses—hundreds of items you can buy for a few cents apiece, or even less if you buy by the dozen.

There are large stuffed animals, even life-size St. Bernards, balloons, paper streamers and bells, banners for every occasion, flags. You must go through these places carefully because there is so much merchandise everywhere. And think about taking small children to such wondrous caverns of affordable playthings on a rainy day when everyone is out of sorts. Kids snap back fast. So do their parents.

Todi Toys
3329 Eastern Ave. (East End)
871-7750

Brazel Novelty Co.
4176 Apple St. (Northside)
541-1318

Brown Novelty Shop
312 W. 4th St. (downtown)
421-0064

The Becksmith Co. supplies toys not only to school fairs but also to hospital gift shops, so you'll find larger-than-usual novelty items here. There are many rack toys, too, such as the ones you'd find in a drugstore. (Note: you must have a tax-exempt number to buy here. So if you represent a religious or school organization, Boy Scouts, etc., check out this place for your next function.)
The Becksmith Co.
5005 Barrow Ave. (Oakley)
531-4151

Toys and Novelties

Novelty Gifts

You Name It is pricier than the other novelty companies. It's a frisky gift shop full of trendy, humorous all-occasion cards, T-shirts, one-of-a-kinds like glasses with windshield wipers, headbands with mistletoe attached. Whatever is new and hot is here, and what you buy is not necessarily something you use, but it may make you laugh.

You Name It
2646 Erie Ave. (Hyde Park)
321-0872
414 Walnut St. (Mercantile Way Bldg., downtown)
381-0872
208 E. 6th St. (Gwynne Bldg., downtown)
651-0872

Outdoor Fun

Swings & Such sells such heavy-duty outdoor play equipment that they guarantee it will last for twenty-five years. These playscapes are modular. You can start with a swing set, add climbing gyms, playhouses—go take a look.

Swings & Such
298 W. Crescentville Rd. (Springdale)
671-6111

Yards of Fun and Fitness sells commercial-quality equipment such as basketball goals, galvanized metal swings, small shelters, shuffleboard courts—on and on. Call for a catalogue or visit the showroom to see the inventory in person. There is much preschool play equipment such as wooden swings, picnic tables, sandboxes, climbing gym sets, playhouses, indoor equipment, too. They sell to day-care centers and schools, so the variety is large and everything is made to take a beating.

Yards of Fun and Fitness
11699 Chesterdale Rd. (Springdale)
771-8182

Children's Accessories

Marianne Plotnick makes all sorts of personalized children's accessories, such as growth charts, painted-to-order oak rockers, decorated coat hangers, wooden chalkboards, puzzle racks, even a wooden stool whose seat is a puzzle made of the child's name.

Marianne has birth announcements, even calling cards for tiny tots to take to birthday parties. Phone her to ask about all of these specialties, which you may see by appointment.

The Glass Rainbow
984-5154

Judy Ruben personalizes and decorates all sorts of items for children: rulers, scissors, umbrellas, canvas totes, T-shirts, baby bottles, mugs, and picture frames. Phone her for a catalogue picturing these items and others.

Just For You
793-7363

Lisa James and Barbara Marowitz hand paint children's furniture and gifts. I saw little pink Windsors decorated with Peter Rabbit scenes, stools, rockers, bookends, and tables. These women will also hand paint by special order, even continue their designs on nursery walls, on dresser drawers, on anything you wish, to coordinate the entire room. Phone them to see what they already have on hand and to discuss custom orders.

Periwinkle Rabbit
Lisa James
751-3239
Barbara Marowitz
559-9348

Off-Price

You can find off-price merchandise most anywhere these days. Retail stores have sales constantly, often undercutting factory outlets. And what's a true factory outlet anyway? Many sell other manufacturers' merchandise as well as their own, making them close cousins to regular retail stores. You'll find factory outlets scattered throughout this book, as well as many other specialty stores that sell at a discount. They are listed in chapters dealing with the specific merchandise they offer.

So what stores are featured in this section? Big department-store-type outfits that offer "off-price" merchandise on a day-to-day basis. But not everything on their shelves always costs less than other stores in town. You know that! They are beat out regularly when competitors slash prices to give customers special deals on selected items. That's why you, as a smart shopper, must do your homework. By checking out prices before you go shopping, you'll always be able to spot the best buy.

When this French-style hypermarket first opened in Mt. Carmel, shoppers flocked to Bigg's by the carload to take advantage of low grocery prices. But stunned supermarket chains fought back by offering coupons and double coupons to regain defecting customers. Still, you save money at Bigg's on a changeable variety of items. Plants are discounted in season. I bought a pair of shoes for $12 that I saw at Bloomingdale's for $20. Packs of rainbow-colored socks and pantyhose are often nice buys. Bigg's bakery products, especially French bread and crusty rolls, draw raves.

Bigg's has everything from dishes to microwaves. And this huge store has spawned a mall and many satellite stores you may want to check out when you're in the area.
Bigg's
4450 Eastgate Blvd. (Mt. Carmel)
753-7500

Makro is a giant trade center selling everything from food to office equipment at between regular retail and wholesale prices to the business public. That means you must own a business, work for an organization or business that will give you a letter of authorization, be a professional, or qualify in some way for a Makro card enabling you to make purchases. Call Customer Registration and see if you're a candidate.

Makro announces specials weekly that are often hard to beat. Whether it's a five-pound wheel of cheese or a popular-name television, the store's ability to buy in volume and pass the savings to customers makes for spectacular deals. And customers' being able to make case purchases on items such as paper products and pet food, as well as buy commercial-size canned goods, is also a big draw for Makro.
Makro
10765 Reading Rd. (Evendale)
554-3144

Swallen's is prime for buyers of big-ticket appliances, while camera aficionados check out the store's equipment regularly. So does everyone else . in town, whether they're hunting anything from records to hardware. Swallen's prices are always competitive.

Many scratch-and-dent floor models and discontinued appliances are displayed at the Spring Grove store. If you need a freezer or refrigerator, it's a good place to look. Check your phone book for Swallen's many locations.

Off-Price

Lazarus Home Clearance Center is filled with furniture and appliances—floor samples, scratch-and-dent models, discontinued merchandise—all sorts of good buys that get even better when the store holds its once-a-month sale. At these crowded weekend events people snap up home staples—couches to VCRs, carpet to television sets—at substantial savings.
Lazarus Home Clearance Center
Winton Rd. & Spring Grove Ave. (Winton Place)
853-7154

McAlpin's Warehouse is open only during their once-a-month sales, not daily. Watch newspaper advertisements for sales of carpet, furniture, mattresses, lamps—floor samples, end-of-the-season, and discontinued merchandise from McAlpin's department stores.
McAlpin's Warehouse
9440 Seward Rd. (Fairfield)
870-1200

Sears Surplus Store is filled with overflow catalogue merchandise, not leftovers from the retail stores. Expect to find anything you'd see in the catalogue—clothes to hardware, vacuum sweepers to sewing machines. New arrivals often!
Sears Surplus Store
6253 Glenway Ave. (Western Hills)
662-8900

You'll find overstocked and discontinued merchandise from the J.C. Penney catalogue and retail stores at this outlet store. Anything from shoes to paint—at good prices—is likely to turn up here.
J.C. Penney Outlet Store
8770 Colerain Ave. (Groesbeck)
385-9700

Service Merchandise has catalogue showrooms throughout Greater Cincinnati (check your phone directory for locations). Go to any one of the stores, select what you want to buy from the catalogue—toys to gold chains, clock radios to hair dryers—fill out an order, and your purchase rumbles down a conveyor belt within minutes. Nice prices, but check around town to make sure they're competitive.

Value City Department Stores can have exactly what you're looking for or nothing even close, depending on the day you go shopping. The company buys merchandise from stores that are going out of business, have leftover merchandise, meet with any kind of physical or financial disaster.

Devotees pick up biggest-name designer clothes and shoes, great children's wear, robes, housewares, furniture—all sorts of goodies. Announcements of arrivals of well-known brands are made in the newspapers. On those days, plan to get to the stores early, before the racks are decimated. Check your phone book for locations.

Outlets, Ltd. is the factory outlet mall located near Kings Island. Since it opened several years ago, there has been a large turnover in occupants, and now many stores that are tenants are part of national chains that simply offer goods at a

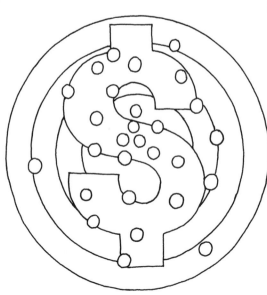

discount. There are endless shoe stores in the mall and much low-end clothing. But there is a handful of stores so truly attractive they make a visit worthwhile. These include Pottery USA, a yarn shop, a wonderful paper supply store, a totes outlet, and an outstanding Proctor-Silex/Wear-Ever Outlet that could outfit your entire kitchen. You'll find out more about these individual enterprises in the chapters dealing with the merchandise they sell.

Outlets, Ltd.
5300 Kings Island Dr.
421-5532

The Shapely Outlet Center is a conglomeration of stores—including an outlet for Shapely merchandise (women's separates), a Polly Flinders children's clothing outlet, a discount shoe store that has moderate to good quality footwear, a small party-paper outlet, some men's clothing stores, and an outlet for Head sportswear—all under one roof.

Shapely Outlet Center
2430 E. Kemper Rd. (Sharonville)
771-7733

To save money on everything from shampoo to toothpaste, people head to the Drug Emporium. These stores offer an abundant variety and, best of all, lots of promotional-size items that fit snugly into a cosmetics travel kit. Find the store closest to you in the phone directory.

Tri-State Jobbing Co., the closest thing to an old-fashioned dry-goods store in this town, buys close-outs, manufacturers' overruns, and going-out-of-business stock from retailers in the area. Just about anything from blankets to overalls, infants' to adults' oversize clothing can surface on Tri-State's shelves—sooner or later.

Tri-State Jobbing Co.
23 W. Court St. (downtown)
621-4500

I am a dime-store fan, and the downtown Newberry's is my personal favorite. But then, the Woolworth's a few blocks away runs a real close second. Where else can you find such an array of plastic fruit and polyester flowers, dollar cosmetics including all sorts of fake fingernails and fuschia lipsticks? Toy racks are filled with uncomplicated playthings like paddles with balls, bubble pipes, jump ropes, and jacks. In the housewares section, there are '40s-style flowered aprons, even salt and pepper shakers in the shape of tomatoes. Pure kitsch!

While the aroma of popcorn entices you, you can seriously consider bags of multicolored hair ribbons, cards of barrettes in the shape of ducks and rabbits, packs of knee highs in shades of hot pink and lavender. Maybe you can't buy much for a dime at these places anymore, but you can sure stretch a dollar and have fun doing it.

Newberry's Department and Variety Store
6th & Race (downtown)
621-1833

Woolworth's
26 W. 5th St. (downtown)
721-6654
Check the phone directory for suburban locations.

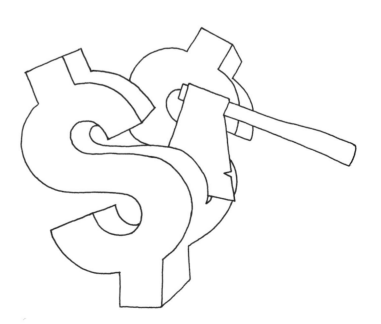

Auctions

106 Main Auction Galleries holds a weekly auction every Tuesday morning at 10:30 (previews are the day prior to the sale), drawing regulars from all over town. But it's not just what goes up for bids that's a crowd pleaser at Main. The Karp family—Phyllis, her husband J. Louis, and their son Jay—keep up a Woody Allen-type running patter during sales that is as lively as their ever-changing inventory.

Since 1910, the Karps have purchased entire estates (they are also appraisers), so anything from fine art, period furniture, and silver to just plain furniture and china can turn up here. Auction buffs snap up everything from couches to crystal, rugs to ruby rings. Many people have furnished whole houses with assorted Tuesday pickings.

Main also holds quarterly fine arts auctions where you can bid on rare Rookwood pieces, fine paintings, furniture, and more. The date of their once-a-year book auction is circled in red on the calendars of area book lovers (more on this in "Reading Matter," page 122). Ask that your name be added to the Karps' mailing list so you will be apprised of all their upcoming events.
Main Auction Galleries
137 W. 4th St. (downtown)
621-1280

Columbia Auction Gallery holds once-a-month auctions of antique furniture (all periods), as well as paintings, rugs, antique and modern jewelry, pottery, silver, china, and furs. Look for ads announcing their auctions in the newspapers, or call and ask to be placed on their mailing list.
Columbia Auction Gallery
3500 Columbia Pkwy. (Tusculum)
321-8210

Lots of Cincinnati antique lovers as well as those from all over the country flock to Garth's Auctions, Inc., in Delaware, Ohio, on the outskirts of Columbus. Many of Garth's auctions offer early American furniture, accessories, stoneware, and pewter, though European furniture and accessories, glassware, and paintings often turn up as well. Catalogues (available by subscription, which costs $70 per year) will keep you advised of all upcoming auctions. And if you don't feel like traveling to Columbus, you can enter absentee bids.

Note that auctions at Garth's can provide major-league excitement. When big-time dealers join the bidding, record prices are sometimes set. At the same time, people are able to come away with real bargains, when what they covet is not as appealing to the rest of the crowd.

Garth's Auctions, Inc.
2690 Stratford Rd.
P.O. Box 369
Delaware, OH 43015
614-362-4771 or 614-369-5085

If you're a car buff, you can try your luck at finding a great buy at the Cincinnati Auto Auction. This public auction of cars repossessed by banks is held every Thursday at 11 A.M. Viewing begins at 8 A.M., and you can start the cars you're interested in but not take them out for a test drive. Also, you must come up with the cash for your purchase by 2 P.M. the next day. Look for the list of cars to be auctioned off each week in the auto section of the Monday newspapers.

Cincinnati Auto Auction
4969 Mulhauser Rd. (West Chester)
874-9310

All the unclaimed items gathering dust in the Cincinnati Police Department's property room are auctioned off twice a year, usually on the second Saturdays in October and April at noon at the Convention Center. However, dates can vary, so check the auction notices in newspapers as time draws near, or call the police property room for information.

What is likely to go up for bids? Anything under the sun that has been stolen and left unclaimed, but always expect lots of bicycles, radios, television sets, stereos, sporting goods, and musical instruments. No cars or guns, though. An hour before the auction you may inspect the items, but you buy everything "as is." No checks are accepted—cash only. And you can remove the item you've bought only after you pay for it.

Cincinnati Police Auction
352-3580

The Hamilton County Sheriff's office holds a yearly auction at its patrol headquarters, usually at 9 A.M. on a Saturday in September. The auction is always advertised in the newspapers a few weeks before it is held, so look for announcements. The most popular items—again, unclaimed stolen merchandise—are bicycles, tools, clocks, radios, skates, you name it. You may view what's available an hour before the auction.

Hamilton County Sheriff's Office Auction
Communications Center and Sheriff's Road Patrol Headquarters
11021 Hamilton Ave.
632-8801

Auctions

The Hamilton County Park District holds an annual spring auction in the maintenance complex in Winton Woods, located south of the golf course off Springdale Road. Typical items are boats (from pedal to rowboats); used ranger cruisers and trucks; a wide assortment of maintenance equipment such as mowers, tractors, weed eaters, and lawn spreaders; even golf clubs that have been rented and are now being retired. Everything is sold "as is," and checks or cash will be accepted. Inspection hours precede the sale, which is generally held the third Saturday in April, but phone ahead for the exact date and time.
Hamilton County Park District Auction
521-PARK

The United States Customs Service's annual auction is alternately held in Cincinnati, Louisville, and Indianapolis. Items that tourists and companies buy abroad, have shipped to the United States, but don't claim are held for a year and then auctioned off. Expect to see such things as a driftwood coffee table, a carton of ski suits, Mexican pottery, handicrafts from Africa—anything in the world. Call the U.S. Customs Service local office and ask to be placed on their mailing list. You will receive announcements two weeks in advance listing the items to be auctioned, the location and time.
U.S. Customs Service Local Office
684-3528

The Internal Revenue Service also holds auctions about twice a month. The date depends on when property is seized from people who do not have the cash to pay Uncle Sam. Items do not accumulate for a period of time as they do at the Customs Service but are sold shortly after they are acquired. Disposal of the property is by either public auction or sealed bids and is advertised in local publications on the same page where legal notices appear, ten days before the sale. Merchandise can range from a single auto to the entire contents of a store. To learn about auctions in advance, ask to be placed on the bidders list, stating your name, address, and the types of items you are most interested in. You will then begin to receive notices in the mail.
Special Procedures Staff
Internal Revenue Service
P.O. Box 1579
Cincinnati, OH 45201

The General Services Administration auctions off everything from surplus government land to boats to clothing. To obtain bid information, write to:
Personal Property
Distribution Division
Federal Supply and Services
General Services Administration
Washington, DC 20406

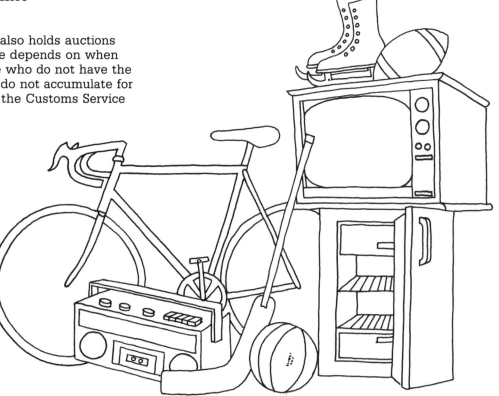

Department of Defense

The Department of Defense has more than 5 million items in its supply system, which is fifty-seven times the size of what's in the Sears catalogue. Mind boggling. And this department auctions a wide variety of its retired and out-of-date equipment—everything from clothing to airplanes. Know that you buy everything "as is/where is," which means that if you buy a truck, you must drive it from wherever it was auctioned back to your house. Also note that when Uncle Sam retires equipment, it may definitely need to be put to rest. On the other hand, you may find some incredible surprises.

Department of Defense auctions are held at military bases all over the country. If you're interested, write to the following address and ask to be placed on the national bidders list. You will be sent information about how the program works, along with forms to fill out to let authorities know what articles you're interested in and how far you're willing to travel to purchase them.

Defense Surplus Sales
P.O. Box 1370
Battle Creek, MI 49016

For information about Department of Defense auctions near Cincinnati (you may want to attend some close, on-site auctions in person), write to the following regional offices and ask to be placed on their regional bidders list. The regional offices will determine, from your address, where the auctions closest to you are.

Defense Property Disposal Region Office—Columbus
3990 E. Broad St.
Columbus, OH 43215

Defense Property Disposal Region Office—Memphis
2163 Airways Blvd.
Memphis, TN 38114

A good Department of Defense auction many Cincinnatians travel to is held once or twice a month at Fort Knox, south of Louisville, Kentucky. You can find clothing, chairs, desks, tables, typewriters, cars, pickup trucks, whatever is likely to turn up on an Army base. Inspection is held during the five days before the sale and you have five days after the sale to remove and pay for what you've bought with cash, a money order, or a cashier's check. For information about the Fort Knox auctions, phone for specific information on when they are scheduled.

Defense Reutilization and Marketing Office—Fort Knox
502-624-5755

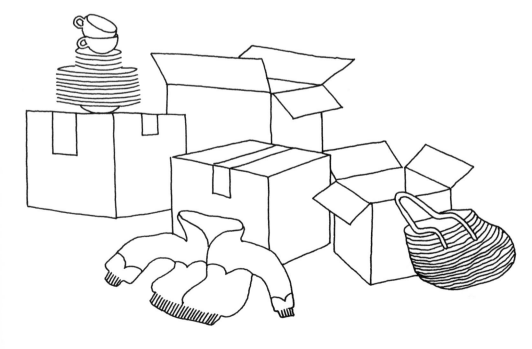

Then and Again

Spotting a fine cherry table amidst a pile of chrome dinette sets or snapping up a mint condition cashmere sweater in a stack of sorry-looking synthetics takes a good eye and perseverance—just what you need to uncover treasures in trash. But it also helps to know where to look. So, this chapter is made up of a couple of secondhand stores, a few consignment shops, some pawnshops, a sprinkle of flea markets, several suggestions for finding extravagant house sales—it's a secondhand soup made from my favorite junque recipe. Yes, I do know that the charitable thrift stores and secondhand shops that abound throughout the city—everyone has his favorite neighborhood place to prowl—are choice for treasure hunters. I haven't included them here because there are just too many. Your secrets are safe.

Used and Abused

Hospital trays, exit signs from a theater, a bench from a church, rows of lockers from a bus depot (great for stashing kids' toys in after you paint them primary colors), student desks, one-arm desk chairs, fire hose, ladders, hatchets, wooden post-office cubbies, garden tools are all haphazardly and comfortably piled together at Liquidators Sales Co., which I always think of as the best permanent garage sale in the city.

Liquidators buys merchandise from going-out-of-business businesses or from those that are remodeling or have had some internal or external disaster forcing them to get rid of equipment. New old items turn up here constantly, so it's possible to find just about anything in the many rooms of this cavernous place.

Liquidators Sales Co.
1610 Reading Rd. (Mt. Auburn)
621-7543

Star Building Materials has yards filled with used bricks at its two locations, and you may buy ten or enough to build a house. At the Walnut Hills location, you are apt to come across house innards such as radiators, doors (turn them into desk tops), windows (they make good hotbeds for gardens), and if you're lucky, a fireplace or mantel. You never know what's going to turn up at Star.

Star Building Materials
2326 Florence (Walnut Hills)
281-2799
8319 Dixie Hwy. (Florence)
525-8882

If you are sorry to see some of Cincinnati's historic buildings demolished, you will be happy to know some of their architectural artifacts have been saved and you can find them for sale at Wooden Nickel Antiques. This place is a catacomb of treasures, and if you have a good eye for making use of old pieces, you can give second life to what you dig up here.

There is a plentiful supply of wrought-iron fencing and gates. Think about the hoop and spear design as a headboard for your bed. The same goes for the tops of old mantels. Standing sentinel against the wall, they can double as a headboard. There are mantels, leaded glass, light fixtures, big Victorian cabinets and sideboards, sometimes tables. Look for bannister spindles, stacks of doors (from Victorian exterior to French interior), marble sinks, wooden window shutters, hanging grates, even chimney pots with fluted designs that once graced the roofs of old houses. The contents of the Wooden Nickel will change with your every visit.

The owners often buy the rights to gut the interior of a building slated to be demolished and are interested in hearing about any architectural contents that are for sale. So if you have these kinds of items available, give them a call.

Wooden Nickel Antiques
1408 Central Pkwy. (Over-the-Rhine)
241-2985

Tucked in the back of The General Store is a cache of Model T and Model A Ford parts that owner Tom Puehl has collected over the years. Since he bought his first Model T in high school, car buff Puehl has been fascinated with rebuilding these cars. If you are, too, this is the place to find new and used parts—everything from ignition cables to steering wheels—plus all the how-to books you'll need for help. Puehl also likes oil lamps and has an extensive line of Aladdin lamps and all their parts, plus his own blend of scentless lamp oil he promises won't smoke when burned.

You'll find a case filled with brass dresser pulls. Besides this caseful, Puehl says he has boxes of them. In fact, boxes of things are piled everywhere. Look behind the counter. Cigar boxes are stacked floor to ceiling, each containing something different. In one, I found dozens of old fountain pens including one gold and pearl beauty. There are boxes of Cincinnati postcards, eyeglasses, pocketknives, cuff links, padlocks, even railroad items such as old tickets and train schedules.

The General Store is not a true antique store. On the other hand, it is packed with vintage items. What it does have is a little bit of everything. Allow yourself some time and explore.

The General Store
818 Elm St. (downtown)
721-4445

While the Seven Hills Clothing Exchange is a haven for preppy clothes shoppers (more about this in "Wearables," page 26), it is also a fine place to pick up all sorts of furniture and home accessories. People setting up first apartments on a budget and those who have fine-tuned antennae for valuables routinely get great buys on couches, silver serving pieces, fine china (Limoges, Spode, Haviland), crystal goblets, antique chairs, crewel-embroidered couches—many refugees from stores like Closson's and Herschede's. Refrigerators to rugs (maybe an Oriental), art glass to lamps—try to beat the dealers to the goodies at this place. The professionals comb through here regularly.

Seven Hills Clothing Exchange
5466 Red Bank Rd. (Madisonville)
271-7977

Secondhand Rose (more about this store in "Dress-Ups," page 153) takes furniture and household appliances on consignment at its Finneytown location. That's where you should go to look at chairs, dinette sets, nice sets of dishes, maybe a $10 blender that is new and perfectly fine except the bride-to-be received two others like it and this one came from an out-of-town store. Secondhand Rose doesn't have large pieces of furniture, but it does have a nice selection of odds and ends you'll want to check out regularly.

Secondhand Rose
8286 Winton Rd. (Finneytown)
521-1384

Betty Orr of Germania Antiques has consignment furniture on the first floor of her shop—nice antique tables and chairs, quilts, baskets, crystal, china. But be sure to pull out the drawers on the wall. They're filled with beaded evening purses, scarves, lace collars, and jewelry. Ask Betty to take you downstairs. There's more furniture, books, old silver, lots of nice surprises.

Germania Antiques
29 E. 12th St. (Over-the-Rhine)
241-2231

If you're a '50s fan and you adore deco, you'll be glad to know about Flashback! This shop has clothes, furniture, radios, lamps, sconces, dishes, glassware, bric-a-brac, and a case filled with funky jewelry. Owners Greg Jones and George Moore are out gathering new items constantly.

Flashback!
903 Race St. (downtown)
784-0943

Then there's Outrageous! This place has all sorts of collectibles. On my sweep through the store I found purses, a Red Goose Shoe sign, a voodoo doll in a casket, furniture, glassware—a little bit of everything. You may hit real pay dirt here.

Outrageous!
100 E. Court St. (downtown)
621-7044

Pawnshopping

Pawnshops are places where people can exchange a diamond ring, a television set, or a stereo—maybe even a camera—for ready cash. But smart shoppers have been scouring pawnshops for years to find great buys on these same items. Much merchandise is never redeemed by the people who pawn it. After a specified period of time, it goes up for sale. Some items are purchased outright by pawnbrokers. Stock builds up until these shops become gold mines of treasure for people who like to dig for it.

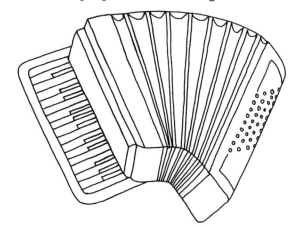

Then and Again

Most pawnshops are located in neighborhoods where people are likely to need small amounts of quick cash to tide them over until they get their next check. But all kinds of people pawn items. Pawnshop owners see spouses who have spent too much money on an indiscretion they need to cover up so they pawn a nice piece of jewelry to pad the budget. College students who want to go to Fort Lauderdale during spring vacation may hock their fancy skis or stereo so they can hit the beach. Gamblers who run into a losing streak visit pawnshops to get enough dough to tide them over until Lady Luck smiles once again. Because the kinds of people who patronize these establishments are varied, so is the merchandise. Television sets, stereos, radios, cameras, musical instruments, and jewelry are the most common items you'll see. But if you're a serious jewelry buyer, be sure to let the pawnbroker know. He'll show you some amazing pieces he keeps in the safe, where the expensive items are always stored.

Always remember, cold cash will buy you more than credit cards at pawnshops. And never accept the first price as the final word. Brush up on the fine art of friendly bargaining before you go shopping. If you're worried you might buy stolen goods at pawnshops, it's not likely. A person who pawns goods must provide complete identification, generally with a photograph. Then a ticket on the merchandise is written, a copy of which is filed with the police. The information is fed into a computer so that if any item is hot, the police will know immediately. The pawnbroker is notified and the item cannot be sold.

Now that you know the rules of the pawnshopping game, it's time to hit the streets. Here is a sampler of some of the Queen City's best stores.

Reliable Jewelry and Loan Office is owned by third-generation pawnbroker Eugene Spiegel, who always has many cameras and outstanding jewelry. There are trays of gorgeous old pocket watches priced at $100 to $3,000 as well as many men's 14-karat gold watches that were restored by Eugene's father in 1940. There are all sorts of rings, pins, brooches, and bracelets as well.

Eugene, a camera buff, specializes in optics. He has classic German cameras for professionals and collectors, telescopes, binoculars, microscopes, and lovely mother-of-pearl opera glasses. He also has violins, vintage radios, new stereos, and a couple of sewing machines.

Reliable buys 85% of its merchandise outright and because the shop is small, there are mostly small items. But what is here establishes Reliable as a gourmet pawnshop. It's a must on your list.
Reliable Jewelry and Loan Office
819 Main St. (downtown)
241-2016

Will's Pawn Shop is the granddaddy of pawnshops. Anything that could possibly pass through a person's life can turn up here and usually does. Will's has a multitude of television sets and stereos and a variety of musical instruments (flutes, piccolos, clarinets, trumpets, and violins). According to Robert Richshafer, Will's son and one of the store's managers, music students to professional rock groups come here to buy instruments. When Kiss comes to town, they always check out the shop's collectible guitars.

Jewelry is also a specialty at Will's. The stock ranges from a 14-karat gold ring in the shape of King Tut complete with ruby eyes to all sorts of gold religious medallions. There are hundreds of watches and wedding-ring sets priced from $100 to $15,000.

In addition to the classic and current cameras, Will's has golf clubs, skis—even microwave ovens. In June a lot of couples who have received duplicates of wedding gifts bring them in here. If they're unused, Will's buys them outright. So, if you're looking for a small appliance like a Cuisinart, remember to check out Will's in June—though any time is prime time in this ever-changing place.
Will's Pawn Shop
Gilbert & E. McMillan (Walnut Hills)
861-2223

Wacksman's Loan Office is not large, but it is well stocked. You'll find a case of jewelry (I spotted some antique gold cuff links studded with amethysts priced at $49 that owner Fred Wacksman says would cost $125 in a retail store), a nice supply of television sets, musical instruments including many guitars and cases, boxes of tools, and stacks of new suitcases.
Wacksman's Loan Office
1113 Vine St. (Over-the-Rhine)
241-5367

Harry Kaplan, of Central Loan, has been in the business for sixty-four years. His store is loaded with interesting goods: fishing poles, a rack of leather coats, a wall of guitars, a room filled with

television sets, stereos and radios, tools (electric and hand) plus all kinds of beautiful jewelry. Central is a superb place to investigate.
Central Loan Co.
1233 Vine St. (Over-the-Rhine)
241-2468

Barr's Pawn Shop looks like a small department store. Check out the jewelry case if you're looking for vintage pocket watches or the supply of guitars if you're interested in hard-to-find Gibsons and Fenders. Barr's has many drums and roller skates, typewriters, hunting rifles, and shotguns.

One-of-a-kind items I saw include a Mickey Mouse telephone, boxing gloves, a home computer, and a beautiful French horn the owner said is worth $1,900 that he'd sell for around $800.
Barr's Pawn Shop
1724 Vine St. (Over-the-Rhine)
721-0088

Flea Markets

Flea markets and garage sales burst upon the spring scene and you'll see signs advertising them tacked up on telephone poles, in supermarkets, and in other neighborhood stores all over the city. But besides these informal sales, these three big flea markets are regularly patronized by aficionados.

Burlington Flea Market (five miles west of Florence Mall) is held the third Sunday of every month from April to October. Antique lovers swoop through here to find oak tables, dressers, chests and trunks, chairs—wicker armchairs to cherry rockers—quilts, jewelry, sometimes stained glass.

Booths are set up in a field outside, though the event is held rain or shine. One person who wouldn't miss a flea market here told me rainy days can be a pain, but can also prove to be profitable. Though some dealers don't show up and others have plastic spread over everything, you can often get the best prices.
Burlington Flea Market
Boone County Fairgrounds (Burlington, KY)
922-5265

A friend who visited Ferguson's Antique Mall and Flea Market says the place looked to her like an Oriental bazaar. Anything you can dream of can turn up in one of the 120 booths here—vintage furniture, glassware, dishes, dolls, toys, silver, Rookwood, clothes. Markets are held Wednesdays through Sundays, year-round.
Ferguson's Antique Mall and Flea Market
3742 Kellogg Ave. (East End)
321-7341

Trader's World Flea Market (at I-75 and Rt. 63) is huge. There are hundreds of dealers at this place selling new and used merchandise, antiques and collectibles outside and inside the building. One flea market fan says this place always has some good things, but a lot of, well, stuff that you have to go through. Trader's World is open only on weekends.
Trader's World Flea Market
601 Union Rd. (Middletown, OH)
1-424-5708

House Sales

If your house is overflowing with all the great finds you've accumulated over the years, or you're moving to smaller quarters, or you have to get rid of a relative's estate, an easy solution is to call in a team of professionals to run a house sale for you. There are a number of such firms in the city.

For a percentage of the proceeds of the sale (discuss how large with the owners), they will go through everything on the premises, set prices, spruce up items so they look their best for customers, advertise the sale in local papers, bring security guards, run the entire operation, and leave your home broom-clean afterward. It's a painless way to get rid of an entire household—clothing to furniture, paintings to appliances. However, if you're in the market to buy, you can uncover real prizes at these sales. But the word is out! These events draw hundreds of people who watch avidly for classified ads in the local newspapers announcing their whereabouts. Lines of early birds form around the block to get first crack at what's inside, while bargain hunters wait until late in the day because that's when prices are dropped.

Watch for ads of the following firms if you're interested in shopping these house sales. Paring down? Call the same people to get rid of your surplus.

Sellout by Elaine
Elaine Goodstein
791-4041

Past Pleasures
Laurie Patterson
Nita Siereveld
574-8585

Helping Hands
Sis Alsfelder
271-5971
Donna Remme
271-7363

Home Work

Tools, hardware, odds and ends you need to fix things around the house—here's where to pick up some great buys.

Tools and Hardware

At Skil's Cincinnati Service Center, you will find new tools from discontinued stock, as well as tools that have failed in warranty and have been rebuilt. There are always lots of drills, chainsaws, and weedeaters, but you can usually come upon routers, planes, and belt sanders—just about any tool a handyperson might need.

Skil Corp.
1245 Tennessee Ave. (Bond Hill)
242-0244

If you are in the market for power tools, you will definitely want to check out the Black and Decker Factory Service Center. This is where reconditioned Black and Decker tools that have failed in warranty are sold at 30% off their original prices. New discontinued products can be bought here at a savings as well. Expect to find anything Black and Decker manufactures, from lawn edgers and hedge trimmers to jigsaws and drill bits. Stock varies constantly according to what's sent in from the factory.

Black and Decker Factory Service Center
2310 E. Sharon Rd. (Sharonville)
772-3111

If rummaging through a jumbled barnful of tools and hardware sounds like fun to you, you can spend happy hours and come up with a savings on assorted items at the Bargain Barn. Hammers, flue pipes, rope, paint supplies, automobile parts, fire extinguishers, plugs and extension cords, light bulbs, garbage cans, locks, pots and pans, glass and brass coffee tables, canning jars, irons—I've just scratched the surface.

Bargain Barn
9204 Reading Rd. (Reading)
733-9770

You have your favorite neighborhood hardware store. Or maybe you buy all your supplies at one of the warehouse discount supply stores sprinkled through the city. Still, you should know about Aufdemkampe. It's an old Cincinnati hardware store, one its loyal customers swear by. It stocks all sorts of home-supply sundries and employs salespeople who know how to help you make intelligent selections.

Aufdemkampe Hardware Co.
2000 Central Pkwy. (downtown)
381-3200

Electronics

The industrial division of URI Electronics sells parts, tubes, and electronic supplies to service industries—just about anything that relates to a stereo, radio, television, or computer. But URI is good about letting people off the street buy here, too, which is a real bonanza if you're adept at repairing the innards of these kinds of equipment but have a hard time finding parts. Just bring in the part number you need or the malfunctioning piece, and a URI salesperson will bring a replacement out of the warehouse.

One of the most unusual features of URI is its seemingly limitless stock of radio receiving tubes (URI was founded when radio was born). Some tubes in the warehouse are more than fifty years old. URI has parts for early and contemporary televisions, too, but no picture tubes.

URI Electronics
Summit Rd. & Reinhold Dr. (Roselawn)
761-4030

Industrial Rubber

Both Netherland Rubber Co. and Pennington Rubber Co. are industrial suppliers of rubber and safety products, and what they sell is definitely made to hold up under heavy wear. You can buy rubber matting by the yard, which you may find useful during slush months or to protect your carpet in high-traffic areas. Look at the rainwear—from car-wash aprons and slickers that construction workers wear in bad weather to lightweight plastic rainsuits. Rubber hosing and fittings for just about any hose that exists can be picked up at these places, too.

Netherland has forty different types of boots, a wall of work gloves—from heat-resistant to surgical—and foam slabs they will cut to your specifications. Both places are happy to work with basement inventors and do-it-yourselfers, so if you need a part made, bring in your specifications and they'll try to fill them.

Netherland Rubber Co.
629 Burbank (Walnut Hills)
221-4800

Pennington Rubber Co.
4676 Paddock Rd. (Bond Hill)
641-0211

Industrial Mats

Banner Mat, Inc. is an industrial matting and specialty floor-covering supplier—whatever you see on office and store entranceway floors can be found at this place. So if you need tough carpeting of any kind, stop in and take a look through Banner Mat's catalogue. You'll find all sorts of rubber-backed carpet that can be scrubbed, hosed down, or vacuumed. It is available in runners of all sizes, or it can be cut to order. Some carpet is designed for absorption, some for scraping. A sampling includes galvanized spring steel wire link mats that can surely scrape the mud off your shoes, tire link mats for the same purpose, all-weather synthetic materials of all kinds and colors, cocoa matting made from tough coconut fibers, which absorb moisture and perform a brushing action.

Some carpets are ready to go, if the size you want is in stock; others, cut to specifications, may take a day or two. Ask if there are discontinued items available in the warehouse. If there are, you'll get great buys if you're not too picky about colors and exact dimensions.

Banner Mat, Inc.
538 Reading Rd. (downtown)
721-4096

Building Supplies

Outdoor construction materials have endless indoor decorating possibilities if you look at them with an imaginative eye. And you will find yards full of round and square cement pipes of all sizes and shapes, plus zillions of other cement products at building material suppliers throughout the city.

Home Work

For instance, ask for land tile, farm tile, or even field tile and what you'll wind up with is a red clay pipe either three or four inches in diameter and twelve inches long. Buy them in quantity (the four-inch diameter is better), lay them in rows, and you've built yourself a wine rack. Stack the tiles between shelves or build them from the floor up. Sewer pipe has a bell on one end and comes in six-inch or four-inch diameters. It is two feet long and looks terrific stood on end as a plant pedestal. Clay flue liners could be spectacular table bases topped with glass.

Also check out building-material suppliers for sand you can buy by the garbage can-full—just bring your own empty container. You can fill a sandbox for a lot less money than you would with the already bagged kind.

Though there are many building material companies in Cincinnati, here are a few names to get you started.

John Mueller Co.
400 E. Wyoming Ave. (Lockland)
821-0071

Nurre Building Materials Co.
4686 Paddock Rd. (Bond Hill)
242-3225

Western Hills Builders Supply
2309 Ferguson Rd. (Westwood)
451-1400

Newtown Supply and Lumber
3543 Round Bottom Rd. (Newtown)
561-7465

Marble

Mees Distributors imports truckloads of Italian marble each month in as many colors as Howard Johnson has ice cream flavors. Besides making fireplace hearths, vanity tops, and window sills, Mees can have anything made from marble, from a tabletop to a bust of yourself. Photos or drawings are sent to the artists in Italy, who complete the work there and then ship it here.

For candy-making and cheese-serving marble, Mees sells leftover cutoffs of mostly white with a gray vein. Some pieces I saw stacked in the back room were fourteen by twenty-three inches, twenty-two by twenty-four inches (you may have them cut to the size you wish) and were priced according to their thickness per square foot. Look for boxes (and you must buy by the box) of windowsill cutoffs, which come in random sizes six to eight inches wide and of varying lengths. Thinking of laying a marble entrance hall? Here's where to gather the materials.

Mees also sells ceramic tiles. Hand-painted ones from a variety of European countries are abundant. I saw delicate Italian flower bouquets and flower-patterned tiles from Portugal. They are gorgeous. For down-to-business tiles to cover walls and floors, Mees has discontinued styles and colors at 30% to 40% off.

Mees Distributors
1541 West Fork Rd. (Northside)
541-2311

Ohio Tile and Marble has a pile of windowsill cutoffs you are welcome to pick through. Most pieces are six inches wide and of varying lengths, and you can buy whatever quantity you need. Two similar pieces could quickly qualify for fine marble bookends, or you can load up enough to do the floor of a room. For larger, working-surface pieces, look around for leftover slab cutoffs, which will be cut to the size you wish.

You'll find ceramic tiles here, too, and discontinued patterns at half price. There may be a few pieces to use as wall accents or enough of one kind for a whole room.

Ohio Tile and Marble
Spring Grove & Elmore (Northside)
541-4211

Home-Improvement Products

Basco, manufacturer of aluminum and fabricated plastic products, insulating glass, and mirrors, generally has a yearly warehouse sale in May or June that warms the hearts of do-it-yourselfers. The items Basco makes are sold at home improvement centers throughout the country so what you'll find at the warehouse sale are discontinued patterns of products such as vinyl-covered shelving, storage racks (the kind you hang on the back of kitchen cupboard doors to hold canned goods), shower doors, tub enclosures, framed mirrors, cutoffs of glass, plastic, and mirrors in all sizes and lengths.

Much of the plastic is in decorative colors and can be used for divider panels. Generally it's available in four by eight foot sheets. But a variety of scraps are piled up in the warehouse for the sale and if you have a creative eye, you'll be able to put them to good use. Prices on fabricated products are about half of what you'd pay at a retail store; much else is sold at cost. Phone Basco in the spring to see if and when the sale is scheduled.

Basco
11440 Grooms Rd. (Blue Ash)
489-1900

Woodworking Equipment

For people who like to putter with expensive woodworking equipment but don't want to buy it themselves, The Wood Gym is the answer. This place has every tool you'd need to make serious furniture, shelves, cabinets, or simple toys and puzzles.

Professionals pay a monthly fee to use the facilities during the day. Many are cabinetmakers who don't want to sink a lot of money into setting up their own shop, so they work out of The Wood Gym for a whole lot less. In the evening, hobbyists can use the facilities for a monthly fee. If you're a novice do-it-yourselfer, you can get help from an instructor who is always on the floor (although he does not stand over you for step-by-step instructions). Even if you are more advanced, you can turn to a professional for advice. Everyone is trained to use the machinery, and you are shown how to adapt individual pieces of equipment to your particular project.

The Wood Gym has a store on the premises where you can find displays of wood and laminates to order for your projects, as well as hardware, glues, abrasives—everything you need to work with.

The Wood Gym
10379 Julian (Woodlawn)
772-4441

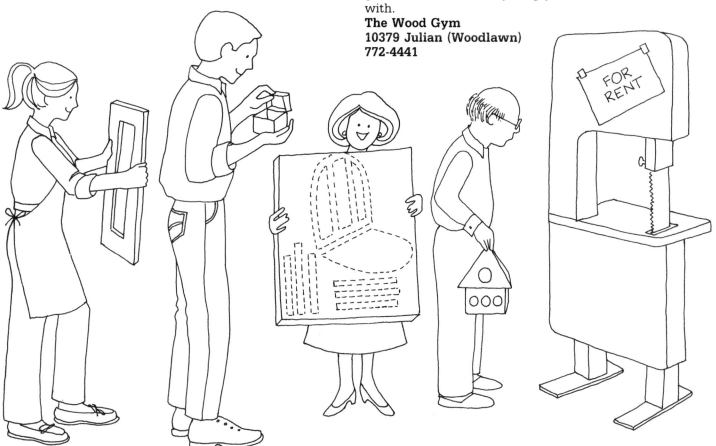

Films

You love to go to the movies, but your kind of entertainment means foreign flicks, vintage classics, low-budget shoots starring little-known actors who later turn out to sweep all the awards. Sounds like you have good taste. But where do you find these kinds of films in Cincinnati?

A good place to begin is The Movies Repertory Cinema. This downtown movie house plays five or six different films a day (from approximately noon to midnight)—anything from *A Room With a View* and *Children of a Lesser God* to *My Beautiful Laundrette* and *Kiss of the Spider Woman.* You'll see films from many foreign countries, American classics, even animated movies. Some films play a few days in a row at different starting times; others pop on and off the schedule over a month or two. If Movies fans respond glowingly to a film—and lines at the box office reflect their ardor—it will be brought back for reruns.

This is a very civilized theater. You can buy Perrier and Graeter's ice-cream-and-cookie sandwiches in addition to more traditional movie-theater fare. And the ticket price is $3—a bargain, considering what you'd have to pay around town to see a current chainsaw massacre.

Get on The Movies mailing list by signing up in the lobby or phoning the theater. You'll receive a two-month schedule complete with film synopses, so you can mark your calendar and not miss favorites. Or watch the entertainment sections of the newspapers for daily announcements.

The Movies Repertory Cinema
719 Race St. (downtown)
381-FILM

The Mt. Lookout Theatre also runs fine films and classics—both American and foreign. You'll find its schedule among the movie listings in the daily newspaper.

Mt. Lookout Theatre
3187 Linwood Ave. (Mt. Lookout)
321-3598

Watch what plays at The Carousel Cinemas. As popular theaters go, The Carousel usually books the more sophisticated mainstream movies, such as Woody Allen's and, on occasion, foreign films like *The Official Story* and *Shoah.* Schedules are in the daily newspapers.

The Carousel Cinemas 1 & 2
8000 Reading Rd. (Roselawn)
761-2270

The Emery Theatre, whose fate is uncertain at this writing (it may be sold and not used as a theater), houses a Wurlitzer organ salvaged from the Albee Theater and owned by the American Theatre Organ Society, prime renter of the Emery. (Spokespeople for the society told me the organ may move to another theater if the Emery meets its demise.) The organ is played as accompaniment when silent films are shown, and there are organ recitals before and after performances and during intermission of other vintage American films. You'll see American movies from the '30s to the '60s—like *The George White Scandals, The Barclays of Broadway* (which featured Fred Astaire), lots of Laurel and Hardy pictures. Watch for newspaper advertisements of the Emery's schedule, or pick up a flyer at the theater and fill out the form that will get you on their mailing list.

Emery Theatre
1112 Walnut St. (downtown)
721-2741

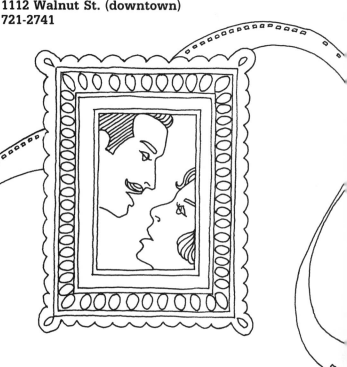

Consider joining the Cincinnati Film Society ($10 will cover it) to see many independently made films—foreign ones, documentaries, and American classics, not products of big studios. Membership entitles you to reduced admission price, a bimonthly newsletter that previews the films, entrance to two members-only films per year, and invitations to receptions for visiting filmmakers whose projects are being shown. Most CFS movies are also open to nonmembers. Find out what's playing by watching the newspapers (films are shown at the theater in the Natural History Museum). Movies are generally scheduled three weekends a month, but hopes are to have them every weekend.

Cincinnati Film Society
P.O. Box 14182
Cincinnati, OH 45214
381-5157

Want to know where an old-time neighborhood movie theater is thriving? Sayler Park. It's home to the Parkland Theater, whose fame is reaching a lot farther than the *immediate* neighborhood. PG movies only are shown—movies like *The Sound of Music, Shane, The Wizard of Oz, The Birds*—on Friday and Saturday nights at 7:15 and at 2:00 on Sunday afternoons. Along with the main feature, there's always a cartoon and a Three Stooges or Laurel and Hardy short—all for the price of $2 for evening tickets, $1 for matinees. And, oh yes, a small popcorn goes for 20¢ here, the large for 40¢, and it's made before your very eyes. For those with a sweet tooth, even candy is sold for 40¢.

Owner Denis Clark is a true movie fan, and you'll find out more about him and his other business venture by reading the next listing. If you want to know what's playing at the Parkland—and movies change weekly—you'll have to call him at his other store or drop by the theater and take your chances. The Parkland has no phone and does not advertise. It also has no air conditioning, which is why it's closed in June, July, and August.

Parkland Theater
6548 Parkland Ave. (Sayler Park)

If you're a movie buff, you'll love Denis Clark's second venture, aptly named Movie Madness. For sale are more than 6,000 movie posters—contemporary, vintage, American, and foreign. There are even foreign posters of American films. Look for lobby cards, press kits, even movie scripts. When a film is made, about 1,500 copies of the script are produced for the entire crew. These scripts are coveted by collectors, so if you would like to memorize the dialogue from *Star Wars* or *The Rocky Horror Picture Show*, ask for them here. Also ask for videotapes of operas performed anywhere in the world. But if it pertains to movies, Movie Madness has it or can get it for you. They have a mail-order business that covers the international market.

Movie Madness
6595 Gracely (Sayler Park)
941-5429

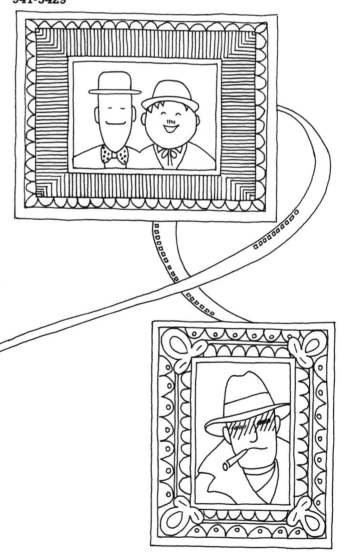

Reading Matter

You can buy books and magazines at many fine stores in Cincinnati—and thankfully, the number is steadily growing. Since supermarkets have made book departments as standard as salad bars, you can put a best-seller in your shopping cart along with your celery. Stores that are part of national book chains are downtown and in every suburban mall. Then there are the smaller neighborhood bookstores, where a friendly owner will take the time to tell you what's good to bring along on vacation, save your favorite author's newest release—even phone you to tell you it's come in. Since those stores are right under your nose, I've devoted this chapter to presenting harder-to-find places book lovers love finding out about—musty secondhand stores you can spend hours browsing through, the best annual book sales, where to find rare books and out-of-town newspapers, even paperback book and record exchanges.

Newspapers

If your idea of a perfect Sunday means curling up with a stack of newspapers, you'll be happy to know you can buy all sorts of out-of-town editions at two local stores that carry forty to fifty different newspapers. While other newsstands and bookstores around town carry *some* out-of-towners, these two carry the most Sunday editions and dailies.

Fountain News
426 Walnut St. (downtown)
421-4049

Duttenhofer's Book Treasures
214 W. McMillan (Clifton)
381-1340

You like service—daily home delivery of your favorite out-of-town newspaper. Here is what's available.

To receive the daily *New York Times* as well as the fat Sunday edition, or only the Sunday paper, phone 1-800-631-2500. Delivery is dependable—your newspaper arrives in good shape and well before breakfast, unless you arise before the birds.

The *Washington Post* can be delivered daily, only it's the previous day's edition. Phone the Times Distribution Co., Inc., at 861-9191 to arrange this service. This is the same company that delivers the daily *New York Times*.

To receive the *Wall Street Journal*, phone 891-7600.

For *USA Today*, call 821-8770.

Book Sales

In the spring, you'll see barrels appear in the downtown public library and all the branches so that patrons can fill them with books, records, and prestige magazines like *National Geographic*. Then all of these donations are sorted, boxed, and taken to Fountain Square for one of the best annual book sales in the city, sponsored by the Friends of the Public Library. It always takes place during the first week in June and runs Monday through Friday.

More than 10,000 new and used books are arranged on tables by category and prices range from 10¢ for paperbacks to $2 and $3 for first editions. On the last day of the sale, you can fill a bag with your choice of books for a dollar or two—and this day is everybody's favorite. Many people who donate books to the sale come downtown to stock up all over again. Phone for more sale information or to request that volunteers pick up your books if you have a large number to donate.
Friends of the Public Library
369-6972

Volunteers work on the annual Brandeis University Book Sale all year round to make it the successful event it always is. Held on a Thursday through Sunday in early fall at the Business Men's Club in Montgomery at 7777 Sycamore St., you can pick up great buys on fine books in twenty-seven categories—fiction to travel. There are collectibles, many of which are pre-1900, a good collection of sheet music and records, lots of paperbacks. All books are individually priced until the last day of the sale, which is bag day. Fill a shopping bag for one low price.

All proceeds from the sale benefit the Brandeis University Library in Waltham, Massachusetts, so if you want to donate books, place them in the many barrels you'll see in businesses around town or call to have yours picked up. Also phone for the exact dates of the sale and to see if there is a change in location.

Brandeis University Book Sale
489-8746

The University of Cincinnati Bookstore has two sales a year, generally during the second or third week in May and October. The May sale is held under a tent on the quadrangle right outside the bookstore; the October sale is in Tangeman Center. Both yield great Bearcat bargains, which include old inventory from the bookstore as well as special buys. Expect to find tables of books categorized by subject, plus books you can buy by the pound. There are records, video and cassette tapes, art supplies, plants in May, U.C.-imprinted clothing such as T-shirts and sweatshirts, plus other wearables like bathing suits and jogging suits, all sorts of gifty items and one-of-a-kinds. Phone the bookstore to find out the exact sale dates.

U.C. Bookstore
475-2844

What better home for books than with people who love them? And some of the most long-lasting love affairs between book owners and their collections take place between University of Cincinnati professors and the volumes they gather during their teaching careers. But when a professor retires, leaves the university, or dies, a proper home for his collection is sought. One of the most popular repositories is the University of Cincinnati library. However, this generosity can create problems for the library if the donated books are duplicates of those already on library shelves. What happens then? The U.C. Library has a sale of superfluous books on the first Wednesday of every month from October to June. The money generated from the sale is then used to purchase needed books for the library's collection.

Anything is liable to turn up at the sales in the lobby of the central library on the corner of St. Clair and Woodside, across from Burnet Woods—hardbacks, paperbacks, records, magazines, even prints suitable for framing, fiction, scholarly works, books written in all languages, dictionaries, encyclopedias, mysteries, cookbooks, as well as first editions in mint condition complete with dust jackets. Students find this a good place to pick up texts. Sale prices are a bargain and can range from 25¢ to $2.

U.C. Library Book Sale
475-2407

Reading Matter

Main Auction Galleries has a once-a-year book auction on the first Sunday in December that is always quite an event—the variety of books up for bids is extensive, and the quality is prime. Expect to find first editions complete with dust jackets, leatherbound sets, books on virtually every subject imaginable, as well as postcards, paper memorabilia, and generally some wonderful old Valentines.

Exhibition days, which precede the sale, are when you can go through the books and put aside those you want to bid on. They will be tied together and the bundle numbered. There is a five- to eight-book minimum on those you can put together in a package of this sort, but you can put together as many packages as you wish. All other books will be sold by the bookcase (which contains five shelves) or by the individual shelf.

There is something for everyone at this book auction. The trick is to come early so you can dig out the best ones. And be sure to get on the mailing list for this event so you will always know when the book auction is scheduled.

Main Auction Galleries
137 4th St. (downtown)
621-1280

Rare and Used Books

Ohio Book Store and Acres of Books, which is almost across the street from it, are two Cincinnati standbys for used books—some rare, some first editions. Both stores have multiple floors of books where you can browse the day away without being bothered, and neither has changed much over the years I've been stopping by. Ohio has more *National Geographics* than anyone else in town, from 1913 to the present, and *Life* magazines from 1936 to 1980. There is a table on the first floor full of out-of-print Cincinnati books that Ohio has reprinted and given a second life. Both stores buy books, but you must discuss exactly what is or is not wanted with the owners. Both will buy whole collections and act as appraisers.

Ohio Book Store
726 Main St. (downtown)
621-5142

Acres of Books
633 Main St. (downtown)
721-4214

Robert Richshafer has a rare collection of books and related items, and for years, his largest customers have been libraries and museums. Recently, he's become more accessible to smaller clients so now you can see his treasures—by appointment only.

Robert's largest selection is in Americana and a good part of that deals with the history of the Midwest. He also has a wonderful photo collection, which includes many nineteenth-century Cincinnati scenes, cookbooks from the 1600s, colonial almanacs, letters and signed manuscripts of authors and other celebrities, maps, wood and steel engravings, political prints from the 1830s and other prints of historical significance. Robert has the original team documents from the Cincinnati Reds, even letters of William Henry Harrison. He will do a book search for you if he doesn't have what you want, but that is unlikely given the depth and breadth of his material.

Robert Richshafer Americana
421-BOOK

Duttenhofer's Book Treasures has a good selection of rare and used books in their store along with one of the most interesting selections of current magazines in Cincinnati.

Duttenhofer's Book Treasures
214 W. McMillan (Clifton)
381-1340

Significant Books has a nice selection of photography, European history, math and science books, and four bookcases of fiction and nonfiction. Prices range from a few dollars to sizeable sums for rare texts. They'll do a book search if you're after something especially hard to find.

Significant Books
3053 Madison Rd. (Oakley)
321-7567

In addition to buying and selling fine books, Barbara Agranoff has an amazing supply of what she calls "ephemera"—railroad timetables, steamship menus, advertising trade cards—all sorts of vintage papers that were often thrown away. Leafing through her collection, I saw sheet music from the Ziegfeld Follies, pinup calendars from the '20s through the '40s, old calling cards, elementary school awards of merit, even an ad for a concert in Burnet Woods that had to be rescheduled because of the assassination of President McKinley. There are drawers filled with postcards from the early 1900s through 1920s, many of which pertain to Cincinnati. Prices on these range from $1 to $10, depending on their rarity.

Barbara is interested in buying ephemera, too, so the next time you swear you're going to get rid of all those papers and scrapbooks that have been taking up space in the basement or the attic, call her first. You may have saleable treasures. Barbara is available by appointment only—for buying and selling.

Barbara Agranoff Books & Old Postcards
281-5095

If you're a paperback trader, try your luck at one of The Book Rack stores. Terms are: you get one paperback for two of yours if they have the same cover price. Or you can get a credit for your books, and the ones you choose will be deducted from your account. You can buy used paperbacks at half their cover price, new books for 20% off retail, and you can rent hardback best-sellers for $2 a week. This is a good deal because public library waiting lists for hot new releases can be long. But be careful how you treat these rentals. If you read while you eat and you have an accident, the book will be yours. Look in the phone directory for the Book Rack store nearest you. There are half a dozen in the city.

Restoration

If the pages of your prized family Bible are crumbling, or a first edition you've purchased needs to be completely rebound to look like its original condition, there are several firms in Cincinnati that do this kind of meticulous work. They can restore disintegrating newspaper pages, maps, etchings, engravings, and documents. They can bind your own collection of poems, or your college master's thesis. Discuss the particular job you need done with the owners of the three following places to see which can best fill your needs.

Archival Conservation Center
8225 Daly Rd. (Finneytown)
521-9858

Cincinnati Binding
2838 Spring Grove Ave. (Camp Washington)
542-8590

Ohio Book Store
726 Main St. (downtown)
621-5142

Comic Books

Enough of this serious book stuff. You love comics. Well, check out Book World's three stores because they have a huge selection of used comics that sell for 25¢ on up to $1,000! They have comics from the 1940s including early Supermans and Planet comics, and many from the 1950s and 1960s. The stores will buy comic books, too, so you might want to bring in yours to see what they're worth. Book World also sells new comic books. Call the hotline for all three stores—541-0083—and you will hear a recorded message telling you all the new titles that have just arrived—there are tons of them.

Book World
7130 Turfway Rd. (Florence)
371-9562
3805 North Bend Rd. (Cheviot)
662-0440
5551 Colerain Ave (Mt. Airy)
541-8002

Reading Matter

The Phantasy Emporium has a large selection of new and used science fiction books, comics that date back to the '50s (Dick Tracy to *Mad Magazine*), and lots of underground ones.
Phantasy Emporium
117 Calhoun St. (Clifton)
281-0606

Record Exchange

So your taste in music has made a radical change from Judas Priest to Pavarotti? You want to get rid of a shelf filled with albums by heavy-metal groups and buy some classical ones? Where can you unload the oldies? Where can you stock up on some gently used records at great prices? Record exchanges. Some in the city will buy, sell, and trade for great deals.

Most store owners are particular about the kinds of records they buy and their condition. All check for warpage, scratches, and chips. Some care more about the jacket condition than others. All are subjective about the categories they will purchase, and that changes constantly according to their current stock. If a store owner has three albums just like the one you're trying to sell, no matter if yours is in terrific shape, you may have to take it someplace else. But what do you have to lose? Here is a rundown of some places to try your luck.

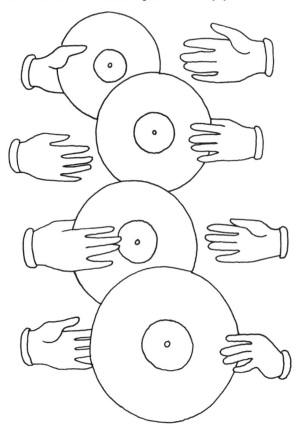

Mole's was the first record exchange in the city, and the store now has about 12,000 albums in stock. Prices range from 50¢ to $4.50 if you're interested in buying. If you're selling, the exchange will pay you half of what clerks feel they can get for your album. For trades, you get two-thirds of the album's selling price. Stock includes reggae, blues, classical, oldies, heavy metal, gospel, movie soundtracks, poetry, and a large amount of rock-and-roll. This store prides itself on its wide selection of jazz albums. It will buy records in all of these categories, but not what managers consider "elevator music." Compact discs and cassettes are also available in the store.

This place is a great information exchange; notices and posters announce what bands are playing where. Owner Jess Hirbe says, "We feel the conversation that goes on in our store is as important as the records we sell."
Mole's Record Exchange
2615 Vine St. (Corryville)
861-6291

Ozarka Record Exchange pays half of what it can sell an album for, and most albums sell for $2.50 to $4; a few are 50¢ or $1. Rock-and-roll is the bread and butter here, but this store also has jazz, classical, opera, bluegrass, blues, folk albums and compact discs. Clerks are most interested in buying rock-and-roll and classical, least interested in "easy listening."
Ozarka Record Exchange
115 Calhoun St. (Mt. Auburn)
751-0345

Everybody's Records is especially interested in buying rock, jazz, and rhythm-and-blues from the '50s and '60s. The store does not want easy-listening (which managers define as Lawrence Welk types) or disco. Frank Sinatra and Barbra Streisand are fine. There are about 10,000 albums here, ranging from reggae, rock-and-roll to maybe the largest blues collection in town. There are collector's items such as interviews with musicians, as well as new wave, compact discs, and cassettes. Everybody's pays half of what it can sell an album for, and will give you a little more for your money on a trade.
Everybody's Records
6106 Montgomery Rd. (Pleasant Ridge)
531-4500

Libraries

Cincinnati has a comprehensive public library system, as well as many specialized libraries. The following resources are right at your fingertips.

The Public Library of Cincinnati and Hamilton County offers 4 million books to avid readers through its main library downtown and its satellite branches. Besides a world-class collection of books, the library has outstanding recordings—from children's stories to foreign languages. You can rent movies—Shakespeare, silent classics, instructional films that show how to wire your house or become a creative writer. The library subscribes to many daily U.S. newspapers, as well as notable foreign ones, and has more than 1,000 phone books, plus that many college and university catalogues.

Activities sponsored by the library include storytelling hours for children and lectures on a variety of subjects. Join the Friends of the Public Library for $10 to receive *Guideposts*, which contains news about everything that's going on and a handy calendar of events.

The information service of the public library does yeoman duty. I have heard staff who answer the phone at 369-6901 give patient, intelligent, complete responses to amazing questions.

**Public Library of Cincinnati and Hamilton
County—Main Branch
800 Vine St. (downtown)
369-6000**

You can join the Young Men's Mercantile Library, the third oldest library in the United States, for $35 per year per family. This entitles you to check out books from the library's general collection, which contains the latest fiction and nonfiction, or peruse on the premises the 100 or more periodicals in residence, as well as the fine assembly of first editions.

This library has the feel of an English club and is a comfortable respite when you're downtown. However, staff will send members books by mail along with a return envelope, one of the most helpful services I've heard of these busy days.

**The Young Men's Mercantile Library
414 Walnut St. (downtown)
621-0717**

The Cincinnati Art Museum Library is open to anyone who pays the museum entrance fee, but only art museum members, staff, and Art Academy students and faculty may check out books. Others may use them on the premises. You will find books and bound periodicals to back up the museum's collection on subjects including art history, sculpture, painting, decorative arts, drawings, prints, and photography.

If you're an art collector, you will be interested in the museum's compilation of art auction catalogues and sale-price lists from major auction houses, as well as biographies of artists and an extensive collection of clippings from newspapers about artists, plus their exhibition announcements. If you like to know about what is happening at other art museums throughout the world, you'll find bulletins, catalogues, and selected publications from many that will keep you up to date.

**The Cincinnati Art Museum Library
Eden Park
721-5204**

The Cincinnati Historical Society Library yields in-depth material on the history of Greater Cincinnati. Photographs, maps, manuscripts, pamphlets, books, and newspapers from 1788 to the present may be studied on the premises by Cincinnati history buffs.

**Cincinnati Historical Society Library
Eden Park
241-4622**

Libraries

The Lloyd Library is one of Cincinnati's best-kept secrets, though it is certainly no secret to students of botany and pharmacy. One of the few libraries in the nation devoted to those subjects, it houses magazines, journals, periodicals, scientific and trade publications, and an admirable collection of modern and historical books in eighty different languages. One of the oldest dates from 1493. This library is the place to study exquisite hand-painted floral illustrations in sixteenth- and seventeenth-century volumes. More than 100 years old, Lloyd Library is open to the public, but books do not circulate.
Lloyd Library
917 Plum St. (downtown)
721-3707

The Civic Garden Center of Greater Cincinnati has the largest horticultural collection in Southern Ohio, Indiana, and Kentucky. If you're searching for information on soil conditions peculiar to our growing area, how to landscape with shrubs, or grow herbs, flowers, or vegetables in Cincinnati, this place surely has how-to books on the subject. Members of the Garden Center may circulate books; nonmembers may use books on the premises.
Civic Garden Center of Greater Cincinnati
2715 Reading Rd. (near downtown)
221-0981

The Frank Foster Memorial Library collection focuses on Appalachian history, geography, social problems, folklore, and famous people. The library's large selection of videotapes includes Appalachian history, the urban Appalachian experience, culture, music, crafts, religion, folk tales, community organizations. Following receipt of a library card, you may check out materials.
Frank Foster Memorial Library
Urban Appalachian Council Bldg.
2115 W. 8th St. (Lower Price Hill)
251-0202

City Hall Libraries
The Municipal Reference Library houses books and magazines dealing with the complex subject of how to run a city. This is where public officials find the most current material on police work, fire prevention, city planning, public works, public utilities, and mass transit. Though books may not circulate, the library should be open to anyone who wants information on how cities solve problems.
Municipal Reference Library
City Hall, Rm. 224
901 Plum St. (downtown)
352-3309

The Office of Planning and Management Support Library houses documents regarding the planning and development of neighborhoods within the city limits. You can see what has been done in the past, what is planned for the future. You can follow changes in building structures from when they were constructed, when they were remodeled, when they were demolished.
Office of Planning and Management Support Library
City Hall, Rm. 141
901 Plum St. (downtown)
352-3441

College and University Libraries

The Walter C. Langsam Library, the main library at the University of Cincinnati—Clifton Campus on St. Clair Street, has a good collection on humanities and social studies. However, there are eleven separate libraries in the U.C. system containing outstanding books on more specialized subjects, such as music-related tomes at the College Conservatory of Music Library, the rare-book archives housed in the Blegen Library located next to the Law School, the world-renown classics and modern Greek collection. Phone the reference number to ask about these libraries, their locations and hours. The information number recording states main library hours, which vary according to the university's calendar.

Walter C. Langsam Library
Information:
475-2535
Reference:
475-2212

The Klau Library of the Hebrew Union College has current and historical collections of Judaica and Hebraica—about 300,000 volumes, some of which may be circulated. This library has a wealth of material on how to teach Hebrew, many juvenile books, rare and ancient manuscripts, much material on the Holocaust and Christian-Jewish relations. The Bamberger collection spans the period from the Renaissance to the end of the nineteenth century, and concentrates on significant thinkers such as Spinoza.

Also on the campus is the American Jewish Archives, a primary source for genealogical material from the Western Hemisphere. Seven million pages, much of which date back to the sixteenth and seventeenth centuries—the beginning of Jewish life in this country—are open for study on the premises to those interested in tracing Jewish family origins.

The Klau Library at the Hebrew Union College
3101 Clifton Ave. (Clifton)
221-1881

Besides its general collection, the Steely Library of Northern Kentucky University has books, manuscripts, documents, and memorabilia dealing with Kentucky history.

Steely Library of Northern Kentucky University
Louie B. Nunn Dr. (Highland Heights)
Information:
572-6312
Reference:
572-5456

The strength of the Xavier University Library collection is in Roman Catholic theology, but it has a good collection of European philosophy and the classics. Serious researchers may be interested in viewing the rare collection of early Bibles and materials on the history of the Jesuit order.

Xavier University Library
3800 Victory Pkwy. (Evanston)
745-3881

The Learning Resource Center of Cincinnati Technical College is open to people who want to use books on the premises. The collection includes texts on engineering technology, business and office management, computers, hotel and restaurant management, and cookbooks—from gourmet to those dealing with all sorts of special dietary and nutritional needs.

Learning Resource Center of the Cincinnati Technical College
3520 Central Pkwy. (Clifton)
569-1606

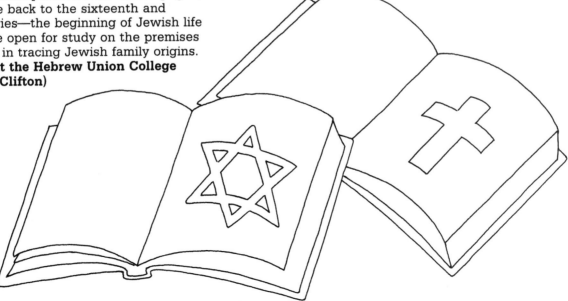

The Queen City's Crown Jewels

The museums, the Zoo, the Nature Center, the Historical Society—all the places mentioned in this chapter make up a pretty diverse group. But they fit together perfectly in the integral role they play in the community. For without institutions that preserve art or animals or the natural environment or history, a community is flat, lifeless, without cultural backbone. The Queen City is lucky to have such sparkling jewels in her crown. They are a beautiful mélange of places where people can visit and feel better for what they see and come away enriched by the experience.

Becoming a member of any of these institutions is that much more of a bonus. For a minimal yearly fee, membership entitles you to openings, lectures, movies, special tours, educational programs—you will be able to participate in any number of events that interest you. And you will always know about them well in advance through newsletters and bulletins you will receive.

There are more than a hundred galleries in the Cincinnati Art Museum which review the visual arts of almost every major civilization of the world over the past 5,000 years through painting, prints, sculpture, drawings, musical instruments, costumes, period rooms, decorative arts, and photographs. To complement the permanent collections, the museum offers a wide variety of temporary exhibitions throughout the year.

Public and special group tours are offered as well as educational programs for adults and children. You must call the museum to find out about its myriad activities. And, if you want food for the body as well as the soul, have lunch at the Terrace Court Restaurant. During the summer, you can dine outside in the Sculpture Garden—just phone for reservations in advance.

Cincinnati Art Museum
Eden Park
721-5204

The Contemporary Arts Center presents continually changing exhibits (eight to fourteen a year) to highlight all aspects of contemporary art: drawings, paintings, sculpture, photographs, architecture, mixed media, and video installations. There are free guided tours, but membership in the CAC entitles you to participate in exciting out-of-town trips that take an inside look at museums, private art collections, and architecture that may not be open to the general public.

Contemporary Arts Center
115 E. 5th St. (downtown)
721-0390

The Taft Museum has been preserved as an outstanding example of Federal architecture, and houses an art collection including paintings by Gainsborough, Goya, and John Singer Sargent, which blend perfectly with the Duncan Phyfe furniture, Regency and Empire fabrics and hangings, Chinese porcelains, and French painted enamels. As a complement to the permanent collection, there are changing exhibitions of varied artistic and historic themes. Guided tours are available as well as a speaker's bureau. There are often lectures. The Taft Museum Garden, a Franco-Dutch style urban oasis, welcomes noontime picnics. What better place to enjoy the downtown sun?

The Taft Museum
316 Pike St. (downtown)
241-0343

The Cincinnati Fire Museum, located in an historic firehouse, exhibits early fire-fighting equipment including hand-drawn pumps, leather buckets, old tools, and firefighter's uniforms. Kids can slide down a fireman's pole, learn about fire safety rules in the home, see a film on how the fire department grew with the city. This is a wonderful place to take children.

Cincinnati Fire Museum
315 W. Court St. (downtown)
621-5553

The Cincinnati Historical Society houses a fine reference library of historical materials on Cincinnati and plans to have a living history museum when they move to Union Terminal. This will include a replica of an early Cincinnati machine-tool shop with actors costumed as tool workers to interact with visitors and answer questions. An authentic reproduction of the Cincinnati Public Landing will contain a life-size steamboat that museum visitors can board. Again an actor/captain in uniform will talk about life on the river. This museum/library will show all aspects of life in Cincinnati: the arts, music, sports, and industry. Sounds exciting!

Cincinnati Historical Society
Eden Park
241-4622

When you walk into the Natural History Museum and find yourself face to face with a dinosaur, you're hooked. There are so many high-quality natural-science exhibits here! Other favorites include a simulated cavern with a dark, dripping lifelike interior and their wondrous planetarium. The museum offers a multitude of programs for adults and children from introductions to fossils, birds, and venomous snakes to anything about the stars. The Edge of Appalachia Preserves, 5,000 acres in Adams County, offers on-site sessions (often week-long) so people can learn about the natural sciences firsthand.

Museum of Natural History
1720 Gilbert Ave. (near downtown)
621-3889

The Cincinnati Nature Center, located on 755 acres of field and forest, cut by streams and dotted with ponds, is a nonprofit institution specializing in environmental education for adults and children. The Long Branch Farm, a division of the Nature Center, is an educational farm with programs concentrating on modern agriculture and beef production, sources of food and fiber and what is required to produce them, the relationships of man, animals, and the land. Both divisions offer a multitude of programs and classes for school groups, but adults may participate in workshops and sessions as well. If you simply want to walk the fourteen miles of trails peacefully alone, or if you want to learn about natural science—anything from herpetology to wildflowers—sign up for any of the programs the Nature Center sponsors.

The Cincinnati Nature Center
4949 Tealtown Rd. (Milford)
831-1711

The Cincinnati Zoo, one of the best in the nation, offers visitors a chance to view rare and endangered animals as well as unique exhibits such as Insect World, the Children's Zoo, and Big Cat Canyon—home of the white Bengal tigers. It also offers a wide variety of programs such as movies, lectures, and educational opportunities for children and teenagers. Guided tours of the grounds, which are a horticultural masterpiece as well as home to the animals, are available.

Cincinnati Zoo
3400 Vine St. (Avondale)
281-4701

The Krohn Conservatory has spectacular plantings, including an ever-changing array of orchids, citrus trees, a tropical palm house, and a rain forest. A walk behind the waterfall delights children of all ages. There are six special shows a year that draw huge crowds, especially the Christmas show, featuring a tree bedecked with handmade natural ornaments, and the Easter show, overflowing with lilies. Arrange guided tours with the Park Board volunteers who happily use the "smell-this, touch-the-bark-of-that" technique to get their points across.

Krohn Conservatory
Eden Park
352-4086

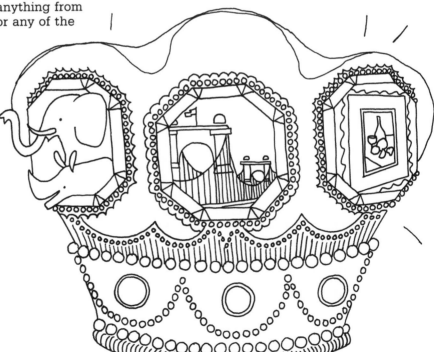

The Queen City's Crown Jewels

The Hebrew Union College's Gallery of Art and Artifacts exhibit suggests you are entering an archaeological site. As a visitor, you "walk through the past," learning the history of the Jews and the ancient cultures of the Near East by viewing pottery, weapons, tools, coins, and jewelry that tell you about the people who fashioned and used them. Besides this permanent exhibit, there are always rotating displays and programs. Call the gallery office to request a guided tour.

Hebrew Union College—Gallery of Art and Artifacts
3101 Clifton Ave. (Clifton)
221-1875 ext. 243

The Harriet Beecher Stowe House, the Cincinnati home of the author of *Uncle Tom's Cabin,* is a cultural and resource center for black history. Exhibits change every four months.

Harriet Beecher Stowe House
2950 Gilbert Ave. (Walnut Hills)
632-5120

The William Howard Taft National Historic Site is the birthplace of the twenty-seventh president of the United States and is being restored to reflect his life and career. Restoration should be complete by late 1988. However, there is presently an exhibit next door to the home.

William Howard Taft National Historic Site
2038 Auburn Ave. (Mt. Auburn)
684-3262

Historic Southwest Ohio operates the John Hauck House, a fine example of Italianate architecture. Once the home of a prominent Cincinnati brewer, it has been restored to its past elegance and is open for tours.

John Hauck House
812 Dayton St. (downtown)
563-9484

Sharon Woods Village is also under the auspices of Historic Southwest Ohio. A model of a typical nineteenth-century village, it is made up of restored buildings that have been moved from their original locations all over Southwestern Ohio. From a Greek-revival farmhouse and a log cabin to a train station and barn complex, this village is a charming walk-through outdoor museum.

Sharon Woods Village
Sharon Woods Park, Rt. 42 (Sharonville)
563-9484

Cary Cottage, home of the poets Phoebe and Alice Cary from 1832 to 1850, became the first home for blind women in Ohio in 1903. After it outgrew these small quarters, the permanent residence for the blind was constructed next door. Cary Cottage has been restored and is open to the public Sunday afternoons only, or for group tours during the week. Clovernook Home and School for the Blind, which is next door, is also open for tours. You'll see a large Braille printing plant and the home's weaving shop.

Cary Cottage/Clovernook Home and School for the Blind
7000 Hamilton Ave. (College Hill)
522-3860

If you're a radio fan, you'll love The Gray History of Wireless Museum. It houses antique radio receivers, transmitters, battery sets, early wire and tape recorders—all sorts of broadcast equipment. One room is a replica of an early 1920s broadcast studio. Admission is free. Tours are by appointment.

The Gray History of Wireless Museum
Crosley Telecommunications Center
1223 Central Pkwy. (downtown)
381-4033

The Vent Haven Museum houses more than 600 ventriloquists' dummies—including Jimmy Nelson's Farfel the Dog of Nestle Quik commercial fame, replicas of Edgar Bergen's Charlie McCarthy and Mortimer Snerd, novelty items like talking purses and canes. The historical perspective is emphasized through pen and ink sketches from the 1700s to the present plus a tape that demonstrates how ventriloquists' dummies are made. The museum is open from May 1 through September 30 by appointment only.

Vent Haven Museum
33 W. Maple Ave. (Ft. Mitchell)
341-0461

Extras from Sports and the Performing Arts

The Cincinnati Symphony Orchestra, the Playhouse in the Park, the Reds, and the Bengals have a lot to offer besides fine entertainment. Sports teams and cultural institutions provide well-known and sometimes little-known extras that do much to enliven the community. And that's what makes up this particular chapter—the extras. However, it would be impossible to list the benefits of every institution or group devoted to the performing arts in the city. So this small cache of cultural pluses is designed to get you on the phone to find out what else is available. See "The Queen City's Crown Jewels," "Libraries," and "Stopoffs" for more ideas.

Music

Hearing a chamber music concert in the grand ballroom of the Taft Museum overlooking its formal gardens is a lovely way to spend a Sunday afternoon. There are five such free concerts every season which are sponsored by the Cincinnati Musician's Association. Watch for newspaper announcements, or phone the Taft to find out when these events are held. If you're a Taft museum member, you'll automatically receive invitations.
Taft Museum Chamber Series
241-0343

The Cincinnati Symphony Orchestra sponsors two Lollipop Concerts per year at Music Hall. Held on Saturday mornings, children four to nine years old and their parents learn about all the instruments in the orchestra, then hear an hour-long program. Neighborhood posters and advertisements in the newspapers announce the Lollipop Concerts, as well as all the wonderful symphony concerts played in city parks that anyone can enjoy free during the summer.
Cincinnati Symphony Orchestra
621-1919

The Ensemble Company of the Cincinnati Opera Association (ECCO) performs throughout the city for school, civic and business groups, even for private parties. The group introduces novices to opera by bringing scenes to life, and can delight opera veterans with more sophisticated programs. The Ensemble Company performs at concerts in the parks—a real treat in warm months. Watch the newspapers for announcements of these events or call the Opera office to learn more about ECCO.
Cincinnati Opera Association
721-8222

Dance

The Cincinnati Ballet Company introduces youngsters to ballet as well as entertains senior citizens with their hour-long Sampler Series Performances. Announcements of these events go to schools and senior citizens centers. But if you don't fall into either category and still want to see if you can attend, phone the Ballet office.
Cincinnati Ballet Company
621-5282

Extras from Sports and the Performing Arts

Theater

Through a program called Interact, the Playhouse in the Park sponsors performances of its interns in area schools, for community groups, and at private parties. What is performed depends on what the interns are working on at that particular time; it may be a one-act play, a performance with masks, other imaginative theater segments.

At 7:30 on the Monday evening prior to the opening of a new play (opening nights are *always* on Tuesdays), there is a discussion of the play by Playhouse staff that is free and open to the public. In the future, hopes are these discussions will turn into ''meet the playwright'' sessions. And if you go to preview performances that are sometimes held before the regular run of a play, tickets will cost less than the full price.

When the Playhouse cupboards runneth over, which is every few years, spectacular costume and stage set sales are held. You can pick up fun duds, even furniture. Watch the newspapers for announcements of all these events, or phone for information.
Cincinnati Playhouse in the Park
421-5440

Ensemble Theatre of Cincinnati is midway between a professional theater company such as the Playhouse in the Park and community theater groups. This troupe specializes in performing new works of local and national playwrights—about five productions per year. If you love theater, you'll want to call or write to get on their mailing list.
Ensemble Theatre
Memorial Hall
1225 Elm St.
Cincinnati, OH 45210
352-3656

ArtReach tours the city performing fairy tales to dramas in schools, for civic and social groups. They'll even conduct workshops with children after performances if you desire. You need only provide a large gym, cafeteria, or auditorium for this professional ensemble of adult actors to delight you.
ArtReach Touring Theatre
351-9973

Cincinnati Children's Theatre has been performing fairy tales and the classics for school children in Cincinnati for more than forty years. However, on the last performance day of the run of a play, which is always Friday, a public performance is held at the Taft Theater. Phone for information on when these are scheduled and how to purchase tickets.
Cincinnati Children's Theatre
321-9041

The Carnegie Arts Center sponsors concerts, recitals, plays, art exhibits—get on the mailing list of this beehive of activities.
Carnegie Arts Center
Robbins & Scott Sts. (Covington)
491-2030

Enjoy the Arts

Any full-time student—elementary school to postgraduate level—can join Enjoy the Arts. Members receive two tickets to symphony, ballet, opera, and Playhouse in the Park performances, plus reduced ticket rates at thirty art and entertainment institutions as diverse as the Classical Jazz Society and Riverbend.
Enjoy the Arts
P.O. Box 19195
Cincinnati, OH 45219
751-2700

Sports

The Cincinnati Bengals have a twenty-five-minute, 16mm color/sound film of the highlights of their most recent season available, free of charge, to groups or gatherings of any kind. Call the Publicity Office to make arrangements to borrow it.

If you're a real fan, you may want to see the Bengals play at training camp (admission is free), held from the middle of July through the middle of August on the Wilmington College Campus—about forty-five miles from Cincinnati. Practices run Monday through Friday, twice a day, but starting times vary. From August 1 on, practices run mostly from Tuesday through Friday because the Bengals are generally off playing exhibition games over the weekend. In any case, before you drive to Wilmington, call 513-382-6661, and ask someone in the Bengals office to confirm there is a practice session. Schedules can be iffy and the Bengals don't want to disappoint anyone. If the Bengals are playing, take along your autograph book. Players are pretty receptive to fans at open practice sessions.

Cincinnati Bengals
621-3550

Gordy Coleman, Cincinnati Reds Hall of Fame first baseman, is the Reds spokesman and a natural storyteller. He makes more than 200 speeches a year—free—and can entertain any group from Cub Scouts to attorneys. (He'll bring along a film if you wish.) Write to the Reds office well in advance of when your group wishes him to speak.

You may borrow films free of charge from the Reds for your group's pleasure: highlights of previous seasons, films of the World Series of 1975 and 1976, ones of the All Star Games—but all of these 16mm films may be kept only twenty-four hours because they are in such demand.

Always dreamt of being a pro baseball player yourself? You can spend a week, aptly titled Dream Week, with the Reds at their spring training camp and take part in practices, instructions, and games. Dream Week is open to both men and women. Talk to those who have participated. They go on and on (and on!) about the wonderful time they had rubbing elbows with their baseball heroes.

For information on all of these programs, write or phone the administration office.

Cincinnati Reds
Riverfront Stadium
Cincinnati, OH 45202
421-4510

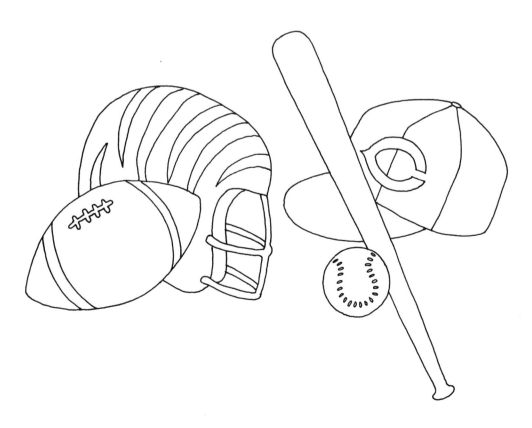

Universities

Cincinnati is fortunate to have so many colleges and universities that enrich the community. You can choose to be educated, entertained, or stimulated from the avalanche of programs they present—programs not just for students. Many of the lectures, seminars, movies, plays, concerts, and art exhibits are open to the public, and free.

Call the university or college whose activities you are interested in and ask to be placed on mailing lists so you can be aware of current campus events. Be specific and state whether it's piano recitals or design students' exhibits you want to know about, but track down the department whose field of expertise sparks activities that would appeal to you.

Every college I spoke to has a continuing education department that offers all sorts of courses or workshops on a noncredit basis. For instance, Northern Kentucky University has Telecourse, classes you can tune in on a Kentucky educational television station. Xavier offers summer workshops such as "Contemporary Women and Their Art," while sports buffs can sign up for noncredit courses in aquacize, weight lifting, racquetball, and karate at the Sports Center.

Check out the University of Cincinnati's Communiversity Program—an extravaganza of short-term classes in an ever-changing array of subjects. Get on the mailing list of U.C.'s College Conservatory of Music, to find out about upcoming plays, student recitals in almost every instrument, and orchestra, jazz ensemble, and chamber music concerts. The Union for Experimenting Colleges and Universities administers bachelor and doctoral degrees earned on a mentor concept in any discipline. You design—with the Union—a self-directed program you can pursue on your own.

Is your appetite whetted? I hope so, because you can surely add much to your city existence if you investigate what the following institutions offer.

University of Cincinnati
2624 Clifton Ave. (Clifton)
475-8000

Xavier University
3800 Victory Pkwy. (Evanston)
745-3000

College of Mount St. Joseph
5701 Delhi Rd. (Delhi Twp.)
244-4200

Hebrew Union College
3101 Clifton Ave. (Clifton)
221-1875

Northern Kentucky University
Louie B. Nunn Dr. (Highland Heights)
572-5100

Thomas More College
2771 Turkeyfoot Rd. (Crestview Hills, KY)
341-5800

Union for Experimenting Colleges and Universities
632 Vine St., Suite 1010 (downtown)
621-6444

Stopoffs

Hopscotching through Cincinnati, you'll find scenic streets, clusters of interesting shops, historic landmarks, and islands of serenity. Just walk through Findlay Market, an open-air food market that looks like a movie set. Notice the buildings that surround this historic area. Many have their original facades and wrought-iron balconies. Findlay Market is a wonderful place to take visitors to absorb Cincinnati history, as is Court Street Market. See "Edibles," page 7, for specifics.

Bring a brown-bag lunch to the steps of the Serpentine Wall in Yeatman's Cove on the riverfront. You'll have a first-row seat to watch river traffic while you soak up the sun. Stroll through Lytle Park at Fourth and Pike Streets, downtown. Notice the photographic plaques explaining the background of the area and the people who lived there. The Taft Museum and the Literary Club are just two of the historic buildings in this section.

Cross the river and visit Devou Park in Covington, which hosts a dramatic view of the Ohio River and the Cincinnati skyline. Pause at the Behringer Crawford Museum of Natural History located on the park grounds. It has wonderful archaeological and geological exhibits.

Poke through the shops on Covington's Main Street. Covering about five blocks, Mainstrasse Village is a restored nineteenth-century German neighborhood housing shops selling handcrafted gifts, vintage clothes, antiques, and collectibles. There are a number of good restaurants in Mainstrasse Village and on Covington's waterfront. This city has preserved much of its authentic river charm, and is a favorite stop for Cincinnati residents and visitors.

What you've just read is only a snippet of the city's sights. But to write about everything of interest in town and in the surrounding area, this chapter would wind up being book length. So I'd like to point you to some excellent sources of information.

If you want to know the most current activities taking place in the city, phone the Cincinnati Convention and Visitor's Bureau Information Line at 421-4636. You will hear a recording that recites a vast number of entertainment possibilities. Call the Downtown Council's Hotline (241-9091) and you will tune into a recording listing the week's activities downtown. To connect with a live person who can steer you to historic spots, special events, a Chinese restaurant should you be in the mood, phone 621-2142.

The Convention and Visitor's Bureau has an excellent guide to the city titled *Cincinnati Official Visitor's Guide* which is free and available from their office at 300 W. 6th St., downtown.

So that you won't miss any of the exciting places surrounding Cincinnati, look in the bookstores for a handy paperback guide entitled *Day Trips from Cincinnati* by David Hunter. From architecturally perfect Columbus, Indiana, to the incredible horse farms in Kentucky, this book contains good descriptions of places that are not more than a few hours drive away, directions on how to get there, even maps.

Tour Guides

To arrange a personally guided tour of Cincinnati conducted by informative guides, contact these services.

Heritage Tours, which highlight the city's history, can be arranged through the Cincinnati Historical Society. They will be customized for specific groups which can tour by bus, van, or horse-drawn carriage. You can even book walking tours for small numbers of people in areas of the city you want to learn more about. Schedule tours at least a month in advance.
Heritage Tours
241-4622

Jean Middlekauf and Dorothy Rockel of Guidance Systems personalize all sorts of city tours for their clients. You tell these two women what you want to see—cultural institutions, historic spots, various neighborhoods—they'll arrange it for a few people or a group.
Guidance Systems
Dorothy Rockel
474-3462
Jean Middlekauf
321-4771

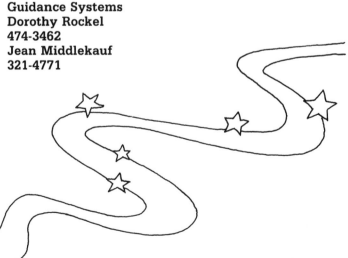

Stopoffs

Tourcrafters professionally coordinates tours for any number of people throughout Cincinnati and the surrounding area. They offer about sixteen packages including visits to city landmarks, walking tours of the downtown area, exploring famous estates and gardens, trips to Lexington horse farms or historic Lebanon. Tourcrafters offers many personalized tour services. Inquire about them.
Tourcrafters
721-8230

Bring Along the Children offers tours designed to delight a minimum group of thirty kids by transporting them to museums, the zoo, on a riverboat ride—they can tailor all sorts of treks. Ask for details.
Bring Along the Children
242-6541

River Tours

Taking in Cincinnati's sights while cruising the river is taking advantage of one of the city's best points. Phone these riverboat companies to inquire about the many tours they offer. Some travel to historic places, such as BB Riverboats' "Cruise to Times Past"—an all-day adventure to nineteenth-century river towns including Rabbit Hash, Kentucky, and Rising Sun, Indiana. All will book customized group tours and parties.

BB Riverboats
261-8500

Jubilee Riverboats, Inc.
581-0300

Queen City Riverboat Co., Inc.
292-8687

Plant Tours

We all know Cincinnati is a manufacturing town. But did you know that you can actually watch the products the city is famous for being made? Many companies offer free tours of their plants; just phone ahead to make the necessary reservations.

Ask about what size group is required and whether there is a minimum age for children. Here's a sampling of some of the Cincinnati plants open for tours. Phone the Chamber of Commerce (579-3000) for a complete list of what's available.

Procter & Gamble
Ivorydale Plant
5201 Spring Grove Ave.
Arrange tours through Tourcrafters:
721-2674

Frisch's Commissary
3011 Stanton Ave.
559-5288

Meier's Wine Cellars, Inc.
6955 Plainfield Rd.
891-2900

Cincinnati Enquirer and Post Production Facility
1531 Western Ave.
721-2700

Shapely, Inc.
2430 E. Kemper Rd.
771-7733

IBM
580 Walnut St.
762-2500

WCET (TV 48)
1223 Central Pkwy.
381-4033

Greater Cincinnati International Airport
Donaldson Hwy., Boone County, KY
283-3144

Cincinnati Water Treatment Plant
5651 Kellogg Ave.
231-7825

Music Hall
1243 Elm St.
621-1919

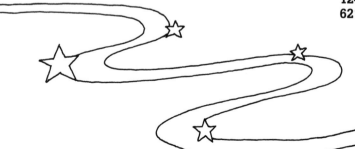

Going Out of Town?

Leaving town? Whether it's for pleasure or business, these travel aids should make your trip much easier.

Will it Rain?

First, you'll want to know what the weather is wherever you are heading, so you can pack accordingly. Phone Banana Republic. This mail-order travel and safari clothing company has set up a Climate Desk you can phone toll-free to inquire about weather most anyplace in the United States and the world (Monday through Friday, 8:30 A.M. to 5:00 P.M., Pacific Standard Time). Two hundred weather stations covering most of the large cities in the world report to them daily. You can ask what the temperature is in San Francisco or Boston, Bangkok or Paris on any particular day, what the humidity level and average rainfall are for that time of year. You can ask for visa information on countries you are planning to visit, and staffers will let you know if one is necessary and give you the proper phone numbers to call to obtain it. State Department advisories on which countries are chancy for travelers are kept up to date as well as immunization information. You can even ask what weight clothing is proper for where you are going.

Banana Republic Climate Desk
1-800-325-7270

Map It Out

If you plan to go camping, hiking, or fishing in a part of the United States you've never explored before, you'll need a detailed map of the area. Topographic maps can be purchased from the National Cartographic Information Center. Each state is broken into quadrangle maps to show, in detail and in color, the contour of the terrain and all the physical characteristics. This is just one example of the huge bank of charts and maps kept on file by this agency. For free indexes of maps and for more information on what you can ask for, write to:

National Cartographic Information Center
U.S. Geological Survey
509 National Center
Reston, VA 22092

Duttenhofer's Map Store sells maps for most anyplace in the world, maps in foreign languages, wall maps, road maps, city, state, and regional maps, atlases, even a number of U.S. topographical maps such as the ones mentioned above. Whether you're visiting the Caribbean Islands or New Zealand, Thailand or France, you can pick up travel information at Duttenhofer's to help you better plan a trip.

Duttenhofer's Map Store
210 W. McMillan St. (Clifton)
381-0007

Safe and Sound

In addition to your travel passport, pick up a copy of *Passport To Nutrition*, a valuable travel booklet put out by the Greater Cincinnati Nutrition Council. It contains a diet to prevent the symptoms of jet lag, complete with instructions on exactly what to eat the day before you take a long plane trip and en route. In addition, you'll find tips on how to maintain good nutrition while you eat on the road and on the run, even lists of popular restaurant foods and the calories they contain. Write for *Passport To Nutrition* and enclose $1.95, which covers its cost plus postage and handling.

Greater Cincinnati Nutrition Council
2400 Reading Rd. (near downtown)
Cincinnati, OH 45202
621-3262

Going Out of Town

The Medic Alert Foundation can give you peace of mind if you have a medical problem and are traveling. Many people join who have diabetes, heart conditions, allergies to medicines, or wear contact lenses. Membership includes an emblem, to be worn as a necklace or bracelet, engraved with your problem, the association's phone number (which can be called collect from anywhere in the world, day or night), and your membership number. If you have an accident or are taken ill and are separated from the identification and medical information in your wallet, the person aiding you can call Medic Alert and obtain your medical history, which is kept on file along with the phone number of your private physician.

Medic Alert
Turlock, CA 95380
1-800-344-3226

Doggone Reservations

If you are planning to take your dog along when you travel, *Touring With Towser*, a directory listing thousands of hotels and motels in the United States that accept guests with dogs, should prove invaluable. This guide also gives tips and etiquette suggestions for traveling pups and their owners. To obtain *Touring With Towser*, write to the Gaines Co., enclosing a check or money order for $1.50.

Touring With Towser
P.O. Box 8177
Kankakee, IL 60902

Home Away From Home

House swapping with someone who lives in a part of the United States or a part of the world you especially want to visit can be a unique travel experience. Find agreeable traders through the Vacation Exchange Club, which publishes a Home Exchange Book each February and April listing homes all over the world, from mid-Manhattan apartments to Irish castles. These books are available to members who write to each other to formalize trade arrangements. Write to the Vacation Exchange Club for information on membership fees.

Vacation Exchange Club
12006 111th Ave.
Youngtown, AZ 85363
602-972-2186

Travel Ohio

The State of Ohio Department of Travel and Tourism is brimming with all sorts of information about traveling within the state. Staff can send you booklets on where the best campsites are, point you to places of interest—from museums to day-long festivals—even tell you how you can take a vacation on a working farm. The numbers to call: 1-800-BUCKEYE for all information; 1-800-282-5393 provides information and makes reservations for the following state park lodges: Burr Oak, Deer Creek, Hueston Woods, Punderson Manor, Salt Fork, and Shawnee.

Travel Planners

You need to have good chemistry with the person who makes your travel plans. You need to have similar tastes. Since your travel agent is going to advise you on countries to visit and accommodations, if you prefer small country retreats and his idea of peaceful is Acapulco—you're in trouble. So I asked people who travel a lot, for business and pleasure, in this country and all over the world, who they trust to make their travel plans. The names of these agents cropped up most often.

Ellen Wyler cares about every detail of each trip she plans, and mother hens her clients to special places all over the world. She's never let me down.

Ellen Wyler
Provident Travel
2800 Atrium Two
221 E. 4th St.
621-4900

Vicky Mary went to school in Switzerland, has globe-trotted for years, and has even been to India half a dozen times. Arranging trips there is just one of her specialties. She provides her clients with such information as what clothes to take, what sights to take in. Her helpful "insider tips" are based on solid experience.

Vicky Mary
Victoria Travel
3330 Erie Ave., Suite 10
871-1100
250 E. 5th St., Suite 1572
762-7677

Joan Baily and Jean Middlekauf are impeccable travel consultants. They can put you up in a castle, tell you where to eat the best lunch on the backroads most anywhere in the world, provide you with a complete portfolio of sights to see, restaurants, and shops. I'd put myself in their hands anytime.

Traveling Tips, a division of Pier and Port
Joan Baily
321-3573
Jean Middlekauf
321-4771

Besides selling a full line of camping equipment (more about this in "Sports Equipment and Clothes," page 159), staff at Wilderness Trace can help you plan any wilderness expedition you have in mind. Those who work in the store have hiked, camped, or climbed mountains just about everywhere in the world—or know someone who's been where they haven't.

Manager Chris Nicholson says they help customers conceptualize trips according to their skills by digging into their file of wilderness areas. So if you want to climb in Nepal or Alaska, explore the Everglades or walk creek beds and ridges in the United States, Nicholson and his co-workers can recommend guide services or agencies along with the names of contact people to plan the trip. Chris also told me there is no charge for these services, but most people who are wilderness types outfit themselves at the store anyway.

Wilderness Trace
3441 Michigan Ave. (Hyde Park)
321-6800
11582 Lebanon (Sharonville)
563-4774

Bag It

Bankhardt's Luggage Shops have a full range of suitcases, hanging bags, duffels, and all sorts of accessories, like plug-in cups to heat water for instant coffee in your hotel room. From modest luggage to the blue-ribbon brands, there is always a fine variety. Look in the phone directory for the downtown and suburban mall locations.

The American Case and Luggage Co. operates a factory outlet store that sells twenty-eight brands of luggage at a 20% discount. Hartmann, Samsonite— all the big names are here. This company also manufactures custom travel cases—mostly display cases so salesmen can safely globe-trot with the tools of their trade. They make travel cases for musicians, technical cases to safely ship computers and delicate tools, jewelry cases—they'll design whatever you need.

American Case and Luggage Co.
25 W. 12th St. (Over-the-Rhine)
621-1399

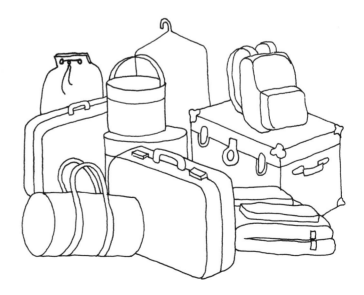

Going Out of Town

140 The totes Company makes all sorts of soft luggage, hanging bags, cosmetic cases, fold-up-into-handkerchief-size rainwear, packable shoe protectors that are sold at the outlet store on the factory premises. Choose from dozens of varieties of collapsible umbrellas (perfect to tuck into a travel bag or purse), rainscarves, and my favorite—their small, flat, zippered bags you can stick inside your suitcase, then unzip to transform them into carry-on size luggage to hold all the wonderful purchases you make during your travels.
totes Outlet Store
10078 E. Kemper Rd. (Loveland)
583-2390
totes Kiosk
Outlets, Ltd. (Kings Island)
398-0258

Wilderness Trace (see above) carries North Face luggage, which you should check out before you make any other serious luggage purchase. These soft bags have so many zippered compartments, are so sturdy and versatile, you can endlessly stuff them and still have room to spare. They come in several sizes, one you can put under an airplane seat as well as a duffel. North Face Luggage is expensive but worth it.

Expecting Visitors?

Say you are expecting guests from out of town and you don't have enough room to put them up with you. You want to find them someplace charming to stay. Phone Ohio Valley Bed and Breakfast, which represents dozens of unique accommodations in this area. These include a hundred-year-old Covington row house, a turn-of-the-century farm house in Clermont County, an 1890 Clifton home complete with a turret and curved porch, a Victorian home in Hyde Park, two homes in historic Metamora, Indiana, an apartment in Maysville, Kentucky, which overlooks the river.

Owners Nancy Cully and Sallie Parker Lotz will give you complete information on all the bed and breakfasts in this area, including exact locations, prices, and what kind of food and hospitality to expect. Join the Guest Network, their nationwide bed and breakfast reservation system (annual fee is $25), and membership entitles you to an unlimited number of reservations plus assistance with your travel arrangements throughout the United States and Canada. Nonmembers can use the service for $15 per reservation.
Ohio Valley Bed and Breakfast
6876 Taylor Mill Rd. (Independence, KY)
356-7865

Learn Your Lesson

You need something new in your life. You've always wanted to learn to speak Italian. Or maybe you'd like to take up fencing, yoga, learn how to write poetry, paint with watercolors. Where do you find teachers, look for classes in such varied activities? In the following places. (For additional classes, see "Herbs and Spices," pages 41 to 43, and "Arts and Crafts Supplies," pages 147 to 149.)

Education Centers

All of the universities in Greater Cincinnati have continuing education departments that offer a multitude of noncredit programs. Turn to "Universities," page 134, for names and phone numbers and ask that class catalogues be mailed to you. Also look through "The Queen City's Crown Jewels," pages 128 to 130. Museums, the Nature Center, the Zoo, other institutions have education departments that present programs for adults and children. Besides all these, here are additional sources for you to investigate.

The Discovery Center, a lifelong learning center, offers more than 100 entertaining and stimulating courses each session taught by experts in each subject. And the subjects include conversational language instruction, all sorts of exercise (aerobics to swimnastics), dance (ballet to jitterbug), how to make a career change, wine tasting, finance and investments, assertiveness training, calligraphy, a variety of computer courses, even white-water rafting. To ask for a catalogue and to register, write or phone.
Discovery Center
1700 Madison Rd. (East Walnut Hills)
221-6800

The Great Oaks Joint Vocational School District offers adult education classes through the individual schools that make up this district. There are classes in floral design, landscaping, pet care and grooming, air conditioning and heating, auto body repair, typing, the concepts of word processing, so many more. Look in the White Pages under Great Oaks Joint Vocational School District. You will find a complete listing of the addresses and phone numbers of all the schools in this system.

Find out what is being offered at the YMCA or YWCA nearest you. Ask about classes, exercise programs—each branch offers a different assortment. Parents and children can often participate in lively activities held at the same time. Or there are classes they can take together. Check the phone directory to find your neighborhood "Y." Through its education department, the Cincinnati Art Museum offers a world of programs in fine arts and art appreciation for children and adults. Its sister institution, the Art Academy of Cincinnati, sponsors creative art classes for preschoolers on Saturdays during the school year and daily during the summer. Adults can sign up for classes in life drawing, photography, painting, many more. Inquire about the full range of these programs.
Cincinnati Art Museum Education Department
721-5204
Art Academy of Cincinnati
721-5205, ext. 232

A small sampling of classes held at the Arts Consortium: "Rhythm and Jazz," "Introduction to African Dance and Drum," private voice instruction, modeling, photography, ceramics, clay modeling/sculpture, independent record producing. Phone for their brochure.
Arts Consortium
1515 Linn St. (downtown)
381-0645

The Cincinnati Recreation Commission publishes a quarterly guide that lists the multitude of programs they offer and the centers where they are held. Pick one up at the center nearest you. And note, the Recreation Commission was created to serve every conceivable population segment through every conceivable art discipline. For anything from classes in weaving and ceramics to dramatics workshops and jazz ensembles, phone the commission, state your particular interest, and staff will point you to the right program. The commission also sponsors a galaxy of sports activities. Inquire about those, too.
Cincinnati Recreation Commission
352-4000

Learn Your Lesson

The University of Cincinnati's College Conservatory of Music offers instruction for adults and children in dance and music, and drama for children only. Pick an instrument you want to play—there is an instructor or a class available. One bonus for children who take music lessons at CCM is that instead of just taking lessons and going home to practice, CCM teachers involve students in groups that play for each other, even orchestras. Music is fun, not a chore. That's what most parents are after.

College Conservatory of Music
Preparatory Department
475-2595

Contemporary Dance Theater holds classes for people of all ages in modern dance, jazz, ballet, tap, creative movement. Enrollment is continuous—you can sign up anytime during the year.
Contemporary Dance Theater
751-2800

Star Gaze

The Cincinnati Observatory, operated by the Physics Department of the University of Cincinnati, is open to the public on most Thursday evenings throughout the year. These popular "Astronomy Thursdays" include slide presentations about astronomy or space science, then, if the weather is clear, viewing celestial objects through one of the observatory's large refractor telescopes. Astronomy courses covering a huge variety of topics and lasting from one to six weeks are also offered. You must sign up well in advance.
The Cincinnati Observatory
321-5186

Water Sports

Can you canoe? It's a big sport on all the rivers that spiderweb the countryside around Cincinnati. Many of the following firms give lessons in canoeing and tubing, offer excursion trips by busing you upriver and letting you float or paddle back to home base, have places where you can camp or fish to take an off-the-water break. Phone for more information on the activities sponsored by the following outfits.

Bruce's Loveland Canoe Rental
200 Taylor St. (Loveland)
683-4611 or 683-4604

Little Miami Excursion Co.
110 Wooster Pk. (Milford)
831-0888

Morgan's Canoe Liveries
Fort Ancient Livery
Brookville Canoe Center
Mad River Outpost
1-800-WE CANOE

Thaxton's Canoe Trails
Rt. 2, Box 391, Hays Station Rd. (Falmouth, KY)
606-654-5111

Novices can learn to sail and race enthusiasts can improve their techniques from instructors at Sailboats of Cincinnati, which also sells small boats on up to thirty-footers.
Sailboats of Cincinnati
9514 Princeton-Glendale Rd. (Hamilton)
874-2126

Strictly Sail Inc. offers lessons when you buy a boat. They also offer sailing lessons in the summer through the Discovery Center. See the Discovery Center listing under "Education Centers" in this chapter or phone the store for more information.
Strictly Sail Inc.
10766 Kenwood Rd. (Blue Ash)
984-1907

Believe it or not, you can learn to scuba dive in Cincinnati. That way you'll be a pro by the time you hit the Caribbean. The Cincinnati Diving Center teaches diving, night diving, diving to explore underwater wrecks, underwater photography at local pools, lakes, and quarries. The center sponsors diving excursions all over the world, sells, rents, and services a complete line of equipment.
Cincinnati Diving Center
8412 Winton Rd. (Finneytown)
521-DIVE

As long as you're going to use water as your sports playground, you want to play safe. Learn lifesaving techniques, basic sailing techniques, and other water-related safety rules from the American Red Cross.
American Red Cross
579-3080

The Cincinnati Power Squadron teaches four fourteen-week class sessions each year on all facets of boating safety. These are free, open to the public, and are held at various schools throughout the city.
Cincinnati Power Squadron
271-8383

To learn of the three classes given by the United States Coast Guard—basic boating, basic sailing, coastal piloting—phone their toll-free number, Boat U.S. It's operated by the Coast Guard Auxiliary. A local call won't get you the information you need.
Boat U.S.
1-800-336-BOAT

Fly Me to the Moon

Your head's in the clouds. Take flying lessons from one of the firms mentioned in "Arrive in Style," page 80.

However, if you're even more adventurous, soaring may be the sport for you. Learn to become a glider pilot from instructors at the Caesar Creek Soaring Club. Then if you're hooked by the thrill of piloting a sailplane— which enthusiasts compare to the combination of sailing, surfing, and skiing above the earth—you can join the club, which is operated by its actively participating members.
Caesar Creek Soaring Club
5385 Elbon Rd.
Waynesville, OH 45068
1-932-7627

En Garde!

In three sessions a year, instructors who are members of the Cincinnati Fencing Club offer classes that meet once a week for ten weeks. There are twenty to thirty people (teenagers and adults) in a class at the Clifton Community Center, which provides the basic equipment beginners need. Then after students pass beginner status, they can join the Cincinnati Fencing Club, which has four major tournaments a year drawing people from six states.
Cincinnati Fencing Club
Clifton Community Center
320 McAlpin Ave. (Clifton)
961-5681

Skating Along

Novice ice skaters—children and adults—can sign up for classes at Northland Ice Center. Groups are divided by age and ability. For private lessons ask for the Northland Skating Academy. Eight pros offer private instruction for children and adults.
Northland Ice Skating
10400 Reading Rd. (Evendale)
563-0008 or 563-0001

Roller skating more your speed? Call the Fun Factory to learn to navigate on wheels.
Fun Factory
1631 Sherman Ave. (Norwood)
631-1311

Ski Cincinnati

Slopes near Cincinnati? Ski enthusiasts can brush up on their technique and beginners starting at age three can take lessons at Perfect North Slopes in Lawrenceburg, Indiana. There's a special program for three- to twelve-year olds on Saturday mornings called Ski Doodles, evening lessons for those who can't get away during the day, private lessons in addition to many group packages. Bring your own equipment or rent it until you decide you like the sport enough to invest in skis of your own.
Perfect North Slopes
812-537-3754

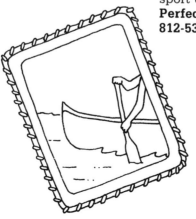

Learn Your Lesson

144 ## Riding High

If you'd like to learn to ride, there are a number of stables in town that offer group and private lessons. Some specialize in English style only, hunting and jumping. Some teach basic horse grooming, how to care for tack, as well as riding techniques. Some have more rigid teaching styles, others are more relaxed. Phone the following places to find the one that suits your style.

Childress Rodgers Stables
1632 Apgar Rd. (Milford)
575-2194

Derbyshire Stables
7730 Camp Rd. (Camp Denison)
831-2587

Miljoie Riding Academy
7333 Main St. (Newtown)
561-9887

Red Fox Stables
1342 Hwy. 50 (Milford)
831-5010

Winton Woods Riding Center
10073 Daly Rd. (Springfield Twp.)
931-3057

Kick Up Your Heels

You're a klutz on the dance floor. You can't even fox-trot or waltz. Well, no more sitting on the sidelines. Call Bud Walters. He'll give group lessons for adults or children in jitterbug, tango, rhumba, samba, cha-cha, fox-trot, waltz, even disco.
Bud Walters
542-4064

You like country-style dancing. Well, the Stone Valley Dance Barn is the place to learn how to square dance and clog (the Appalachian version of tap dancing). Adults can begin once-a-week classes in September that continue for nine months. Tom Stone, the owner, will give you more information on classes, or kindly point you to other square dance clubs that offer lessons closer to where you live if you feel Stone Valley is too far away from your home.
Stone Valley Dance Barn
Rt. 3, Box 1 (West Harrison, IN)
637-5183

How about vintage dances? The mazurka, schottische, galop, quadrille, Charleston, all the ragtime dances—phone the Flying Cloud Academy of Vintage Dance and owner/instructor Richard Powers will send information on classes and workshops. They're for newcomers who want to learn the basics and for more advanced students. All classes are held on Wednesday evenings at the University YMCA on Calhoun Street in Clifton, and everyone who participates has a wonderful time. Once you join this lively group you'll know when historic balls are held—everyone dresses in authentic clothes, and shows off their steps.
Flying Cloud Academy of Vintage Dance
321-4878

What's Cooking?

The Culinary Emporium offers cooking classes (many in the evening) at their Kenwood and Tricentre stores: Cajun basics, Mexican classics, French, Chinese, and Italian dishes, how to make homemade pasta, prepare fresh fish and other tasty low cal dishes. The stores also sponsor cook's tours—trips to historic spots combined with a gourmet meal. Get on Culinary Emporium's mailing list so you will know about all of the activities, classes, and demonstrations the stores sponsor.
The Culinary Emporium
Kenwood Towne Centre
793-2783
11439 Princeton Rd. (Tricentre)
772-1510

The Fourth Street Market Cooking School, held at the downtown L.S. Ayres store, is directed by Marilyn Harris, who gives classes herself and also arranges those given by visiting chefs and cookbook authors. There are morning classes, some given in the evening, but ask about the Lunch and Learn Series held at noon. They're convenient if you work downtown and want to learn about food as well as nibble a delicious midday snack. Phone to get on the mailing list for notification of schedules or watch the newspapers for announcements.
L.S. Ayres Fourth Street Market Cooking School
352-5271

Lazarus Creative Kitchen, directed by Barbara Lauterbach, offers year-round morning, evening, and Saturday classes as well as forty-five-minute lunchtime programs, which are a great noon deal since you get to eat the dish that's been taught. Visiting chefs and cookbook authors lead classes that you will know about in advance if you get on the school's mailing list. Otherwise check the newspapers for Lazarus' monthly ads announcing the schedule.
Lazarus Creative Kitchen
369-7556

Dora Ang teaches Chinese cooking—classic dishes representing various provinces—in sessions of three classes held in students' homes. You form your own group of from eight to fifteen people, depending on the size of your kitchen (Dora demonstrates; class members gather 'round in chairs to watch). Dora brings all the food and utensils. All you must supply is the space.
Dora Ang
761-9504

Whole Foods Cuisine owners Gale Howe and Valaree Hemighaus (see "Home Entertainment," page 86, for information about their catering service) teach private lessons and group classes in macrobiotic and vegetarian cooking. You'll be familiarized with whole foods ingredients and a whole world of hearty, healthy dishes and specialty items.
Whole Foods Cuisine
Valaree Hemighaus
681-9272
Gale Howe
861-4440

Learn to make candy in hands-on classes of twelve students, as well as special-occasion cake baking and decorating at the Party Cake Shop. These are offered year-round.
Party Cake Shop
1785 E. Galbraith Rd. (Reading)
821-6161

Mind Your Manners

If facing a formal table set with assorted sizes of forks, knives, and spoons throws you into a cold sweat, despair no more. Sign up for one of Marja Barrett's etiquette classes, which can put a shine on your professional image. Her adult etiquette classes, taught at the Omni Netherland, cover invitations, introductions, how you present yourself at the table as well as your manners. Marja leads the class through a four-course meal. She also teaches table etiquette classes to children during a five-course lunch—such staples as how to use a napkin, when to say please and thank you, how to order, much more. Ask about Marja's other classes including "Company Manners for Everyday" (tips for business luncheons, how to address colleagues, clients, and superiors) and "Polish Pays" (how to make a good impression visually and aurally).
Marja Barrett
651-1521

Parlez-Vous?

This time you want to speak the language when you go to Spain. Or Japan. Or Italy. Or anywhere in the world. Take lessons at any of the following places.

Traveler's Aid
632 Vine St., Suite 505 (downtown)
721-7660

Berlitz
503 Race St. (Skywalk)
381-4650

Inlingua
602 Main St. (400 Gwynne Bldg., downtown)
721-8782

Tri-State German American School
961-7976

Learn to Sign

Learn lip reading and sign language at the Cincinnati Speech and Hearing Center. Class sessions last ten weeks; there are not more than twenty people in a class.
Cincinnati Speech and Hearing Center
3021 Vernon Pl. (Mt. Auburn)
221-0527

Learn Your Lesson

Testing, Testing

If you want to prepare yourself for entrance exams to college, law school, really the whole world of qualifying tests, call the Stanley Kaplan Educational Center. Ask for a brochure listing all the courses they offer, including speed reading.
Stanley Kaplan Educational Center
1821 Summit Rd. (Roselawn)
821-2288

At a Sylvan Learning Center each person is tested to ascertain his skill level, then a program is written to increase his basic skills or to enrich them. Instructors work with preschoolers to adults on an individual basis. Also, those who must take college preparatory tests—ACT and SAT—can sign up for pre-test help. Look in the phone book for the center in your part of town.

Lisa Collins of Word of Mouth Tutoring Service employs teachers to work one on one with students in subjects such as math (from elementary to calculus), French, German, and Spanish, biological sciences, and social studies. Teachers can help two-year-olds recognize shapes, learn the alphabet. Some teachers are even certified in special education. You can arrange for at-home tutoring, or if you live too far away for a teacher to come to you, a neutral meeting place such as a library can be arranged.
Word Of Mouth Tutoring Service
683-9498

Bridge, Anyone?

Get two or three tables of people together and phone the Queen City Bridge Club to set up lessons.
Queen City Bridge Club
761-0448

Janet Dorger offers an eight-week series of bridge lessons—beginner and intermediate, day or evening—to no less than eight people at a time.
Janet Dorger
871-1114

Antiquities

If you want to learn more about American antique furniture and decorative arts, Sue Studebaker, a graduate of Winterthur Institute for Advanced Studies, is a fine instructor. Take her ten-week course at the Warren County Historical Society, where you should phone to see when classes are scheduled and to register.
Warren County Historical Society
105 S. Broadway (Lebanon, OH)
1-932-1817

Don't Forget to Write

For private or semiprivate lessons in calligraphy and illumination, phone Holly Monroe. She'll custom tailor classes to individual students' needs, which is a great way to learn.
Heirloom Artists Calligraphy Studio
771-2737

Living Free

Jim Schenk, director of Imago, says his organization's prime aim is to show people how they can live more gently on the earth and not be so destructive to the environment. Says Jim, "We assist people in transitioning to a humane, sustainable way of living that is self-reliant, cooperative, interdependent, and conscious through workshops and private consultations." These include organic gardening, solar heating, conservation, food usage and preparation, care of aging parents, many more.
Imago
553 Enright Ave.
Cincinnati, OH 45205
921-1932

Arts and Crafts Supplies

Serious artists to Sunday painters—they've shared their supply sources in this chapter. You'll also find crafts materials such as knitting yarns, wool for rug weaving, gold for jewelry making. Some of the stores that sell these supplies also offer lessons which are mentioned in this chapter as well.

Fine and Commercial Art Supplies

Artists recommend these stores for brushes, handmade Japanese and European paper, paint—anything for any fine or commercial art medium.

Prince Reproductions, Inc.
708 Walnut St. (downtown)
621-0726

Sterleen's Art Materials
810 Sycamore (downtown)
241-1225

Suders Art Store
1309 Vine St. (Over-the-Rhine)
241-0800

Cincinnati Artists' Warehouse
1150 Main St. (downtown)
621-2224

John R. Green Co.
411 W. 6th St. (Covington)
431-5568

Frame It

The following stores are recommended by professionals for their fine work and fair prices.

Frameworks
Valley Center (Roselawn)
821-7499

The Miter Box
7220 Montgomery Rd. (Silverton)
984-4747

Art Preparators
2030 Madison Rd. (O'Bryonville)
321-3729

Sharon Cook Gallery
113 Park Pl. (Covington)
491-4990

Haney Custom Framing
946 Wareham (Mt. Adams)
721-5409

A.B. Closson Jr.
401 Race St. (downtown)
762-5572
7866 Montgomery Rd. (Kenwood)
891-5531

Malton Gallery
2709 Observatory Ave. (Hyde Park)
321-8614

Prince's and Suders' (see previous listings in this chapter) also have good reputations as framers.

At Frame & Save (see the phone directory for their many locations) you can do framing yourself or have work custom done. Note: there are other fine frame-it-yourself centers in Cincinnati. Investigate locations near you.

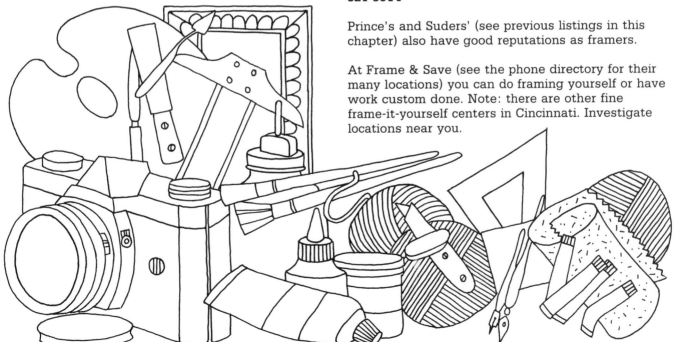

Arts and Crafts Supplies

Photography Supplies

Where do photographers buy equipment and have it repaired?

Provident Camera Shop, Inc.
18 W. 7th (downtown)
621-5762

Pete's PhotoWorld, Inc.
614 Race St. (downtown)
721-7383
7400 Kenwood Rd. (Kenwood)
793-7383

Jack's Camera Center
51 E. 4th St. (Dixie Terminal Bldg., downtown)
721-6458

Norton Photography
2609 Vine St. (Corryville)
281-5002

Swallens
Check your phone directory for locations.

Craft Supplies

If you are looking for rainbow shades of tissue paper, burlap and felt, ribbons, string, Styrofoam balls, dried weeds, silk flowers, seashells, all sorts of interesting objects used for department store displays, such as giant crayons, velvet hands to hold rings, real-looking but not to eat asparagus, garlic, croissants, all sorts of fruit—any kind of raw material for decorations or crafts—try these two stores.

Cappel Display Co., Inc.
920 Elm St. (downtown)
621-0952

Color Brite Fabrics & Display, Inc.
212 E. 8th St. (downtown)
721-4402

Tole and Decorative Art Supplies

The Nearsighted Owl has three rooms packed with quality unfinished wood for those interested in tole and decorative crafts, about 400 books on the subject as well as paint and other supplies. Classes provide much individual attention.
The Nearsighted Owl
406 W. 6th St. (Covington)
491-6000

Art Glass

If you make stained glass, or you'd like to learn how, you can find supplies and take lessons at Merry-Go-Round.
Merry-Go-Round Stained Glass
10829 Montgomery Rd. (Sycamore Twp.)
489-6474

Jewelry Making

Cincinnati Gold and Silver Refining Co. sells gold and silver by the sheet or wire to jewelers, artists, and dentists. Order 10-karat gold, pure gold, even platinum by the ounce a day ahead of when you need it.
Cincinnati Gold and Silver Refining Co.
316 W. 4th St., 5th fl. (downtown)
721-0944

Rope

If your craft includes the use of rope, head out to Industrial Rope Supply. This wholesaler has hemp of all kinds, synthetic rope used for boating, rope to support mattresses if you're looking for some to restore an antique bed, even the kind you can use to make nautical-looking fences. If you can tie it, it's in the warehouse. There are hundreds of varieties and colors you can buy by the foot or the giant spool.
Industrial Rope Supply
5250 River Rd. (near the Trolley Tavern)
941-2443

Leather

Tandy's has everything for leather crafts: skins, leather-working equipment, craft kits, how-to books, rhinestones and beads to decorate garments, bags of leather and suede scraps that make wonderful elbow patches, purse straps, trim, or whatever else you can think of.
Tandy Leather Co.
4077 E. Galbraith Rd. (Deer Park)
984-3434

Rug Making

Pat Nolan, proprietor of The Rug House, teaches rug braiding and weaving workshops. Besides giving individual and group lessons, Pat stocks beautiful woolens that she buys as remnants from coat manufacturers and textile mills as well as Scottish burlap, warp cloth, and monk's cloth for rug backing. You'll also find wool cutters, hooks, and dozens of other rug-making supplies you're welcome to buy whether or not you're a student.
The Rug House
871-0890

Martha Petrie gives classes in traditional rug hooking for novices and for experts who want to brush up on shading and dyeing techniques. She also offers a complete line of supplies.

Martha Petrie
321-9603

For the most beautiful custom rya rug designs and supplies, Greta Peterson has always been a rich resource.

Greta Peterson Galerie
7696 Camargo Rd. (Madeira)
561-6785

Lace Making

Lace making isn't a lost art if you take lessons from Bonnie Kareth. She also sells all the supplies you need for this intricate art.

Bonnie Kareth
341-7289

Smocking

Diane Breth of The Heirloom Shop offers classes in smocking, fagoting, and French hand sewing techniques. All supplies are available as well as exquisite Swiss trim and French lace. Phone for an appointment or a catalogue.

The Heirloom Shop
321-1640

Basketry

Donna Hagenauer teaches all basic basketry techniques for a minimum class of four students, maximum of twelve. Evening and day sessions can be arranged.

Donna Hagenauer
961-3877

Knitting, Stitchery, Weaving, Quilting

There are many fine shops in town that offer luxurious yarn for knitting, crocheting, spinning, weaving, and needlepoint; thread for counted cross-stitch work; quilting accessories; basket-making supplies. Some shops specialize in one craft, such as knitting or counted cross-stitch; most offer supplies for several. All offer lessons and some teachers will design custom patterns for you, finish garments you've made, even do repair. Ask who does what!

Robert Joseph Co.
2533 Gilbert Ave. (Walnut Hills)
559-1704

Clasgen's Yarn Shop
2383 State Rt. 132 (New Richmond, OH)
553-3736

Peach Mountain Studio
7754 Camargo Rd. (Madeira)
271-3191

Creative Needles
8546 Winton Rd. (Finneytown)
522-6952

Knitter's Choice
7796 Montgomery Rd. (Montgomery)
793-5648

Glendale Yarn Shop
27 Village Square (Glendale)
771-0244

Fiber Naturell
9424 Shelly Ln. (Montgomery)
793-4940

Wizard Weavers
2701 Observatory (Hyde Park)
871-5750

The Knitting Bag
2757 Observatory (Hyde Park)
321-6930

Aunt Mary's Yarns
Outlets, Ltd. (Kings Island)
398-1066

The Top Drawer
6880 Wooster Pk. (Mariemont)
271-6691

Stitches 'N Such
702 Nilles Rd. (Fairfield)
829-5188

Cross Stitch Crazy
3639 Glenmore (Cheviot)
661-4551

Fabrics

150   If you're after exquisite fabrics, my first choice for the best selection in Cincinnati is Fashion Fabrics. Owner Bob Kuresman always has Italian silks and challis, incredible paisleys, mohair and cashmere, Pendleton wools, Irish linens, European curtain lace, a wall of Ultrasuede. The rest of the store is packed with less expensive but always tasteful fabrics, as well as a complete line of sewing accessories. Bob and his staff are knowledgeable about which fabrics can be used for which purposes and are always willing to assist you.

Fashion Fabrics
9889 Montgomery Rd. (Montgomery)
791-2395

Banasch's carries a well-rounded supply of fabrics, from top-of-the-line to those with more modest price tags. The store's sewing accessories include a five-star button selection—probably the biggest variety in town.

Banasch's
108 E. 7th St. (downtown)
721-5210

Everyone who has been to Silhouette Fabrics tells me the store stocks a lovely supply of fine yard goods. But every time I've tried to see for myself, the place is closed, and when I phone, no one answers. Still, you may want to stop by. And you may have better luck than me.

Silhouette Fabrics
1979 Madison Rd. (O'Bryonville)
321-6556

House of Laird fabrics are shown by appointment only by company representatives throughout Greater Cincinnati. There are 800 to 1,000 swatches available for you to choose from, silk to Ultrasuede, linen to mohair. This company is known for its impeccable quality and service. Since all of its representatives sew, they can be immensely helpful to you in selecting fabrics, supplies, and patterns. They can also recommend dressmakers if you're not adept at making clothes but still want some custom made. Your best bet is to call Dottie Osmond, area manager, to get on the House of Laird mailing list so you will know when seasonal fabrics arrive.

House of Laird
871-4449

Calico Corners is where everyone heads to buy upholstery, slipcover, and drapery fabric because there is always a huge variety from well-known companies in stock, and new shipments arrive weekly. Fabrics that you need in large quantities can be special ordered. Prices are good on first-quality yard goods, even better on seconds, which you are invited to examine for flaws. Calico Corners also has its own custom workrooms where they will make draperies, slipcovers, and bedspreads for you if you don't want to tackle the job yourself.

Calico Corners
Ridge & Highland Ave. (Gold Circle Mall)
631-8778

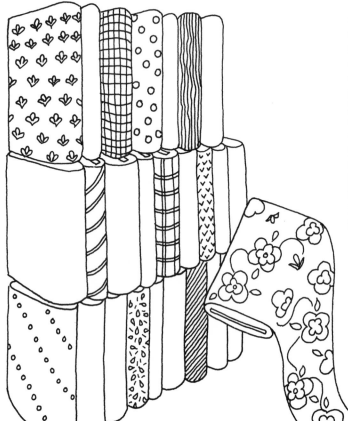

En Provence (more about this store in "From the Frying Pan . . . ," see page 36) has among its exquisite offerings rolls of French provincial cotton fabric—flowered and paisley—as crisp as a French country morning. If you want to make a pillow, a shawl, cover anything, or make clothes with continental flair, this is a charming place to find fabric.

En Provence
2722 Erie Ave. (Hyde Park)
871-9009

Benjamin Hey Mill Outlet sells close-out fabrics from fine wool to cotton and polyester blends, plus yarn which is mostly Orlon. Upholstery and drapery fabric is generally priced at 20% to 50% below retail.

Benjamin Hey Mill Outlet
4142 Airport Rd. (near Lunken Airport)
321-3343

Shor's has been at the same location in Covington for years, selling all sorts of fabrics; a specialty is drapery yard goods. They have their own custom shop and can design and make any kind of window treatment you specify.

Shor's Department Store
30 Pike St. (Covington)
431-0971

If you want to make leather garments, go to Tandy, which carries modest to extravagant quality, supple to sturdy, natural tones to vibrant hues.

Tandy Leather Co.
4077 E. Galbraith Rd. (Deer Park)
984-3434

If you're searching for cotton duck by the yard, go to Queen City Awning Co. and choose from about twenty-five colors of the lighter weight variety they stock. This is the kind you can sew with a standard home machine without breaking the needle. The heavier weight duck—great for making director's chair covers and canvas bags—comes in eighty colors here. Queen City also carries green vinyl by the yard if you need it to cover lawn chairs.

Queen City Awning Co.
318 E. 8th St. (downtown)
241-0437

Dress-Ups

152 You were the good guy. You volunteered to come dressed as the bunny at your neighborhood Easter egg hunt. Now where in the world are you going to pick up a bunny suit? The following places are your best bets for finding one, along with costumes and accessories for any stage production or special occasion.

Theatre House is a huge warehouse packed with more costumes and accessories than you could ever imagine exist in one place. A sampling: suits of armor, sets of spotlights, all kinds of hats from toreador to musketeer, dance footwear, stage weapons, chicken feet, fake teeth, witch's brooms, breakaway bottles, fans, stage makeup. Ask for a club to go with your caveman costume. Someone will reach in a bin and hand you one!

Phone for a catalogue so you can see Theatre House's complete stage line. Then if you still can't find what you want, talk to them about designing costumes and scenery for you.
Theatre House, Inc.
400 W. 3rd St. (Covington)
431-2414

Clown Alley has more than 4,000 costumes in stock, from common ones like witches and devils to elaborate animal suits and 1890s to 1950s period costumes. In stock are about forty Santa Claus suits, along with multiple Frosty the Snowmen and Rudolph the Reindeers.

Clown Alley's owner, Jack Holland, manufactures plastic costume accessories sold all over the world which you can buy at the store: devil's pitchforks, hooks for Little Bo Peep, meat cleavers—take your pick from dozens.
Clown Alley Productions
7855 Glendale-Milford Rd. (outside Milford)
831-8121

Schenz Theatrical Supply always stocks a great array of costumes, from Santa suits to harem garb to official dress for kings and queens. Animal heads, which Schenz makes on the premises, are also for rent at the store. Special orders can be accommodated.

This place stocks a fine line of theatrical makeup, which staff will show you how to use. Many savvy women who want good-quality makeup—(especially eye pencils in a rainbow of colors) at less than you'd pay at a cosmetics counter have been buying at Schenz for years. And anyone who wants to disguise a facial scar is familiar with Schenz's stock because it does the job and stays on for hours.
Schenz Theatrical Supply
343 W. 4th St. (downtown)
721-5600

Stagecraft Costuming, Inc. houses more than 7,000 costumes besides custom making them, especially animal suits worn by mascots for high school or college athletic teams. You can buy accessories here as well.

Stagecraft also manufactures road cases for storing and transporting band equipment, sound equipment, costumes, and props. Say you travel with the football team; how do you get your bear suit from city to city without smashing the oversize head? Or you finally made the marching band and you have to tote your tuba. Stagecraft can design this kind of equipment.
Stagecraft Costuming, Inc.
3944 Spring Grove Ave. (Northside)
541-6803

Secondhand Rose (you'll find out more about them in "Then and Again," see page 111) rents costumes as well as tuxedos and prom dresses. Owner Nelle Gartner says scary costumes are in demand at Halloween, in February and March people are heavy into Mardi Gras and St. Patrick's Day garb, vintage clothes go in and out of the store all year long.

Secondhand Rose
8286 Winton Rd. (Finneytown)
521-1384
1026 Delta Ave. (Mt. Lookout)
321-7525

All That Jazz has wonderful costume accessories such as moustaches and beards, spray cans of hair color, gangster hats, cigarette holders, canes, and sequin vests. There is a fantastic selection of leotards, unitards, tights—all sorts of dancewear and shoes—plus an extensive selection of theatrical makeup. Kryolan, a fine German line, as well as Bob Kelly, well known in New York, are just two lines always kept in stock.

All That Jazz
277 Calhoun St. (Clifton)
961-1900

Loshin's Dancewear is a good place to find leotards, leg warmers, warm-ups, tap, ballet, and toe shoes, even little girls' ballerina costumes like tutus, with or without sequins, in half a dozen colors.

Loshin's Dancewear
260 W. Mitchell Ave. (at Spring Grove)
541-5400

Priscilla Hershberger has made costumes for children's theater, designed sets for productions—she's even written the plays. This imaginative woman custom-makes costumes for rock groups, ballerinas, for anyone for any occasion. Priscilla designs clothes that move with the wearer; they are never constricting. She has an incredible feel for fabric and makes street clothes that are as joyful as her stage creations.

Creature Costumes by Priscilla
681-2249

Every year there is an extravaganza Halloween costume sale at Gabriel's Corner. Priscilla Hershberger and an assortment of her friends bring the overabundance of "stuff" they've collected in their search for stage costumes so people can put together their own costumes from the odds and ends they are welcome to poke through. Choir robes, Indian headdresses, cowboy chaps, formals—picking through this fantasy flea market yields Grade A returns. Call Gabriel's Corner to find out the exact date and time the sale is scheduled.

Gabriel's Corner
1425 Sycamore (Over-the-Rhine)
241-6553

Sparkle Plenty

From jewelry stores that have served Cincinnatians for generations to the recent burst of "by appointment only" businesses that dish up diamonds at a discount, there are wonderful opportunities to buy gems in this city. Aren't you glad?

First: A handful of stores you can depend on whether you're looking for a child's gold locket, a wedding string of pearls, or a fiftieth-anniversary emerald.

Herschede Jewelers
4 W. 4th St. (downtown)
421-6080
3440 Edwards Rd. (Hyde Park)
871-1700
Kenwood Towne Centre
891-4700

Newstedt-Loring Andrews Jewelers
27 W. 4th St. (downtown)
621-9844
2714 Erie Ave. (Hyde Park)
321-3604

Grassmuck-Lange Jeweler
435 Vine St. (downtown)
621-1898

Boris Litwin Jewelry, Inc.
725 Race St. (downtown)
621-1123

Now here's my favorite place, a secret I'll gladly share with you—S&L Jewelry Co. I first came here to have a ring repaired and soon realized owner Frank Jones is a master at bringing any piece— antique or contemporary—back to life. (More on this in "Handiest People in Town," page 56). But Frank creates jewelry, too. Bring him a picture or an idea, and he can come up with whatever you have in mind. Even if you don't have something in mind, Frank has dozens of jewelry catalogues for you to look through. He can order any piece you like, and his prices are decidedly friendly. Or he'll order an array of gemstones for you—then make the jewelry you want using the quality stone you choose (or stones if you're doing something serious). Everyone I've sent to Frank has been pleased with his work and ecstatic with his prices.
S&L Jewelry Co.
37 W. 7th St., 4th fl. (downtown)
241-7359

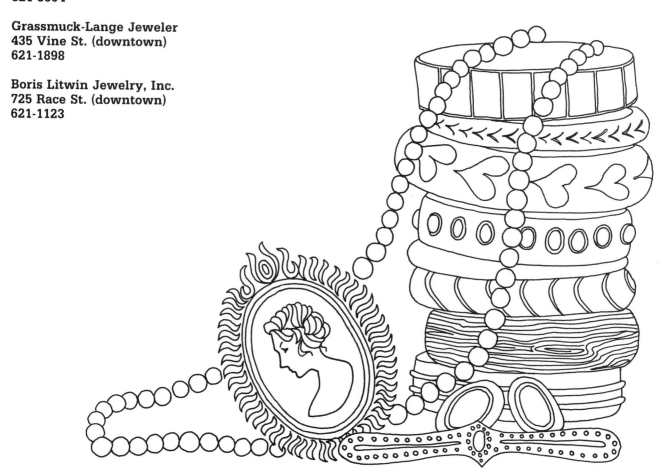

When I ask people where they bought the great-looking pin or earrings they're wearing, a good number say from Raul Haas. This creative man sells antique and contemporary pieces he scouts for all over the world. What he doesn't have on hand he makes. He even has a person on the premises who does nothing but string pearls. Raul calls himself a New York-style jeweler—he buys in the morning and sells at night. He has a good eye, offers good prices, and he's gathered quite a devoted following.

Raul Haas/Hyde Park Jewelers
3434 Edwards Rd. (Hyde Park)
321-7679

Marcia Roesch is an artist who creates contemporary-looking 14-karat gold jewelry inlaid with opals, which are her specialty, as well as other semiprecious stones such as onyx and lapis. Diamonds, rubies, and sapphires show up in some of her understated pieces, and everything she creates is a one-of-a-kind original. Phone Marcia to see examples of her craft, and talk to her about custom designs, which take about six weeks to complete.

Marja Jewelry
871-9528

There is no finer collection of antique jewelry than Bernice Friedman's of Heirlooms, Ltd. She buys only the most outstanding quality pieces from all over the world and has such stunning taste that when you go to make a serious purchase, the choice is agonizing. She carries museum-quality baubles dating from any time between the fifteenth century and the 1940s: cameos, drop-dead deco diamond pins and earrings, French gold chatelaines, Italian inlaid bracelets.

Bernice is knowledgeable about all the jewels she owns and loves them as much as you will. She also stands behind their authenticity. Her hours are by appointment only, although from Thanksgiving to Christmas, she and her security guard are in residence at 307 Dixie Terminal Building, downtown, from 11 A.M. to 4 P.M.

Heirlooms, Ltd.
721-1343

Sparkle Plenty

"By Appointment Only" Jewelry

If what you see at Tiffany's and Fortunoff's is what you'd like to own, but not at retail prices, pay attention to this list of "by appointment only" sellers. They carry "latest-look" jewelry and the more traditional kind. From heavy gold link chains, big cuff bracelets, stylish sterling silver pieces, even semiprecious stones—they have them. And their stock changes constantly as they follow whatever is current fashion. If you're a serious jewelry buyer, definitely check out this list.

If you like the look of Elsa Peretti and Paloma Picasso jewelry, Agnes Richter and Lois Drill buy the same styles. They can also update a plain gold collar with a stone-studded slide and can have older jewelry remade.

The Two of Us
Agnes Richter
631-2826
Lois Drill
791-3380

Besides trendy, top-fashion jewelry, Marilyn Guttman of Golddiggers sells high-style sweatsuits and jumpsuits studded with stones, patches of leather, and lace.

Golddiggers
891-9528

Saundra Kirsh of Simply Elegant leans to the classic styles for gold and silver, as well as semiprecious stones and pearls.

Simply Elegant
891-8995

Sandy Wolfson of Touch of Gold carries traditional to trendy jewelry—$5 bracelets on up to $7,000 diamond necklaces that convert into a bracelet you can wear around your wrist or ankle. She has shows at the Carrousel Inn usually once a month. Phone her to find out when.

Touch of Gold
891-GOLD

Marilyn Randman carries costume jewelry made of brass dipped in 24-karat gold and then studded with semiprecious stones, some pins and earrings made out of antique fabric; some sterling silver bracelets and earrings. If you've shopped at Barney's in New York, you've seen what she sells. Marilyn calls it fun jewelry. Prices range from $25 to about $200.

Marilyn's Jewelry
631-6620

Artware

If you like artist-made jewelry rather than gold and diamonds, investigate the Sarah Squeri Gallery. Sarah represents artists who create iridescent glass necklaces, or work with tiny ceramic beads, even new materials like silicone and paint. Roberta Williamson, one of Sarah's artists, creates whimsical jewelry with silver images of her home life—her dog, hands, hearts—hanging from them. These pieces are so special people who wear them are stopped on the street by admirers. Sarah has a good eye for jeweled art. See what she has; tell her what you like. She'll call you when she comes across pieces that will please you if she doesn't have them already.

Sarah Squeri Gallery
330 W. 4th St. (downtown)
621-1650

Sports Equipment and Clothes

Racing bikes to running shoes, designer tennis togs to plain old sweats—here's where to suit up to work out.

Sweats and Shoes

When the Velva Sheen Manufacturing Company misprints logos on T-shirts and sweatshirts, they wind up at their outlet stores. And that's exactly where people who want clothes they can seriously sweat in put together their wardrobes. You wind up buying T-shirts with all sorts of strange things written on them, which is half the fun of shopping at Velva Sheen. The other half is the great prices. Besides misprints, the stores are crammed with unprinted sweatshirts, sweatsuits, T-shirts, rugby-style shirts, jackets—there are racks of garments. If you are sending a kid to camp and expect him to come home with half his clothes missing, stock up at Velva Sheen. Check the phone directory for the store nearest you.

Just Sweats is opening stores faster than people can jump on the exercise bandwagon, and these stores are terrific. Bins hold heavy to lightweight sweats in plain colors, stripes, and prints. I bought some yellow and black bottoms that looked to me like a distant relative to a Picasso print; they're pretty snappy for a walk in the park. From pocket pants to fleece shirts, university logo sweatshirts to baggy socks, Just Sweats has an ever-changing supply at prices you'll like. Look in the phone book for the store nearest you.

H. Wolf, a wholesale distributor and silk-screen printer of sportswear items commonly found in college bookstores and sporting-goods shops, has a warehouse sale the first two weekends in December and the first weekend in May. This is when Wolf sells salesmen's samples and excess stock at wholesale prices or lower: thousands of T-shirts, sweatsuits, warm-ups, rugby shirts, football jerseys, children's T-shirts, gym shorts, jackets, tube socks, and all sorts of interesting odds and ends. These sales draw big repeat crowds! Call for exact times and to verify the dates.
H. Wolf & Sons
10139 Commerce Park Dr. (Sharonville)
874-8000

Sporting Foot and Things, Finish Line, and Brendamour's blanket the city with stores selling full lines of well-priced athletic gear. You'll find shoes from aerobic to running, warm-ups, tennis togs, T-shirts—expensive designer brands to more moderately priced clothes. Merchandise changes constantly and there are often specials. Says Mike Haffer of Sporting Foot, "I try to buy the right merchandise at the right time at the right price." That's exactly why the customer benefits—when a brand gets hot, Mike goes for it in quantity and drops prices. Finish Line and Brendamour's are competitive, too. So shop these stores for a good range of quality merchandise and value. These outfits have many stores that are located in malls throughout Greater Cincinnati. Check your phone directory for addresses and phone numbers.

Running

Bob Roncker's Running Spot is the hot spot to gather information as well as clothes and shoes if you are a running enthusiast. Bob, a former teacher and coach, has been running for twenty-five years. So besides selling anything a runner might need—from shoes to shorts—he generously shares his knowledge about the sport. Clinics are often held at the store to give people all sorts of information on subjects from technique to diet. Group runs start out from there, and to add to the pleasure, Bob shares little-known routes he's discovered. He even puts out a newsletter containing announcements of upcoming races plus racing tips. Pick it up at the store. Also, pick up applications for Friends-A-Foot. It's a group that matches runners according to their ability and where they live (and run) so they do not have to run alone. This can be dangerous, especially for women.
Bob Roncker's Running Spot
1993 Madison Rd. (O'Bryonville)
321-3006

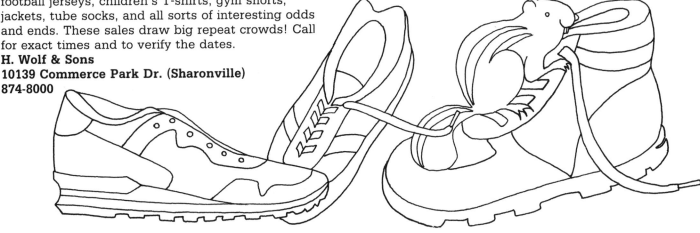

Sports Equipment and Clothes

Tennis

If tennis is your game, here are shops that specialize in equipment for your sport. Some offer snob-appeal brands as well as moderate ones; some sell a wide range of merchandise at a discount. Some sell equipment and accessories, others just apparel; some have racquetball and squash equipment as well.

The Tennis Nook
Valley Center (Roselawn)
761-3400

Tennis and Ski Warehouse
11449 Princeton Rd. (Tricentre)
771-9855
7565 Kenwood Rd. (Kenwood)
745-0099

Head Factory Outlet
2430 E. Kemper Rd. (Shapely Outlet Center)
771-5758

Tennis on the Square
2648 Erie Ave. (Hyde Park)
321-1200

Courtside
29 Fountain Square Plaza (downtown)
579-9050

Golf

For golf club repair, restoration, to have clubs custom built, to buy ready-mades at friendly prices plus all sorts of accessories, tee off at these stores.

Clubworks
5 Main St. (Milford)
831-3454

The Golf Doctor
11119 Reading Rd. (Sharonville)
554-4449

Pro-Golf
11570 Springfield Pk. (Springdale)
772-5758

The Old Golf Shop stocks gifts for golfers: golf prints, glassware with golf themes, brass bookends, ice buckets, some antique golf items, all sorts of tournament prizes.
The Old Golf Shop
325 W. 5th St. (downtown)
241-7789

Soccer

For shoes, jerseys, shorts (the Umbro brand, big and baggy around the legs, is what kids are wearing to school these days), balls, nets, goals—shop these stores.

Ryans Soccer International
10735 Reading Rd. (Evendale)
563-4625
8261 Beechmont Ave. (Anderson Twp.)
474-4366

Off the Ball
6611 Hamilton Ave. (North College Hill)
522-9424

Ski

If you're after downhill or cross-country ski equipment, boots, gloves, ski suits—try these two stores plus Tennis and Ski Warehouse (check the "Tennis" section in this chapter for its locations).

Tyroler Ski Haus
222 Hartwell Ave. (Hartwell)
821-0198

Leisure Ski & Marine
6766 Harrison Ave. (Dent)
574-3456

Bikes

Racing bikes, all-terrain bikes, around-the-block riding bikes, exercycles, helmets, gloves, clothes, accessories—pedal on over to these stores.

Solo Sports
2008 Madison Rd. (O'Bryonville)
321-0882

Campus Cycle and Ski
241 W. McMillan (Clifton)
721-6628

Jim's Bicycle Shop
8015 Plainfield Rd. (Deer Park)
793-1163

Montgomery Cyclery
Check the phone directory for the store closest to you.

Riding

J.B. Schaaf has a complete line of tack. R.J. Becht & Son is a fourth-generation custom clothier. Their fine garments for adults and children are sold all over the country.

J.B. Schaaf Saddlery and Leather Work
3505 Harrison Ave. (Cheviot)
481-9900

R.J. Becht & Son
236 E. 8th St. (downtown)
579-1171

Camping and Climbing

Tents, ropes, shoes, clothes, food—any equipment for rugged outdoor activities anywhere in the world—try these wilderness outfitters.

Wilderness Trace, Inc.
3441 Michigan Ave. (Hyde Park)
321-6800
11582 Lebanon Rd. (Sharonville)
563-4774

Outdoor Adventures
39 Calhoun St. (Clifton)
221-6700

You can buy mats for all kinds of workouts or have one custom made at Queen City Gymnastics. They also sell gloves and other gymnastics accessories. If you are really serious about exercise and want to construct a gym in your own home, staff here will consult with you on what is the best floor to install and the right kind of equipment to buy for your special needs.
Queen City Gymnastics Center, Inc.
11658 Deerfield Rd. (Blue Ash)
489-7575

Jane Fonda wears you out. Debbie Reynolds is too slow. You like exercising with a video but you can't find one that's exactly your speed. Phone for an appointment with Kathy Davis, owner of Workouts. She will make an exercise video especially for you. You pick the music. You tell Kathy how vigorous the exercises should be. You also tell her about any trouble spots (trick knees, a bad back) so she can skip exercises that will aggravate your problems and include ones to improve your health. When she completes the video (cost is $50 to $75), Kathy will run through it with you until you get the hang of it. Kathy also consults on setting up at-home exercise rooms—floors, equipment, the works.
Workouts Ltd. Exercise Studio & Apparel
7426 Montgomery Rd. (near Kenwood)
793-4444

Help: Get It— Give It

There are many excellent helping agencies in Cincinnati. However, such abundance creates the problem of knowing exactly which to call— especially when you're in the middle of an emergency. "I'm in the county. Is this city agency going to help me out?" That's the last question you should have to consider when it's a matter of life or death.

So, with all due respect to the hundreds of caring services, I've pared down my list to the best *referral* agencies I could find—those in the center of the web of human services in this area that quickly get callers to just the aid they're after.

In a fire or crime emergency, your first call should be to the **fire** or **police** department that serves the area in which you live. Always have the numbers posted next to your telephone, ready should you need them. In Cincinnati the police number is 765-1212 (the police also dispatch the life squad) and the fire department number is 241-2525.

Drug and Poison Information Center: 872-5111 is the twenty-four hour, seven-day-a-week emergency number. Pharmacists can tell you what procedure to follow if your child has swallowed a harmful substance or what to do if you have inhaled a toxic chemical.

Besides providing superb emergency services, this agency disperses all sorts of information, such as what the interaction of two drugs you are taking will be, what reaction you will have if you mix a glass of wine with a specific prescription pill, what the side effects of any drug are. If you find your teenager swallowing a funny-looking pill, staff at this agency can help you identify it, even refer you to community agencies that deal with substance abuse. There's also a speakers bureau. Your group can ask an expert to come to talk about drugs or poison prevention.

Rape Crisis Center: 381-5610. This twenty-four hour helpline is operated by Women Helping Women. After office hours, an answering service monitors the phone so they can immediately contact a beeper-wearing counselor who will phone a rape victim within minutes of the attack. The counselor will help the woman through this crisis, advise her to get to a hospital where she will meet her, and stay with her through the examination. Other staffers will accompany the woman to court should she decide to press charges, and give her support to combat rape's aftershock.

Women Helping Women also provides domestic-violence counseling, support groups for adult survivors of incest, are court advocates for children who have been sexually abused, and counselors for their parents. Ask for speakers on subjects such as how to stay alive during a sexual attack, how to keep domestic verbal abuse from escalating into physical violence, how children can protect themselves against sexual abuse. Speakers can bring along an outstanding film on this last subject.

281-CARE is the **suicide prevention hotline** that puts despondent callers in touch with counselors who will talk them through their crisis. If counselors feel callers need further help than they can provide on the phone, they'll try to coax them to come in for a face-to-face session the next day or refer them to agencies who can tackle their problems.

This agency has superb intentions and delivers a much-needed service—when phone lines are open. For a person in deep despair, getting a repeated busy signal can spell disaster. If 281-CARE is tied up when you need help, move to the number listed below—that of the Information and Referral Center—which can provide crisis intervention (and so much more) and seems to have phone lines that are always free.

Your First Call For Help: 721-7900 is the helpline of the United Way Information and Referral service. This service is aptly named. It is the most comprehensive, expeditious referral agency in the area.

According to director Patricia Hiett-Cogan, there are more than 500 social service agencies and 250 child-care agencies in Greater Cincinnati that provide more than 3,000 services. Information and referral specialists keep computerized track of all these services, along with their eligibility requirements, so that anyone who calls for help is given the right person to call at the exact agency that can fill his need on the spot.

For example: You're an older American having trouble balancing your checkbook; call and see if there is someone at an agency who can help you out. You're despondent and need quick telephone bolstering, you're having marital problems, need free legal assistance, cancer support, drug counseling, child care, you're unemployed and need emergency food, shelter, or clothing—there is nothing you can't ask the staff at this responsive agency. Best of all, you will come away with concrete answers if not immediate aid.

The **Disability Services Information Project**, 821-5060, is a one-stop source of telephone assistance (though not emergency help) for people with disabilities from accidents or illness and their families, friends and the professionals who serve them. Staff members assist callers in assessing their needs, whether simple or complex. Then they match needs to services, which are handily computerized, helping them pick options that are best suited to them.

Say you have a child with a lifelong disability and you want to know what support groups are available, what the latest information on the disease is. Staff has access to the American Medical Association computer data base and can send you a printout—the same one available to physicians. Liken this service to a funnel. It's a good entry point to acquaint yourself with the services available for any disability that exists.

You want to give help. Call the **Voluntary Action Center** at 762-7171. It's a clearinghouse for volunteers and the 600 agencies in six counties who need them. If you'd like to volunteer, but don't know where or what jobs are available, staff will discuss possibilities with you. They'll send you lists of agencies—cultural, those that provide emergency services, you name it—along with their needs, so you can plug in where you'd feel most challenged. Director Peg Pauly encourages would-be volunteers to come in for a brainstorming session to get their interests clear if a phone conversation doesn't do it. That way, their skills are matched to organizations who can use them in the most fulfilling way possible.

The Voluntary Action Center also maintains a Board Bank—a service that matches volunteers to serve on the boards of non-profit agencies who have openings. Ask about it.

Keys to the City

Fighting City Hall is a hassle. And it's not too often you come out a winner. While trying to locate the right person to answer your question (let alone solve your problem) at the agency charged with providing the service you're after, it's easy to drown in a sea of red tape.

To prevent that awful fate, use the following list of the city's core headache-solving phone numbers. But there's one disclaimer: how humane the people who answer these phones will be is as chancy as the Ohio Lottery. Some are kind and will honestly go out of their way to help. Others? Don't be surprised by dripping indifference.

The general number for **City Hall** is 352-3000. It's a starting point.

The **Clerk of Council**—who is a fund of knowledge on when committee meetings are scheduled, what issues are being considered, how you can submit or present your problems to council—can be reached at 352-3246.

If you'd like legislative information on the status of bills pending in the **Ohio House and Senate**, phone 1-800-282-0253.

See a traffic light malfunctioning? Call **Traffic Engineering** at 352-3710. This rings at the dispatcher's office and he sends out fixers.

But if you would like a stop sign, a traffic light, or a crosswalk *installed* where there isn't one presently, phone 352-3715.

The Hamilton County number for all the above traffic engineering services is 825-2280.

For **emergency highway problems** that could cause a traffic accident, such as a pothole as large as a crater, call 352-3361.

Street sign keeled over or missing? Phone 352-3378.

Hamilton County Highway Maintenance— which will repair potholes, traffic signs, remove ice and snow, and pick up dead animals, to name just a few of its functions—can be reached at 761-7400.

The **Sanitation Division** is who you should contact for litter control, street and alley cleaning, garbage pickup information and complaints, to report dead animals on city streets, and to arrange special pickup of large items. Note that you may put out three wooden or upholstered pieces—even as big as a couch—on your regular collection day, but no hide-a-beds or metal items (these will be taken away by special arrangement, three to four days after you phone in your request). The magic number for all this is 352-3691.

Smell something strange in the air? Phone 251-8777 (the **Southwestern Ohio Air Pollution Control Agency**) to complain about air pollution whether you're in Hamilton, Clermont, Warren, or Butler County. In Kentucky, call 371-0598.

If you're worried about water pollution, industrial waste, or any hazardous materials, phone the Southwest District office of the **Ohio Environmental Protection Agency** in Dayton at 1-449-6357. There is no Cincinnati number to handle these worrisome problems.

Still not satisfied? To report violations of any Ohio environmental protection laws, phone the **EPA Environmental Hotline** at 1-800-282-0270.

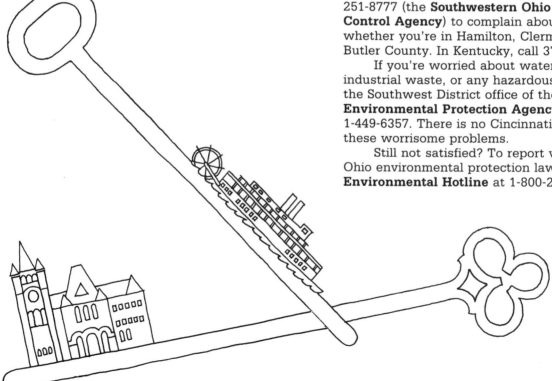

Complaints about building structures, such as broken windows, unsafe floors, or bad wiring (especially if your landlord won't fix them), should be channeled to the **Building Department** at 352-3275.

Need a **building permit**? Call 352-3271.

For **zoning information**, which you should gather before you build anything in any neighborhood, phone 352-3273. This is also the number to call to complain about junk in a neighbor's yard or to report that the person next door is doing business out of his house when he knows it's a no-no.

City **income-tax** questions? Phone 352-3838. Questions about State of Ohio personal-income and withholding taxes? Phone 1-800-282-1780. If you need information from the IRS, phone the Cincinnati district office at 621-6281 or their toll-free number, 1-800-424-1040.

The **Cincinnati Health Department**'s general information number is 352-3100. Specific problems commonly phoned in to this department are: animal bites, 352-3159; insect complaints, 352-3159; rat problems, 352-3153; unsightly trash and weeds, 352-3159. To obtain birth and death certificates, phone 352-3120. For information on sexually transmitted diseases, phone 352-3149.

Street flooded because your sewer isn't functioning properly? Phone **Stormwater Management**. The number is 352-3800.

All water problems including a color or odor more unusual than it regularly is, flooded basements, no water at all, and meter repairs should be phoned into the **Water Works** twenty-four-hour emergency number, which is 352-4623. For billing information, phone 352-4747.

Cincinnati Gas and Electric Company has two twenty-four-hour emergency numbers. For gas problems, phone 651-4466. For electric problems, phone 651-4182. For all other complaints (even billing), call 381-2000.

If you have a question or complaint about investor-owned public utilities and have not found recourse on the local level, phone the **Public Utility Commission of Ohio** (PUCO), at 1-800-232-0198.

If you need postal **zip code information** for anywhere in Cincinnati or the U.S., phone 684-5571. All you need to have handy is the address.

The **main post office delivery station**, at 1623 Dalton Avenue, downtown, has a mailbox in the parking lot whose contents are emptied and sped on their way every hour, on the hour, twenty-four hours a day, seven days a week. Keep this in mind when you have to get a letter out in a hurry.

For information on how to use **Queen City Metro**, phone 621-4455. Staff will mail you bus schedules, even tell you—on the telephone—how to get from where you are to where you need to go.

You've lost track of the time? Phone 721-1700 for the **correct time** of day.

For information on obtaining **driver's licenses and plates**, phone 651-3838. Driving tests to qualify for a license may be obtained at two locations in Hamilton County: 8958 Blue Ash Rd., Blue Ash, 791-1644, and 8078 Hamilton Ave., Mt. Healthy, 522-6600.

Keys to the City

The phone number for information on everything that goes on in the **city parks**, including where they are, nature activities, how to rent a lodge or reserve a picnic area, is 352-4080.

For **Hamilton County Park Board** information—and the activities that are sponsored here range from wildflower- and bird-identification walks to where you can boat or fish—call 521-7275.

The **Cincinnati Recreation Department** sponsors so many activities from arts and crafts lessons to every kind of sports league imaginable, it's mind boggling. The number to tap into all this is 352-4000.

For all City of Cincinnati consumer complaints, phone the **Consumer Protection Division** at 352-3971. The staff handles all sorts of problems such as deceptive sales advertising (like the old bait-and-switch routine) and faulty repairs.

The **Ohio State Attorney General** is also a consumer advocate for citizens. To reach the local office of Anthony J. Celebrezze, phone 852-3497. The toll-free number for his Columbus office is 1-800-282-0515, but the phone rings busy much of the time. If you don't mind footing the phone bill, call 614-466-8831.

More consumer information is available from the **Cincinnati Better Business Bureau**, which will tell you whether a company you are contemplating doing business with has complaints registered against it. Call them *before* you sign on any dotted line, at 421-3015.

Want to know who your state representatives, your county commissioners, your United States Congressman are? Do you need to know where and how to register to vote, how to obtain an absentee ballot? Phone the **Hamilton County Board of Elections** at 632-7000.

For information on **fire prevention**, phone 352-2360. For **crime-prevention** assistance, phone 352-3514. This section of the Cincinnati Police Department will direct you to your proper district so you can ask for a crime-prevention officer to come to your home to assess how safe it is against break-ins and give you suggestions on how you can burglarproof it. Yes, they will! (If you live in the suburbs, phone your local police department and see if there is a crime-prevention officer on staff who can help.)

If you live outside the City of Cincinnati and/or Hamilton County, you may have to turn to your phone directory for some of the important numbers you need. Look under the suburb or county in which you live for the sheriff's office number and for a general information number. You may have to do some digging, and you will probably get shuffled from one office to another, but persist!

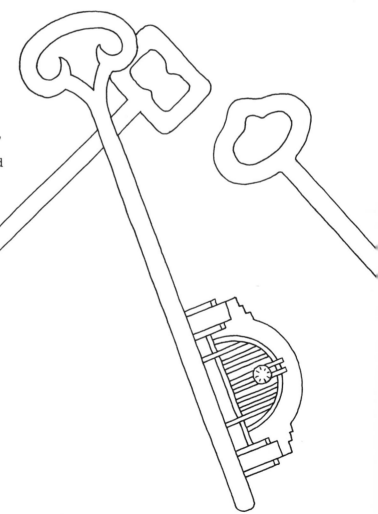

Additional Aid from the Feds

If you need help from the feds, but you're having trouble tracking the exact person to contact at the right agency, phone the local office of the **Federal Information Center** at 684-2801. Staffers cut through the maze of Uncle Sam's red tape, generally have the information you need at their fingertips, but will research your problem and phone you back if they don't.

Your **United States Representatives and Senators** can also help you cut through government red tape. They are first-rate expeditors because they maintain liaisons in every agency and department of the federal government and can quickly get you the answers you need. These include updates on which foreign countries are considered safe or unsafe for travel, helping with emergencies that occur abroad, processing passports within forty-eight hours, obtaining copies of pieces of legislation that come before Congress, arranging VIP tours of the White House, Pentagon, FBI, or Kennedy Center. Find the office numbers of your representatives in the phone directory or call the Board of Elections.

Cancer Information Service: 1-800-4-CANCER. This inquiry service, funded by the National Cancer Institute, supplies the most recent information about cancer and cancer-related resources to the general public and health professionals. You can ask for specific information on particular types of cancer, inquire about local detection, treatment, and rehabilitation facilities, learn about cancer prevention and possible causes of cancer, ask questions about a procedure suggested by a physician.

AIDS Aid. There are three hotlines you can call for information concerning Acquired Immune Deficiency Syndrome.

The U.S. Department of Health Service
1-800-342-2437

National Sexually Transmitted Diseases Hotline
1-800-227-8922

National Gay Task Force AIDS Information Hotline
1-800-221-7044

V.D. Hotline: 1-800-227-8922. This is a referral service on all aspects of sexually transmitted diseases. Staff will refer callers to places where they can obtain confidential, free consultation.

Alzheimer's Disease: 1-800-367-4540. This twenty-four-hour service sends out printed material about the disease and will put you in touch with local support groups.

National Runaway Hotline: 1-800-621-4000. This service refers runaway children who call this well-publicized number to shelters and also passes messages to their parents (if they request it) without disclosing their whereabouts. Parents may also call for advice on what procedures to follow if their child is missing.

Index

Index

Vital Statistics

Lois Rosenthal and Tina Blackburn have teamed up for the third time to produce *Living Better in Cincinnati* to celebrate the city's bicentennial.

Since the first *Living Better in Cincinnati* in 1975, Lois has written a number of local consumer guides as well as national books such as *Partnering: A Guide to Co-Owning Anything From Homes to Home Computers* and *How to Stop Snoring.* She was a columnist for the *Cincinnati Enquirer* for nine years, hosted a popular call-in show for WCKY, and has appeared on radio and television shows from coast to coast, including the *Today Show* and *Hour Magazine.* She is currently writing for magazines such as *Cosmopolitan, McCall's* and *Writer's Digest.* She is a contributing editor to *Sylvia Porter's Personal Finance Magazine.*

Tina Blackburn was an art director with various prestigious advertising agencies including Northlich Stolley and Intermedia when she lived in Cincinnati, and has collected an impressive number of awards for her work. These include a bronze award for the design of the very first *Living Better in Cincinnati* in the 1976 Art Director's Show. When Tina moved to New York with her husband Bruce in 1979, she became a graphic designer and illustrator with Blackburn and Associates, a graphic design consulting firm. While her clients are now mostly in the New York area, she reached back to her Cincinnati roots to help make *Living Better* blossom.

Guide to the Malls

170 Rather than repeat the street addresses and suburbs of well-known shopping areas mentioned many times in this book, I've listed them all conveniently below. All other store addresses as well as the suburbs in which they are located are included in individual listings.

Beechmont Mall Five Mile Rd. and Beechmont Ave. in Anderson Township.
Eastgate Mall I-275 and Rt. 32 in Mt. Carmel.
Bigg's Place Mall 4450 Eastgate Blvd. (I-275 and Rt. 32) in Mt. Carmel.
Kenwood Mall Kenwood Rd. and Montgomery Rd. in Kenwood.
Kenwood Towne Centre (formerly Kenwood Plaza) Kenwood Rd. and Montgomery Rd. in Kenwood.
Outlets, Ltd. 5300 Kings Island Dr. near Kings Island.
Shapely Outlet Center 2430 E. Kemper Rd. (between Mosteller Rd. and Chester Rd.) in Sharonville.
Tri-County Mall Princeton Rd. and Kemper Rd. in Springdale.

Tricentre On Princeton Rd. just south of Kemper Rd. in Springdale.
Northgate Mall Colerain Ave. and Springdale Rd. in Bevis.
Western Hills Plaza Werk Rd. and Glenway Ave. in Westwood.
Valley Center In the 7600 block of Reading Rd., half block north of Section Rd., in Roselawn (it's right across from Bilker Food Market).
Swifton Commons Mall Seymour Ave. and Reading Rd. in Roselawn.
Hyde Park Plaza Between Paxton Rd. and Wasson Rd. in Hyde Park.
Skywalk This second story of downtown Cincinnati crisscrosses a large area. If you're searching for a shop on the Skywalk, phone ahead and ask the store owner to give you exact directions.
Convention Place Mall 435 Elm St., downtown.
Newport Shopping Center Alexandria Pk. and Carothers Rd. in Newport.
Florence Mall I-71/75 and Rt. 18 in Florence.

Get Into Print

If you know of a place, a person, or a service not mentioned in *Living Better in Cincinnati* that should be included in new editions, please share it with me. Write to:
Living Better in Cincinnati
1507 Dana Avenue
Cincinnati, OH 45207

Dear Lois